VAN MEEGEREN:
MASTER FORGER

CONTENTS

PLATES

Acknowledgments

The two most important source books are *Van Meegeren's Faked Vermeers and de Hooghs*, by Dr P. B. Coremans (1949) and *Back to the Truth* (entitled *Retour à la Vérité* in the original Belgian edition) by M. Jean Decoen (1951). I have used both works extensively and have given exact references wherever I have quoted from them. I have included two anecdotes from *The Van Meegeren Mystery*, a biographical study by Maurice Moiseiwitsch (1964), and have incorporated a few short passages from my own earlier book, *The Master Forger* (1951).

Plates 17 and 35 are reproduced by gracious permission of Her Majesty the Queen. The frontispiece, copyright Black Star; plate 3, copyright Fotocommissie, Rijksmuseum, Amsterdam; plate 8, copyright National Galleries of Scotland, Edinburgh; plate 11, copyright Lord Kilbracken; plates 16, 26, 37, 38, copyright Ullstein Bilderdienst; plates 24 and 36, copyright Mauritshuis, The Hague. The author and publishers gratefully acknowledge the help of the Institut Royal du Patrimoine Artistique in supplying plates 1, 2, 4–7, 9, 10, 12–15, 17, 18–23, 25, and 27–34 (copyright A.C.L., Brussels). Acknowledgments are also given to the present owners of the forgeries reproduced, including the Museum Boymans-van Beuningen (plate 7).

I am extremely grateful to Andriette Schoorel for her many careful translations from the Dutch language of articles and news stories; and above all to Gina—without whom this book might never have been written, or might on the other hand have been completed some months sooner.

THE PROTAGONISTS

Han van Meegeren, forger

Johanna, his second wife
Doctor G. A. Boon, M.P., solicitor
Mijnheer R. Strijbis, house agent

VERSUS

Doctor A. Bredius, expert
Mijnheer D. A. Hoogendijk, dealer
Mijnheer D. G. van Beuningen, collector
Reichsmarshal H. Goering, collector
Doctor P. B. Coremans, expert
Monsieur J. Decoen, expert
Mijnheer P. de Boer, dealer
Mijnheer W. van der Vorm, collector
Doctor D. Hannema, museum director
Doctor A. M. de Wild, expert
Herr A. Miedl, banker
Mijnheer R. van Strijvesande, dealer
Herr W. Hofer, dealer

I

Beginnings

TOWARDS the end of 1937, a major work of art came on the market in Rotterdam. Nothing that could be verified was known of its provenance, but it was signed *I. V. Meer* and had been certified in enthusiastic terms by the eminent art historian, Dr Abraham Bredius, as the undoubted work of Jan Vermeer of Delft.* The *Christ at Emmaus*, as it soon became known (plate 7), was bought for the equivalent of some £180,000 in today's money and presented to the Boymans Museum, where it quickly attracted more notice and acclaim than had any other canvas in the museum's distinguished history. Before long it was generally recognized, with only a few dissenting voices, as an inspiring and highly important example—Bredius thought the most important example—of Vermeer's known work.

Two years later, a well-known private collector in Rotterdam, Mr D. G. van Beuningen, paid 220,000 guilders, the equivalent of some £66,000 today, for a small canvas, *Interior with Drinkers* (plate 16), signed *P.D.H. 1658* and ascribed to de Hoogh. It was remarked that it bore a strong resemblance to the same master's undoubted work, *The Cardplayers* (plate 17), which hangs in Buckingham Palace.

In early 1941, the same collector found some half-million guilders—much the same as had been paid for the *Emmaus*—to acquire a smaller and much less interesting canvas, a *Head of Christ* (plate 26), which had been brought to him by Hoogendijk, the leading Amsterdam dealer. It too was signed *I. V. Meer* (the initials being again in monogram) although it appeared to be no more than a study for the central figure of an unknown major work. A few months later Hoogendijk, who had also been involved in the *Emmaus* negotiations, returned to van Beuningen, having found in the meantime the major work in question: a *Last Supper* (plate 25) which was clearly by the same hand and bore the same

* See his certificate, page 62 below.

† A guilder in those days was roughly the equivalent of a U.S. dollar now.

signature. Again no provenance could be established, but van Beuningen paid 1,600,000 guilders for it, the equivalent today of almost half a million pounds. As part of the deal, he returned the *Head of Christ* to Hoogendijk and it remained on the latter's hands.

Later that year another Rotterdam collector, Mr W. van der Vorm, who had put up the major part of the *Emmaus* money, paid 219,000 guilders for a supposed de Hoogh, *Interior with Card-players* (plate 18), again signed *P.D.H. 1658*. Once more Hoogendijk was the dealer.

In April 1942, Hoogendijk sold a second canvas to van der Vorm. It was signed *I. V. Meer* but was much less pleasing than the other three; it appeared to represent the blessing of Jacob by Isaac (plate 30). Van der Vorm paid 1,270,000 guilders for it—the equivalent of about £127,000 then, or of between two and three times that figure now. There seemed to be no surprise that four new Vermeers had now been discovered in less than five years, though fewer than forty had previously been known with certainty.

Six months later, a secret deal was arranged with the occupying Nazis under which Goering, no less, would pay the unprecedented price of 1,650,000 guilders—again, almost half a million pounds in today's money—for another of the strange Vermeers, all with biblical subjects, that were coming on the market with such surprising but apparently acceptable frequency. This was *Christ and the Adulteress* (plate 32). Goering paid in kind, returning some two hundred relatively minor works stolen by the Germans and probably worth collectively rather more than the agreed cash price.

Finally, in 1943, the Netherlands State paid 1,300,000 guilders for a thoroughly bad canvas, *The Washing of Christ's Feet* (plate 31), signed *I. V. Meer* as the others had been. The experts who examined it agreed that it was unimpressive and were to admit later that they 'did not like it',* but it was clearly by the same hand as the others and they wished at apparently any cost to prevent the Nazis from getting it. The total paid for these eight supposed Old Masters was over 7,000,000 guilders, the equivalent of some £2,000,000 today.† It is certain that six, and virtually certain that all of them, were the work of Han van Meegeren, a sharp-witted, sharp-tongued Dutch artist, of erratic temperament and small

---

* See evidence at the trial, page 181 below.
† For summarized data, see Appendix 1.

talent, who had conspicuously failed to make any name for himself except perhaps in the despised field of photographic portraiture.

His case has been discussed and argued in professional and lay circles ever since. It was not only that his fakes had been accepted by the most eminent judges as the work of two greatly esteemed masters—a fact which persuaded some, in particular van Meegeren himself, that he must therefore be their equal. Of much greater significance, he had attacked public confidence in the entire basis of certification, recognition and critique. Several of the forgeries, in particular the *Emmaus* and to a lesser extent the *Supper*, had been extremely widely acclaimed; critics and art historians had been loud, though not quite unanimous, in acceptance and admiration. Either then, it was argued, they must be ignorant and unqualified to judge, or else it must be an unhappy, inescapable fact that it may be impossible to establish authenticity beyond any doubt except in those relatively few cases where provenance is known in detail and with certainty. Doubt seemed to be cast by inference on many other works, certified by experts no less distinguished than those whose opinions had now been proved meaningless.

If the facts disturbed the professional, they fascinated the layman, to whom van Meegeren came to epitomize that heroic figure, the victorious underdog: a little man (as he was both physically and creatively), a forgotten failure and outcast, who had accumulated by guile a vast fortune and fame at the precise expense of those who had refused him recognition. It is hardly surprising that in a public opinion poll soon before his trial he came second to the Prime Minister in national popularity.

Despite their severe buffeting, the experts of the art world quickly regained their self-esteem and prestige to a quite astonishing degree. Perhaps they tended for a while to be just a little less dogmatic in their judgments, but the instinctive, subjective and therefore fallible opinion of one or two acknowledged pundits was soon once more sufficient to decide who painted a 'doubtful' picture, and therefore whether it was worth nothing or half a million. There was the recent case, to take only one example, a van Meegeren in reverse, when a fine-arts auctioneer in London failed to recognize a quite well-known and admirable Rubens, attributing it instead to a minor contemporary. After it had been sold for less than one-hundredth of its value, and the facts came to light, the dealer concerned was completely unrepentant: he calmly commented that he 'still didn't like it'. Comparable events are by no means infrequent, which may seem most remarkable when works of art are changing hands at far higher prices than ever. Yet, in the case of a truly old canvas, there must often be no other way of establishing who painted it; the expert can only inspect it and say what he thinks, and indeed the very continuance of the market depends on such decisions being generally respected.

Moreover if a supposed Old Master is a modern work that has been artificially aged, van Meegeren showed that this may no longer be detectable even if laboratory tests are applied. Almost certainly, deception of this order had never previously been accomplished. Others had tried, only to be exposed when their work came under general scrutiny, or examination by scientific methods which had not been previously developed. Many forgeries have succeeded which simulated the work of a master who was alive, or recently dead; then detection may depend solely on aesthetics, which are merely a matter of opinion. Van Meegeren achieved success on a completely different level: he secured the acceptance of present-day paintings as seventeenth-century works. Yet the French expert, M. Louis Hertig, expressed a commonly held view when he wrote in *L'Amateur de Peinture:* 'A complete forgery is not frequent; with an old painting it is impossible. . . . To paint today a canvas of the seventeenth century can only end in a piece of work that is not viable.' This may indeed have been the case until van Meegeren, after four years of research, developed his remarkable technique, which required not only chemicals that had not long been available, such as phenol, but patience and expertise such as very few would-be forgers possess. It is true that his later forgeries have deteriorated so greatly in the quarter-century since he painted them that by now they might well have been recognized for what they are, but the very fact that the *Emmaus* and the *Supper* are still held by some to be authentic is one clear indication—and there are many others—that these at least would by now have taken their place in Vermeer's accepted *œuvre* if van Meegeren had not claimed them as his own.

However, since his trial, his working methods and technique have been generally ascertainable (and are set out below in some detail). Scientific examination is in any case seldom thought necessary: not one of the van Meegerens was ever inspected in the laboratory, not even X-rayed, till after his confession, and it is still not a normal practice. But even if this precaution be taken, it now seems likely that the work of a determined forger who follows van Meegeren's general principles may be beyond detection in the present state of knowledge. For a while in the twenties and thirties the laboratory technicians may have been in command as new techniques became available, but van Meegeren succeeded in moving ahead of them and staying there.

It may be argued that this is not so, that his forgeries escaped detection only because they were never properly examined, through lackadaisical complacency or unexplained mass hypnosis, and that their modernity became quickly evident and certainly demonstrable when this was finally done. This is a hard position to hold. The *ad hoc* Commission set up by the Netherlands State in 1946 to examine and pronounce upon the eight supposed forgeries comprised two distinguished art historians, who had primarily concerned themselves with aesthetic values, and three eminent scientists, led by Dr P. B. Coremans, Director of the Central Laboratory of Belgian Museums, who had mainly considered technical aspects and had submitted all the canvases to a long series of advanced laboratory tests over a period of some nine months. Their unanimous opinion, confirmed by two leading British technicians who had been invited to check their findings, was indeed that all eight were modern; and at his subsequent trial van Meegeren (as he ardently desired) was judicially proved to have painted all of them.

However, the laboratory work had been greatly facilitated—as will seldom happen again—by the fact that the forger had co-operatively revealed important details of his technique. The technicians not only knew that there was strong *prima facie* evidence of inauthenticity, which encouraged them to use very special care, but had been told by van Meegeren what particular substances to seek. It is easy to confirm the presence of phenol *if it is expected* (because it turns violet with ferric chloride and produces a white precipitate with bromine water), but it would be the purest luck if such very specific tests were applied when trying to identify unknown or unsuspected substances. It is virtually certain that phenol and formaldehyde—the two most incriminating substances used by van Meegeren—would never have been isolated and recognized if the forgeries had been scientifically examined at the time of sale. Furthermore it is an inescapable and highly significant fact that a rival school of thought, led by the Belgian expert, M. Jean Decoen, has always held, and still holds today, on the basis of precisely the same technical evidence, that two of the canvases, the *Emmaus* and the *Supper*, are not only true Vermeers but among his most notable masterpieces. Decoen and his followers have taken each piece of evidence held by the Coremans Commission to prove them modern, turned it around, examined it in a different way, and shown (or attempted to show) that it could equally well prove nothing of the kind. Moreover Decoen has launched virulent attacks against the personal integrity of Coremans. He has alleged in print, for example, that Coremans sponsored the forging by an unknown hand (not van Meegeren's) of two pictures needed to provide confirmatory evidence for his thesis. The position today, despite the most thorough analysis possible, is still that one school of thought believes two highly important canvases to have been painted by perhaps the greatest master of the seventeenth century, whilst most maintain that they are the work of Han van Meegeren.

It is only out of deference to Decoen and his followers that I have described it as no more than virtually certain that van Meegeren painted all eight. I will examine the conclusions put forward by both sides when they differ, and hope to show that I am fully justified in agreeing with this principal finding of the Coremans school and writing as though it were correct, but the existence of the controversy proves that there cannot always be certainty even in the laboratory. There is total agreement that van Meegeren painted the six others, but it is known that he took progressively less trouble with each succeeding forgery so that even this degree of unanimity springs more from his bad workmanship than from investigating skill.

Van Meegeren's aims and motives cannot be set down with certainty or simplicity. Motivation may always differ widely at different levels of consciousness, especially in as complex, devious and neurotic a person as he was, and may change radically with achievement (or lack of it) and with other changing circumstances. Moreover his own statements, on this as on almost everything else, have to be taken with much reserve, and confirmation sought where possible from verifiable evidence, since he took a pathological delight in misleading investigators. He himself always insisted, and his near family have always maintained, that his original intention was clear and indeed legitimate. His aim, he would say, had been to paint one false canvas that would be indistinguishable, both aesthetically and (more important) technically, from a highly important work by a greatly esteemed seventeenth-century master, and to claim and prove authorship as soon as it had been accepted as such and acclaimed. Thus he believed, or pretended to believe, that he would compel the acceptance of his genius as a creative artist, which he knew had been denied, and at the same time show the ignorance and incompetence of the entire *genus* of art critics, gallery owners, art historians and the like, whom he hated as being responsible for that denial. Money, therefore, would have been no consideration; the picture would have to be sold to prove his point beyond doubt, but the cheque would be returned when he had done so. This, however, he would have found impossible when he suddenly became wealthy for the first time in his life; moreover he had at last found work that satisfied and absorbed him to the point of obsession. He therefore continued until extraneous circumstances forced him to confess—to avoid charges of collaboration as a result of the sale to Goering—as he would have planned to do voluntarily, and for a completely different reason, almost a decade earlier.

There are very considerable difficulties in accepting this thesis. In the first place, it is precisely the story he might well have invented to gain sympathy if his true motive had been the sordid, unintellectual desire to make a dishonest fortune. Moreover it is hard to believe that a man of van Meegeren's character and temperament spent four arduous years on research, and a further six months painting the *Emmaus*, if it were intended to bring him no financial reward but only dubious revenge and vicarious acclaim. However, there is certain evidence, though aspects of it are disputed, to persuade me, on balance, that this was in fact most probably the case, or at least that van Meegeren at his mind's most conscious level believed it to have been. The relevant considerations are as follows. Van Meegeren told the police in 1945 that he had painted the *Emmaus* on an authentic seventeenth-century canvas from which he had removed the original painting (a *Raising of Lazarus* by an unidentified minor contemporary of Vermeer's). It had still been mounted on its original wooden stretcher. For the very purpose of subsequently proving his authorship of the forgery, which he had supposed might be disputed in view of its excellence, he claimed to have cut a vertical strip 'thirty to fifty centimetres wide' from the left-hand edge of the canvas. It had therefore been necessary to shorten by the same amount the two horizontal arms of the stretcher. The sawn-off pieces, together with the strip of canvas, constituted his evidence, since he would hardly have cut down a Vermeer and in any case it is obvious that the *Emmaus*, if painted by Vermeer, would not originally have had more space on one side but not the other. He had left these bits and pieces in his Nice villa before departing, never to return, soon before the outbreak of war in 1939. If the police searched the villa, they would certainly find them there.

The police dispatched a team led by Inspector W. J. C. Wooning, and it has to be admitted that they managed to find (after an interval of six war years) only one of the two stretcher fragments and no strip of canvas. However, the fragment found was 49·6 centimetres long and could be proved, not merely by its general texture and colour but also by the exact coincidence of the annual rings in the timber, to be a continuation of the left-hand extremity of the upper horizontal arm of the original stretcher. As a necessary part of his thesis to prove the *Emmaus* a Vermeer, Decoen simply ignores this highly important evidence,* though to me it proves conclusively that van Meegeren did cut down the *Emmaus* stretcher—and therefore the canvas—by the amount he had stated; it would almost certainly prove authorship but not necessarily that he was planning to *claim* authorship. However, I find it impossible to believe that he would have gone to the trouble involved, which was considerable and would not otherwise have been necessary, and run the useless risk of preserving objects that would have been highly incriminating if found accidentally, unless he intended to use them for the purpose stated, though it is possible to suggest that he retained the evidence for a very different reason of very typical cunning, that if his deceit came to light fortuitously (as was to happen) he would be able to claim this false but more laudable motive. It is impossible to know the truth beyond any doubt, but my feeling is that van Meegeren may have persuaded his own conscience that he was going to admit authorship and must therefore retain evidence,

* See below, pages 164-5.

whilst at the same time, in his innermost heart, he may have known that he was quite unlikely to do so.

This would not necessarily invalidate his supposed belief that he would be proving (as he certainly desired) that he was a great creative artist, and the experts both ignorant and incompetent, thus exacting a terrible revenge from them, though it would mean that he was proving it to himself alone and perhaps some intimate friends, not to all the world. In either case, however, this would be a belief, even though he may indeed have held it, that is at best contentious. In the first place, it seems to contain an inescapable contradiction: if he were indeed a genius, as both artist and chemist, and could therefore produce a truly perfect 'creative' forgery—and he came as near to it with the *Emmaus* as is conceivably possible—then the deception of the critics would have been *ipso facto* forgivable. He could not have it both ways. He would rather have proved, though this would itself have been significant, that it was possible for a modern forger, as probably never before, to create a work that the most important critics and scientists, even if they applied their knowledge with the most consummate skill, would be unable to distinguish from a seventeenth-century masterpiece. (It should be noted that the technical problems were greater than the aesthetic.) It was only with his later fakes, because they were increasingly badly executed but still secured wide acceptance and fetched even higher prices, that he at last—and therefore accidentally—achieved his second aim of demonstrating beyond doubt the extreme fallibility of expert thought, but at the same time this bad latter workmanship was proving him much less than a genius. Moreover it is in any case certainly arguable, some would say it is self-evident, that his ability to paint even as fine a work as the *Emmaus* in fact proves nothing whatever, or at best extremely little, about his talent as an artist.

The artist, it is held, must be a product of his times, showing in his work the influence of the whole previous history of art (which he himself may in turn influence if he is great enough). Indeed Matisse has written: 'I have never avoided the influence of other artists and would have thought it a form of cowardice and insincerity to do so.' One reason for van Meegeren's lack of success in his own right had been that he had failed to develop his undisputed early talent to accord with any accepted principles of current artistic thought. His early training and instilled ideals had been on strictly traditionalist lines: at school in Deventer (the home of de Hoogh) and then at Delft (the home of Vermeer) it was these same masters who had been held up to him as incomparable models. And as a traditionalist, consciously ever-faithful to the standards and values of the seventeenth and eighteenth centuries, he had achieved notable successes in the early years of his career. It may then have been partly that 'like many other talented artists surrounded by worshipping admirers, he fell into easy ways; in consequence his talent failed to mature and his work acquired a superficial character, thereafter rarely overcome'.* It was also that he refused to be influenced, even to the smallest degree, by any of the progressive movements of the twenties and thirties, for whose leaders and followers he expressed contempt, or by any meaningful contemporary thought, but withdrew instead into a reactionary, traditionalist backwater of his own.

It was all very well for him to have fallen as a boy under the spell of such as Rembrandt or Vermeer, just as a romantic student today may feel similarly drawn towards Renoir or Cézanne and at first seek to emulate their style, standards and feeling, but such youthful impulses have to be discarded when they have served their purpose. Instead van Meegeren became, in a manner of speaking, an anachronism: he continued throughout his life to owe allegiance to the Golden Age, refusing to abandon the known world of childhood by jumping into the mainstream, or even a minor tributary, of existing thought or progress. It may thus have been true, whether or not van Meegeren was aware of it, that it was *only* by passing off a canvas of his as the work of Vermeer or his like that he could hope for recognition (which was of special need to one of his insecurity) in respect of a canvas painted by him in accordance with his own outdated desires and principles. It may not be completely fanciful to suggest that he was forced to be Vermeer.

For if he had signed the *Emmaus* with his own name, it would have been of no interest or value and would have attracted no attention. This is not surprising nor reprehensible. There is no contradiction in the fact that almost every mature artist today

---

* P. B. Coremans, *Van Meegeren's Faked Vermeers and de Hooghs* (Amsterdam 1949), page 24.

admires Vermeer but none would dream of trying to paint in any way as he did. The *Emmaus*, if offered in 1937 as a van Meegeren, would have been thought nothing more than an extremely curious oddity: a twentieth-century work bearing no relation to contemporary thought, somewhat reminiscent of Vermeer (though by no means of a 'typical' Vermeer) with undertones of Caravaggio. What gave it a very great part of its value was what it told the beholder *about Vermeer*; no one is the least bit interested in whether Caravaggio influenced van Meegeren. It is also true, as was clearly shown by the prices paid for the later forgeries but as would in any case be generally acknowledged, that much value resides in the fact that a picture is the work of a great master, irrespective of its aesthetic qualities. The latter appear, unfortunately, to be of not much more than minor importance when such a canvas is sold.

Van Meegeren had failed to win acclaim as a great creative artist in his own name. So far from doing so by signing his work with another's, many will hold that he detracted from such reputation as he possessed already by painting over and obscuring his own small identity and achievement with the false colours of Vermeer.

2
The Technique

FROM much that is known of van Meegeren's history, it appears that he had already reached an advanced stage of paranoia by 1932. Violently and increasingly resentful of criticism or opposition since childhood, and a rebel against all authority, he had long suffered from a growing and finally obsessive *folie de grandeur* which had led him, without rational justification, to imagine himself a master and thence to the delusion that his absence of success resulted from a sinister conspiracy against him. These are classical symptoms; but it is perhaps not till he begins actively to plan or later to exact—often with diabolical ingenuity and persistence—his terrible vengeance on those he has convinced himself to be responsible for his plight that a paranoiac progresses to the pathological stage. This will often be shown when bitterness and resentment have so accumulated that the sufferer, perhaps as the immediate result of some trivial straw of adversity or of a chance occurrence that happens to suggest a method of revenge, finally despairs of ever finding the one true rational remedy (whatever it may be) for his feelings of inadequacy and turns instead to an act of violence or outrage, directed against the person or persons or a symbol of them, who are the cause (real or imagined) of his adversity.* Such an act may be unconnected with his plight, as when a jealous husband beats his dog to revenge his wife's infidelity. On the other hand the form chosen may bring revenge in a highly relevant way, as in the case of van Meegeren, who would have convinced himself with the very irrationality that must be a necessary part of such an ambition (since it is the impossibility of a rational solution that has led to it) that he would also be proving himself a great artist, the denial of which by his enemies had itself caused his obsessive hatred of them. This was confirmed at his trial by the psychologist, van der Horst, who

* Oswald's shooting of President Kennedy is given as an example in William Manchester's *Death of a President* (London, 1967).

stated as his opinion: 'The defendant's character leads to sensitiveness to criticism, fed by a revenge complex which explains his anti-social attitudes.'

It was in 1932, soon after his move to the South of France from Holland, that van Meegeren began his four years of advanced research and technical experiment before starting work on his first fake, the *Emmaus*, though there is evidence* that he was thinking of forgery at least a year earlier. It would therefore have been at about this time that his paranoia developed to the pathological stage in which, at last despairing of achieving his true aim in life (acceptance as a great artist) by the one true means (painting a great picture), he turned instead to revenge by the irrational but strongly related means of forgery. It cannot be said with certainty what particular event drove him, perhaps across the shadowy border of insanity, to reach this decision, but an informed guess is possible. He had been living for three years in The Hague with his second wife Johanna (always known as Jo), since their long-delayed marriage in 1929, when they decided on a holiday in Italy and drove there in an old and battered car, the first he had ever owned. They went the rounds of the galleries and he almost certainly saw Caravaggio's *Christ at Emmaus* in Rome. It may have been as he beheld this work, which was to contribute so much to the planning of his deceit,† that the resolve and strength came to him.

The move to the South of France was a direct and unplanned result of the same summer holiday. The car broke down in Roquebrune, a charming village by the sea between Menton and Monaco, and they had to spend the night there; by chance they heard of an attractive villa in the Domaine du Hameau on the mountainside above, the Primavera, which was to let furnished at eighteen shilling a week.‡ They took it on the spot, as the *gérant* of the Domaine, M. de Augustinis, who has a role to play in the drama, still clearly remembers. It is known that van Meegeren was already maddened (I use the word advisedly) by Holland and his life there, by the hostility or indifference of the critics and gallery

* See below, page 25.

† See below, pages 41–2. Caravaggio painted three different versions of the *Emmaus*, one of which is in the National Gallery, London. The version that van Meegeren saw is now in the Brera, Milan.

‡ At the time of writing, the Primavera (plate II) is up for sale; the asking price is £30,000.

owners against whom he had long waged a useless losing war, and by growing moral censure. His accumulated resentment now drove him to decide that they would leave Holland 'for ever' and make their permanent home in the Midi. (In fact they would stay seven years: almost six at the Primavera and thirteen months at the much more splendid villa in Nice, the Estate, which he was to buy from part of the *Emmaus* proceeds.) Mercurial and unpredictable to a fault, he had always been inclined to take important decisions lightly; the move to Roquebrune had been typically impulsive.

Today there are over a hundred villas in the straggling Domaine du Hameau. In 1932 there were only twenty or thirty; the Primavera was still completely secluded—a charming two-floored building, yellow-walled, possessing much feeling and personality, in a garden of roses and orange trees—and looked out from its mountain across the village to the sea. Apart from its delight and his distaste for The Hague, van Meegeren must have believed that a secluded home in a completely changed environment, where no friend might drop in unexpectedly and take for granted the freedom of his studio, would be specially desirable for the work that lay ahead. He and his wife returned to Holland to wind up their affairs there, irremediably crashing the car on the way, abandoning it by the roadside and continuing by train, and came south again in October to move in.

At the sunny Primavera van Meegeren settled down, or so he took pains to make it appear, to the kind of life that might be considered normal for an easy-going artist of middle age—he was now forty-three—with a rather eccentric nature and some unconventional tastes, who had, however, to earn a living like everyone else. His marriage, though it was to remain childless, was reasonably satisfactory: his wife, a former actress, was an attractive and sophisticated woman,* of considerable ambition, perhaps rather masculine and dominant, who had been his leading mistress for more than a decade—and the wife for much of it, significantly enough, of a well-known art critic, Karel de Boer—till their eventual marriage. She was now helping to put some stability into his life, at least by comparison with all that had gone before. After early successes, he had lost ground as a painter: to make ends meet, he had been driven increasingly over the previous decade to commercial work and portraiture, much against his inclination, and

---

* See his portrait of her, plate 19.

the latter now occupied the greater part of his working time. He had to support from the proceeds not only himself and Jo, but also his first wife, Anna, who had divorced him in 1923 after eleven unhappy years—they had married when they were both still students—and her two children by him, who lived with her in Holland and whom he saw only very occasionally. Their holiday had taken all his savings and he had, in any case, an extravagant nature and expensive technical needs. There were a good many possible clients among visitors to the Côte, but he seldom commanded more than forty or fifty guineas for his meticulous, out-of-fashion, photographic likenesses in the manner of a Rembrandt *manqué*, so he would have been painting them steadily throughout these four years.

Han van Meegeren* had (plate 13) developed a difficult and complex personality, riven by insecurity and self-doubt, through the consuming neuroses that may be supposed to have grown in him from the emotional conflicts of his childhood.† His neurotic instability not only made the reassurance of public recognition a specially strong need, but at the same time caused weaknesses in his character, some of which had been largely responsible for his failure to obtain it. These included a general inability to concentrate or persevere, a tendency to leave a canvas unfinished (or a woman no longer loved) and move on to the next one, a need to experiment with many different media and techniques, a proclivity to sudden anger and passionate *rapprochement*, and a total unwillingness to abandon or develop his early artistic principles—all obvious symptoms of a failure to mature. He was vain, moody and aggressive. On the other hand he had a wry and special sense of humour and much charm. His attractiveness to women grew more from his gallantry than from physical attributes. He was of slight build, as he had always been. He had sharp features, with an artist's perceptive eyes, at times arrogant, at times shifty, and equally likely to be illuminated by kindness or embittered by cynicism or resentment. His small moustache was almost Hitlerian and his hair was grey and thinning. He gave small attention to his personal appearance and dressed carelessly, even shabbily, often in dressing-gown and slippers; he would never be noticed in a crowd, but had a knack all the same for giving the impression of being a

* He was christened Henri after his father. Han is a common diminutive form.
† See Chapter 5 below.

master, even though unacknowledged, when occasion demanded. In Roquebrune he was always addressed as *maître*.

Van Meegeren was seeking to escape from an *impasse* in his career which he had reached a decade earlier. Until his late twenties he had by any standards been successful. At Delft he won the coveted gold medal that was awarded for the best painting by any student of the past five years; he was then at once offered a professorship at The Hague Academy, which he declined in order to concentrate solely on creative work. His facile talent and clever draughtsmanship soon won him admirers, especially in high social circles. Moreover his two early one-man shows, in 1916 and 1918, were extremely well received and all his canvases on both occasions were sold. At twenty-nine he had already reached his peak, though this he never realized; when he began to lose ground, critical censure or indifference so worked on his over-sensitive nature that he became less and less able to give of his best, even within the ambit of his own outdated principles. He began to take on commercial work such as posters and Christmas cards, which further lessened his reputation, the more so since they were often banal and vulgar. These and his portraits, which were little more than potboilers,* occupied him increasingly, though from time to time he would come up with a canvas that was original and impressive in its way. He remained a painter's painter, with a real knowledge of methods and techniques, especially those of his too-well-loved Golden Age, and of the history and chemistry of art (which may have led him to his occasional work as a restorer, in which he picked up many useful tricks of the trade), but he had now worked for a decade with little imagination and less inspired thought. Lacking a sufficiently strong creative drive and impulse to succeed, he would almost certainly have continued unnoticed in the same humdrum way until his death if inspiration of a different kind had not come to fire him. In Holland he had turned on those who declined to recognize him as the master he fondly believed himself, but nobody had listened to him.

Some might suppose that van Meegeren, having decided how he would force the world to listen, put everything aside when he had settled down at the Primavera and embarked with obsessive passion on the long technical researches that would lead to revenge and self-justification. However, this seems unlikely; apart from

* See for example his typical *Portrait of Schuh* (plate 20).

the fact that he had to earn a living, he cannot even have known when he started his first tentative experiments if they could possibly succeed. It seems more probable that he began them in rather a *dilettante* way—he had always tended to be *dilettante* in all things—and then gave them more and more of his time as he became engrossed, fascinated and finally possessed by them. If so, it was almost certainly the first time in his life that he was eventually driven by a motive of such strength, which would give further reason for his failure to fulfil his promise, as it would help to bring the pre-eminent success that now lay before him.

Van Meegeren's first need was to find a way of creating a work of art that would be technically indistinguishable, if subjected to the most exacting tests in the laboratory, from a painting three centuries old. He was not yet concerned with the aesthetic requirement, the ability to paint in a style that would be generally accepted as that of Vermeer or de Hoogh, which he was quite confident he possessed. Certain matters would involve him in nothing more than research, in a field with which he was already well acquainted. He knew, for instance, that he would have to paint on canvas made in Vermeer's time, since the age and provenance of the canvas itself can be told with much more certainty than may be guessed about the picture, but he could buy a work of that period—in fact he had bought one already—by a little-esteemed or unknown artist and remove most of the paint from it. This would be difficult and tedious but he thought it should be possible. He would have to use Vermeer's pigments, since these are almost always identifiable by chemical analysis or microscopy if not to the naked eye, but this too should be possible, though often the raw materials—which might not always be easy to obtain and would in some cases, especially the lapis lazuli, be very costly—would have to be ground by hand (as Vermeer's were) so that their particles would be heterogeneous under the microscope. But such considerations, though essential, were elementary, at least when compared with the two particular requirements that he knew to be the most difficult of all. These were, firstly, the creation of hard paint; secondly, the inducement of crackle that would be as similar as possible to the authentic age-crackle of all old oil paintings.

Oil paint gives a superficial impression of being dry within a few days of application; that is, it no longer smears or smudges.

Actually it still contains a high percentage of the medium used and is therefore successfully attacked by solvents. It may be fifty years or more before evaporation is complete. In this long drying process, the diminishing volume of paint on the canvas eventually, and increasingly, causes crackle to appear. Its formation will be accelerated by the contractions and expansions of the canvas and its stretcher, caused by changing temperature and humidity, which will not have affected the paint so long as it retained a sufficient degree of its original elasticity. When crackle forms, each crevice may eventually penetrate not only the surface paint-layer but also any undercoats; this is not invariable but will depend upon the pigments used or on factors such as the quality of the paint. As the process continues, more and more 'islands' of paint are formed; the crevices between them become filled with dust and microscopic debris.

Sometimes crackle appears in a relatively modern painting. This will not have been caused by the slow hardening of the paint but by faulty ingredients; it is usually confined to the surface layer. This 'youth-crackle' is at once identifiable as such.

More than Christ's eyes, more than the love of the Apostles, more than lapis lazuli or gamboge—more important by far than such as these did van Meegeren rightly consider this intricate and unintended pattern of hair-lines in the paint. He was confident of tapping Vermeer's inspiration; he believed that he could create God in his own image. All were to no avail if he failed to induce convincing crackle in the creation.

Hard paint and crackle were two distinct but related requirements. Van Meegeren would have tackled the former first, because the manner of inducing crackle would depend on how the paint was hardened. His initial work in the field of forgery, at first probably occupying him for no more than an occasional idle hour in the course of a working day, had therefore this purely technical end. So far from being devoted, as might be imagined, to trial canvases in the manner of the masters, his craft and ingenuity were first directed towards finding how to make paint dry quickly and completely without discolouration or damage. It was obvious that this could be achieved only by some kind of heating process, and it soon became clear that a very special medium would have to be employed to ensure that colours and paint surface were not adversely affected by the heat necessary to cause the drying of a century in a day. Van Meegeren began by experimenting with orthodox media such as linseed oil or poppy oil, subjecting his trial daubs to varying degrees of heat in his first primitive oven.

It cannot be said with certainty whether he worked in secrecy, which would have increased the strain and tension, or whether his wife already knew what he was doing and could help him with sympathy and encouragement. I can only state the relevant known facts. Van Meegeren maintained that he kept her in ignorance throughout, right up to the time of his long-delayed confession. Moreover he was to depose on oath after his confession that he was 'completely alone' at the Primavera for the six months it took him to paint the *Emmaus*: 'During this whole period,' he stated, 'I sent my wife away because I wanted no witnesses. I required perfect solitude to achieve a work of art that would amaze the world and confound my enemies.' Van Meegeren even described how his wife once returned unexpectedly when the *Emmaus* was in production 'to find out what my *retraite* might mean. She departed after looking over the house, which was completely empty, and took away with her a bathing costume which had been the pretext for the unannounced visit of a suspicious wife.' This has a ring of truth about it and his mentioning of the otherwise irrevelent fact that she found the house empty would indicate that her suspicions had nothing to do with his work. He does not explain how, if she searched the house for a hidden mistress, she failed to find evidence of the *Emmaus*, but he might have had time to hide the unfinished canvas. In any case his insistence that he kept her in ignorance was accepted by the Dutch authorities, who preferred no charges against her as an accessory.

It has to be said on the other hand that the story of the 'bathing costume' is just the kind of tale van Meegeren might well have fabricated to ensure this if his wife had been fully *au fait* from the beginning. Of much greater significance is the firm evidence of the unshakable de Augustinis, then the *gérant* of the Domaine, who now has his own business as an estate agent in Roquebrune. He is absolutely positive that van Meegeren was never alone at the villa for 'more than a day or two at the most' throughout his tenancy. He was on intimate terms with the van Meegerens and would visit the villa, he told me, 'at least once a month'. Furthermore it was stated in print as long ago as 1951, without any ifs or buts, that the story of Madame being sent away was 'invented by our forger in all its details',* and this never evoked a denial. We may therefore take it that she was in fact at the Primavera all the time. This in itself does not prove that she knew what her husband was doing, but it makes it very likely.

There is a final consideration. Van Meegeren had required only a small oven in which to bake his trial daubs. As his experiments proceeded, he would need one that was far larger and more elaborate: the *Emmaus* is about four feet square $(45\frac{1}{2}'' \times 50\frac{1}{4}'')$† and the oven, which was electric, had to hold it comfortably without folding or rolling. Such a large and curious apparatus could not easily have been kept hidden nor its discovered presence explained away. By a strange chance, however, it can be asserted beyond contradiction that the presence of an oven in the basement of the Primavera was known at an early stage not only to Jo van Meegeren but also to all the neighbours and indeed to the local police. It happened that a girl disappeared, under suspicious circumstances, at just this time; villagers noticed a plume of smoke rising from the villa although the weather was warm and jumped to the conclusion that van Meegeren—the strange foreign artist up at the Primavera—had done away with her and was disposing of the body. It was one of his very few pieces of bad luck. The police arrived with a search warrant and found the oven in the basement; they could quickly satisfy themselves that the neighbours' conclusions were baseless and accepted van Meegeren's explanation that he was using the oven for certain technical experiments (as he was). His wife must have known about all this; it was the talk of Roquebrune.

However, whilst I hold it to be indisputable that at some stage she became aware, perhaps accidentally, of the nature of his work, it cannot be said when or how this happened.

Whether in solitude or with his wife's knowledge and aid, van Meegeren had to proceed by slow trial and error, since he was exploring an unknown field and had no precedents of any kind to follow. It is known that he was helped to some extent by a book on Vermeer's technique by the greatly esteemed Dutch expert, Dr A. M. de Wild. (De Wild, alas, has a clownish role to play. He was a member of the government committee that advised the Netherlands State to buy van Meegeren's least good forgery, the

---

* J. Decoen, *Back to the Truth* (Rotterdam, 1951), page 22.
† The vertical measurement is always given first.

Washing of Christ's Feet, as a Vermeer; he was then a member of the Coremans Commission which found it and the rest to be indisputably fakes; finally, at the trial, he was to claim with pride, to the vast amusement of the Court, that van Meegeren's success had largely been derived 'from my treatise on Vermeer'.) Of greater help to him was a book by Professor Alex Eibner, *Ueber Fette Oele*. When van Meegeren first tried orthodox media, the paint dried quickly in the oven but he found that the colours lost their brilliance or were changed, or the paint surface was marred by blisters or scorching, or very often both; several canvases caught fire. From Eibner's book he came to realize that essential (i.e. volatile) oils, such as oil of lilacs and oil of lavender, would evaporate more quickly and completely, and tend to have less effect on the paint surface, than the usual fatty oils he had been using. In many months of work he had made small progress; this discovery was an important step forward, but results still fell short of the standard he was seeking.

So, in due course, van Meegeren turned to chemistry. Had he not done so, and had he then not made a completely original discovery which led to a process that no one previously had so much as considered, his entire programme would almost certainly have failed. This, indeed, was the necessary step forward to make possible, almost certainly for the first time ever, such deception as he planned. His problem may be stated simply as the conversion of a liquid to a solid, more precisely as the conversion of a rather volatile liquid—the Vermeer pigments combined with essential oil—to an extremely hard solid without affecting the colours. This led him to examine the growing field of synthetics. His research brought him the knowledge that a new substance, bakelite, had recently been developed which was exceedingly hard though largely employing synthetic chemical liquids. (The first bakelite patent had been taken out by the American chemist, L. H. Baekeland, in 1907, but the product was only now becoming generally available.) Van Meegeren found that bakelite is a carbon compound made from phenol and formaldehyde; phenol (carbolic acid) had first been discovered, in coal tar, in 1834, and formaldehyde was synthetically developed later in the century. The inspired thought came to van Meegeren that if a solution of these two substances could lead to bakelite, they might help him to harden his paint to the extreme degree required. This, it should be emphasized, was a pure invention of his; their use in painting, as an artificial resin, was unprecedented.

So much progress has since been made in plastics that it would now probably be possible to evolve a technique even more successful than van Meegeren's; it is in this direction that today's would-be forger should direct his researches.

The incorporation of a phenolformaldehyde resin with essential oil at once gave van Meegeren much encouragement, though long further experimentation would still be necessary. He began by dissolving the resin in benzene or turpentine and then had to discover how, and in what proportions, the resultant brownish liquid should be combined with which oil. And he now found a new problem emerging: he had to keep his paint manageable, for it tended to dry too quickly owing to the presence of the resin. The precise way in which van Meegeren dealt with this is not known with certainty since two different versions exist.

Coremans holds the view that he would make up a quantity of the full formula in advance, consisting therefore of phenolformaldehyde, dissolved in benzene or turpentine, and the essential oil (he specified 'synthetic lavender oil and/or synthetic lilac oil'), and 'by incorporating various pigments in this liquid, a paint was obtained which was easily handled with a brush'.* There is supporting evidence: two bottles containing solutions of phenolformaldehyde with an oil were to be found by the police in his studio. On the other hand the forger's son, Jacques, himself a painter and well acquainted with his father's techniques, has given me a somewhat different version. His father, he said, would make up his paints by incorporating the required pigments in oil of lilacs (not lavender) and have these ready on his palette. He would prepare separately the correct solution of resin. Then, with each stroke, he would dip his brush in the phenolic solution before taking up the prepared paint from his palette and applying it to the canvas. I prefer the latter version because less danger would exist of a quantity of prepared paint drying hard on the palette, owing to the excessive presence of resin in it, before he had time to apply it. But in fact it seems likely that van Meegeren had no hard and fast rules but employed different methods at different times and may well have used both those described.

* Coremans, op. cit., page 20.

An obvious risk might be thought to lie in the use of phenol and formaldehyde because neither substance was discovered till the nineteenth century. This does not seem to have worried van Meegeren, and his nonchalance would be justified. Not one of the forgeries was ever subjected, as far as is known, to chemical analysis of any kind before his confession. In any case, as he knew, so much of the resin would evaporate in the very complete drying process that only the smallest traces would be left. Besides, as I have indicated, it would be extremely hard to identify the presence of either incriminating substance unless it were suspected, and this would be exceedingly unlikely. Moreover their presence, when eventually confirmed in the paint of his *Last Supper*, would fail to convince van Beuningen that the painting was modern. He and his followers calmly asserted that van Meegeren, in the course of restoring it, must have repainted extensive areas—including the signature, which is admitted to be a forgery—and used the chemicals when doing so, which seems a curious suggestion; for work of that kind they would not have been necessary. Furthermore the conclusiveness of the tests by which the resin's presence was established has in any case been disputed. Decoen quotes the comments of M. Charles Meurice, Director of the Institut Meurice de Chimie in Brussels:

It is established that the synthetic resin found in van Meegeren's studio is coloured violet by means of a solution of sulphuric acid containing one per cent of vanillin [and] that the greater part of the paint on the canvases examined [by the Coremans Commission] possesses the same qualities. The conclusion of the Commission that the canvases were painted with synthetic resin by van Meegeren is a hasty conclusion because (a) a large number of old paintings produce similar reactions and (b) the reaction is not specifically that of phenolic resins, which prove nothing under these conditions, but of products mixed with phenolic resins, which deprives the reaction of every value.*

This statement is of importance even if it shows only that eminent chemists can differ basically on their interpretation of such elementary tests where complete unanimity would be expected and therefore detracts further from the whole supposed value of laboratory examination. Of Meurice's two reasons for dismissing the official conclusion, the second seems nothing more than a quibble. As to the first, it is only possible to marvel that the

* ibid. page 18.

opinions of chemists are apparently as subjective, as inexact and as arguable as those of art historians.

Using phenolformaldehyde and an essential oil, van Meegeren began obtaining such promising results that he must have felt certain of being at last on the right lines. He had found a way, after perhaps two years' work, of keeping his paint manageable, and it dried completely if baked for about two hours at $105°$ Centigrade, leaving a very hard residue which was not attacked successfully by any ordinary solvent. Indeed it is now held by some—though this is disputed by others—that he performed his task too well. This opinion, put forward by the Commission, is based on the assertion that a drop of caustic potash (hydroxide of potassium) which causes old paint to desaponify—and therefore to decompose—has no effect whatever on van Meegeren's forgeries. But once again the experts are at odds. Meurice states categorically that though 'the greater number of old canvases do not stand up to the action of hydroxide of potassium, the fact is far from being general'.* Moreover Decoen has published macrographs† which certainly do appear to prove not only that paint from the forgeries was frequently desaponified by the caustic, but also that paint from certain undisputed old paintings, including works by Rubens and Fabritius, was often in no way affected by it. This must again indicate to the layman, and indeed to the professional, either that knowledge in the technical field is far less perfect than he imagined, or that eminent scientists and art historians are ready to state conclusions that they know to be false if it happens to suit their purposes. Van Meegeren, perhaps not aware of the dangers of overhardness, was content to satisfy himself that the paint was hard enough; he had next to tackle discolouration. It must now therefore have become necessary, if it had not been before, to use Vermeer's pigments.

Virtually all pigments nowadays are synthetic and may be identified. Because they were unknown three centuries ago, their detected presence would prove a painting modern unless it could be seen that they had been used only in subsequent restoration. Van Meegeren had therefore to obtain the raw materials and manufacture his pigments as Vermeer did. Much the most important were the blues, the yellows and the white—above all the blues.

* ibid.   † Decoen, op. cit., plates 178–201.

Vermeer sometimes used indigo, but his most notable blue—indeed his most notable single colour—was ultramarine. This is nowadays always prepared by synthesis: sodium chlorate is heated with kaolin, charcoal and sulphur. Vermeer made it from powdered lapis lazuli and van Meegeren would have to do the same; this presented a special difficulty because the pigment is very expensive and in fact was not easy to obtain in the quantities he needed.

In his statement to the police, van Meegeren said he obtained lapis lazuli 'in the early part of 1931' from Winsor and Newton, the leading London colourmen, who were able to confirm that four separate quantities of natural ultramarine had been sold, totalling $12\frac{1}{2}$ ounces, during that period. The pigment is in such extremely rare demand that van Meegeren is assumed to have been the customer on each occasion, though his name never appeared in the firm's records. He had always enjoyed making his own paints but would hardly have incurred this expense—the price, even then, was four guineas an ounce—simply for the pleasure of painting an ordinary picture with powdered lapis lazuli, when synthetic ultramarine is almost indistinguishable except under the microscope. It is this that indicates he may already have been thinking of forgery then, though he did not start active research for something over a year. Winsor and Newton inform me that they have now been unable to manufacture genuine ultramarine for 'about thirty years', because 'the raw materials occur in only a few remote parts of the world and not all of it is suitable for the preparation of the pigment'. It was supplied, they say, in powder form and it is 'virtually certain' that van Meegeren would then have ground it by hand, to ensure that the particles would not be too homogeneous. Van Meegeren used ultramarine copiously in his forgeries and had to use it in his experiments, since the synthetic product would react differently to chemicals and heat; this must have cost him dear but was inescapable.

Indigo, too, is now almost always synthetic but some natural indigo is still made*—from the juice of certain plants, among them *isatis tinctoria*, used by the ancient Britons for woad—and this would have been quite easily obtainable.

Vermeer's yellows were usually gamboge and yellow ochre: the

---

* I have watched its manufacture in the Yemen, where it is a favourite dye and is also used cosmetically.

former is obtained from resinous gum (also used as a purgative) and the latter, like all ochres, from a native earth which has to be ground and washed. These presented no particular problem. For his white, van Meegeren used white lead, as Vermeer did; this was a paint of special importance because it is the most susceptible to crackle and at the same time the least likely to be penetrated by X-rays. Its drawbacks are that it is poisonous and easily becomes discoloured; zinc white has neither of these characteristics and is nowadays always preferred, but it was unknown till the late eighteenth century and therefore could not be used. For his vermilion van Meegeren had to obtain cinnabar, which is an ore containing mercury; his bright red was burnt sienna (that is, hydrated ferric oxide, manganese dioxide and earthy matter, heated) and he also used Venetian red. His black, which he used sparingly, was carbon black; for his browns he manufactured burnt umber (by calcining umber, an earth containing manganese and hydrated oxides, after washing and drying). All the raw materials necessary for the pigments so far mentioned were to be found by the police in his studio in 1945, so it may be said with certainty that all were used by him. He is believed also to have made carmine, the vividly red pigment obtained by boiling cochineal and adding acid salt, and others such as green earth, whose presence may be suspected in the forgeries, but not proved with certainty by chemistry.

If the pigments used by van Meegeren had been analysed at the time of sale (a safeguard that is almost never taken) one of the forgeries—and one only—could have been revealed as such at once. When painting Christ's robe in the *Adulteress*, he carelessly allowed cobalt blue to contaminate his ultramarine. This pigment, which he must have had in his studio for quite a different purpose, was unknown till the nineteenth century; its presence—discovered by the Coremans Commission—would at once have given the show away if Goering's men had analysed the paint, even superficially. Cobalt was also found in one of the unsold trial forgeries, *Woman Reading Music*, which must also have simply been due to carelessness.

Such identification presents no difficulty with many pigments, especially those such as natural ultramarine that are recognizable to the naked eye or beyond doubt under the microscope, or to a lesser degree those identifiable by spectrography. These include cobalt blue, for the simple reason that it contains cobalt, a well-known and easily verifiable element. The same applies to white lead. Other pigments cannot be so easily detected but have known reactions to certain specific tests. The presence of natural vermilion, for example, may be confirmed by its positive reaction to mercury. Indigo shows its presence 'by partial solubility in nitrobenzene and its discolouration by chlorine', and gamboge by 'the brownish shade obtained with caustic alkali', to quote the official report. Van Meegeren, though an accomplished chemist, may not have known the details of such tests—he was to say ironically at his trial that he found them 'even more extraordinary than the fact that I painted the *Emmaus*'—but he was well aware that they existed.

As has been indicated, the manufacture of many Vermeer pigments was nothing new to van Meegeren. His first teacher, Bartus Korteling, at High School in Deventer, had taught him to despise those who bought their paints ready-made and synthetically prepared. An artist of the old school, Korteling made a point of preparing his own in the manner of Vermeer and encouraged his pupils to do likewise. So if it was Korteling who was indirectly largely responsible for van Meegeren's failure to achieve mature success in his own name, owing to his enduring inability to throw off the traditionalist principles which he had so firmly implanted in him at such an impressionable age, it was also Korteling who had given him much valuable knowledge and experience to put him well on the road to success of a different kind in a project aimed largely at justifying those principles.

When he had assembled sufficient quantities of the most important pigments required, a process which must have given his workroom on the top floor of the Primavera more the appearance of a paint factory than of an artist's studio, van Meegeren patiently continued his experiments until he discovered the exact proportions in which his formula should be combined with them to ensure that no colour would alter in the heating process and also the precise temperature to which they should be subjected and for how long. It was now necessary to consider in detail the difficult and delicate question of crackle, which he knew to be all-important. Crackle of a kind would have appeared spontaneously in parts of the paint surface during experimental baking, owing to the inevitable contraction involved in all evaporation, but it would have been neither uniform nor general, and would seldom have given the true appearance of 'age-crackle'. Moreover, van Meegeren had so far been applying his paint to unused strips of modern canvas; new questions might arise when he used an old one.

His plan at this stage was to obtain a painting by a minor Dutch master of the seventeenth century, remove as much as possible of the ancient paint from it, and then re-use the canvas for his forgery so that it at least could give no possible grounds for suspicion. It was when he began experimenting with paint-removal that he hit upon his highly ingenious solution to the major part of the crackle problem. He was assuming at this stage that he would have to remove the old paint as completely as possible so that no part of it would be visible if the subsequent forgery were X-rayed. Later when he found that on no occasion was it held necessary to check authenticity even by this elementary though not necessarily conclusive test, he saw no reason for useless labour and left large visible areas of the originals: a hunting scene under the *Last Supper*, for example, and a battle with horses and riders under the *Adulteress*, both clearly visible in radiographs (see plates 29 and 33). This was not so foolhardy as it may seem, firstly because X-rays are rather surprisingly seldom used to check supposed Old Masters, and secondly because the detection of an underpainting is, as surprisingly, no positive indication that a painting is false. This is clearly shown by the fact that X-rays have revealed an underpainting in the case of at least one Vermeer which still holds its place of honour with an unequivocal attribution. However, van Meegeren was now still a perfectionist and hoped to remove all traces of the underpainting. He would have to leave intact the bottommost layer—that is, the original ground—since it would be impossible to remove all the old paint down to the very canvas, which would be frail and vulnerable. From this fact, the thought came to him that if he could remove all the paint *except the original ground* in such a way that the crackle in the latter stayed as far as possible intact, he might be able to induce new crackle of an identical or largely identical pattern, which must therefore give a completely authentic appearance, in the paint layer or layers to be imposed on it.

Both parts of this programme presented great difficulties and nothing provides better evidence of van Meegeren's obsessive persistence, ingenuity and skill than the quite remarkable degree of success achieved. The removal of the surface paint was an operation of extreme delicacy and it is still not known exactly how he did it. It has been said that he used solvents, but these would have had to be powerful to attack the old paint and there would have been a serious danger that they would at least partially obliterate the vital crackle in the ground. I was told by Jacques van Meegeren that his father used soap and water with pumice stone, and this may well have been so, but it would have been an extremely long and tedious process even if assisted by a palette knife, a chisel, or some other similar instrument. It would probably have been a question of tackling each individual paint-island in turn, and of these, in a large canvas, there would be hundreds or even thousands.

Having achieved his aim by one method or the other, or by a combination of both, van Meegeren found, as he had hoped, that if he covered the exposed ground with a fairly thin paint layer and baked it, the original crackle would largely reappear. This so-called levelling layer was intended to provide a smooth surface for him to work on. Van Meegeren then found that the same crackle could be persuaded to reappear if he applied a second paint layer and baked it. Coremans refers to this as a 'cellular' layer and describes its purpose as being to 'assist the age crackle on the old canvas in forcing its way to the surface of the modern paint'.* Van Meegeren must next have painted, on surfaces thus prepared, a series of trial compositions using the Vermeer pigments, the essential oil and the resin; he need have taken no pains with these aesthetically since they were for technical purposes only. He found when he baked these that the original crackle would still reappear spontaneously in much of the new pictorial surface layer, though this would be less likely to occur in areas where the paint had been thickly applied.

For induced crackle to be completely perfect, its surface pattern should include *all* the authentic crackle present in the ground. Not only would it then seem equally authentic to the naked eye, but radiographs could give no suspicious indications. It is in this field, rather than in the revelation of underpaintings, that X-rays may be of greatest value in testing authenticity, though even here interpretation is unexpectedly subjective and may therefore be inconclusive. As evidence of this strange fact, it is only necessary to

* Coremans, op. cit., page 16.

mention that the same radiographs of crackle in the *Emmaus* and the *Supper* were held by Coremans to contribute evidence that they were painted by van Meegeren, but by Decoen that they were painted by Vermeer.

In this case, Decoen's opinion need not to taken very seriously. He begins by telling of a meeting with van Meegeren at which the latter was asked how he produced the crackle in the *Emmaus*, and replied: 'I painted over an old canvas and the crackle still visible is that of the old picture.' His questioner then asked him: 'So there is still an old picture underneath it?' Van Meegeren replied in the negative; he had 'scraped it away completely'. Decoen comments: 'Upon this blatant contradiction, the hearing was closed.'

It is not, of course, a contradiction at all, and it is hard to understand why Decoen reacted so foolishly to a quite obvious statement of truth, for he records with some kind of pride that he went on to assail the forger with these words: 'Listen, van Meegeren, you will probably fool many people but you can't fool me.' It was rather that Decoen was making a fool of himself, the more so for later putting it in print. Van Meegeren had merely said, with perfect accuracy, that he had scraped away the old *picture*. This would not include the original ground layer (in which the crackle was duplicated) which he had been most careful to preserve, as Decoen well knew. He later implies that the suggested technique is impossible: 'Could van Meegeren have reproduced all the crackle of the *Lazarus* in the composition of the *Disciples* though the entire painting had been removed?' he asks. 'By what kind of miracle did he preserve, intact and visible, all the crackle over the whole surface of the canvas?' But fortunately, three pages later, with the inconsistency of which he is often guilty, he himself admits that precisely such an effect, miracle or not, could in fact be achieved. 'Of the reproductions of *Isaac Blessing Jacob*,' he writes, 'the first reveals a network of crackles which have an excellent appearance. This indeed is as it must be since they are those of the authentic picture *which have all reappeared.*'*

Crackle will often not be visible at all in X-rays except in a few small areas, especially those where use has been made of a mineral pigment such as white lead. If, where crackle is to be seen, the pattern coincides exactly with that visible in the surface layer, no suspicion can possibly arise. If there are some crevices in the

---

* My italics; Decoen, op. cit., page 31.

surface crackle that are not reproduced in those sections of the radiograph where crackle is visible, there may well be an innocent explanation: these particular crevices, as is sometimes the case, may never have extended to the ground. On the other hand it would be highly suspicious if there were proved to be crackle in the ground that was not reproduced in the surface paint, since it is known that in the normal way it appears first in the latter and works its way downward, not *vice versa* as van Meegeren was inducing it to do.

If, however, some crevices had existed in the ground and van Meegeren failed to persuade these to reappear on the surface, they might well not be detectable in a radiograph, or only as very hazy lines, because their failure to reappear would probably be due either to the crevices being very small, or to the surface paint layer having been too thickly applied, or both. Such otherwise damning evidence might therefore go unnoticed.

Whether or not van Meegeren was aware of this use of radiography (and its many limitations), it must have been obvious to him that he could not hope to achieve the perfect result but must try to get as close to it as possible. If there were areas in the visible surface layer where it seemed that the original crackle had not sufficiently reappeared after heating (and he had no X-ray equipment with which to check this), he could induce additional surface crackle by embossment—that is, by rolling the canvas round a cylinder, bending it back and forth, or often by pressing the back of it with his thumb. Crevices so induced, he found, had a lucky, co-operative tendency to correspond with those underneath that had not spontaneously reappeared. Others might not so correspond, but this, as I have indicated, would not lead to suspicion if the whole surface crackle still possessed a pattern that gave an authentic appearance.

With much practice, van Meegeren became extremely adept in inducing crackle by both these means. And he made an important discovery. He found that if he covered the whole baked surface with a thin layer of varnish, and let this dry naturally, it greatly improved the efficiency of his technique: crackle appeared more quickly and with greater uniformity. The varnish had another important function. Van Meegeren had somehow to ensure that each crevice in his induced crackle-pattern appeared to be filled with the dust and débris of three centuries. He accomplished this as follows. The layer of varnish would itself take on the crackle-pattern. He would cover it—the entire varnished surface—with a layer of Indian ink. If he allowed this to dry naturally and then removed the varnish—and therefore almost all the ink—with alcohol or turpentine, he found that sufficient ink penetrated through the crevices in the varnish to the crevices in the paint and remained there. This ink he discovered to be almost indistinguishable from dust, though it was rather too homogeneous to be perfect. He knew that the hardened paint surface could not be affected by the action of the solvent used; if any ink had unintentionally seeped through to it, he could remove it with soap and water. Finally van Meegeren would apply a new coat of varnish, which Coremans describes as having 'a slightly brownish colour for the benefit of those who prefer their varnish tinted'.*

As things were to turn out, it was this use of Indian ink—rather than the artificial resin, rather than the radiographs, rather than the induced crackle—that first indicated to the investigating Commission in 1946 that the works under examination were indeed likely to be forgeries. The scientists noticed the blackish substance in the crackle and at first took it to be 'genuine' dust and dirt. However, it was then found to be 'of a homogeneous nature, quite different from the heterogeneous type of dirt normally found in the crackle network of old paintings. A study of these crevices in the *Head of Christ* (with the aid of a binocular) proved—e.g., in the forehead of Christ—that they were soaked with a bluish liquid which had diffused into the white lead paint on either side of the crackle. This implied that the paint was porous and that the medium could not be a fatty substance. This naturally led to further investigations and the results showed a definite analogy between the substance of the crevices of the *Head* and in the other pictures . . . Suspicion was aroused.'† This had not needed very great technical skill and it would be remarkable that it had escaped the attention of those who saw the pictures before their respective sales, were it not for the fact that they seem never to have been examined with any attention at all. The mistake made by van Meegeren, which could thus well have led to his undoing, was that he failed to realize that his use of a volatile medium, of which he would have had little or no practical experience, but which was

* Coremans, op. cit., page 21.   † ibid., page 7.

necessary for the technical reasons already given, would result in a paint more porous than he realized. The ink would therefore seep into it to an unforeseen extent. If this had ever been noticed, it would almost certainly have been fatal to him, since no rational explanation could have been offered for the presence of ink in the crackle of a Vermeer.

Having progressed thus far in his long and arduous experimentation, van Meegeren at last reached the moment, in 1934 or more probably 1935, when he felt ready to start work on a series of increasingly careful trial forgeries. These probably included the four canvases never offered on the market, which were to be found by Wooning a decade later in his long-abandoned Nice villa. It is possible that one or two of these were painted after the *Emmaus*, but Coremans indicates that all four date most probably from 1935-6* and circumstantial evidence confirms this. One of these was a *Woman Drinking* (30¾″ × 26″) in the manner of Hals and signed *F.H.* (plate 6); one was a small unfinished *Portrait of a Man* (12″ × 9¾″), unsigned, but clearly intended as a Terborgh (plate 5). The two others were also unsigned but were obviously after Vermeer. They were a *Woman Reading Music* (22½″ × 19″) and a *Woman Playing Music* (25″ × 19¼″)—the latter unfinished (plates 1 and 4).

All four were painted on genuine old canvases from which all but the original ground had been carefully removed; in all, the phenolformaldehyde formula had been used before baking, and crackle had been induced quite satisfactorily. Moreover only seventeenth-century pigments had been used, except for the cobalt in *Woman Reading*. The fact that van Meegeren made no attempt to sell any of them, even though the two 'Vermeers' in particular may be considered most successful, is of considerable significance, especially since the likely reasons provide confirmatory indications of his motives and intentions.

The 'Hals' and the 'Terborgh' are little more than sketches. Coremans was to describe the former as being 'reminiscent of *Malle Bobbe*', adding that it is 'as good as any of the works of Hals' pupil, Judith Lyster', whilst of the latter he wrote that 'the expression of the face is excellent, but the texture leaves much to be desired'.† But neither, however admirable, could be considered a major work. Their suppression by van Meegeren would confirm

* ibid., page 28.   † ibid., page 38.

the supposition that his aim at this stage was to create a forgery that would be accepted not merely as the work of a great seventeenth-century master but as an extremely significant work of his. These could have had no such pretensions and probably van Meegeren was no more than amusing himself and was primarily concerned with observing the effect of his ageing process on more or less finished canvases which embodied the right pigments.

The two false Vermeers are in a different category. Both are carefully painted and excellent compositions. It has been suggested that van Meegeren may not have been satisfied with their technical quality and it is true that the crackle in *Woman Playing* appears to be crude and gives the definite impression (with the great benefit of hindsight) that it was created by rolling the canvas, rather than that it developed spontaneously in the heating process, as is much more desirable. Coremans goes so far as to write that 'although the photograph may give it the appearance of being a good work, the texture of the painting can mislead no one'.* In *Woman Reading*, as already mentioned, cobalt had been used, but van Meegeren may not have been aware of this. Otherwise it was painted with extreme technical care: when subjected in 1946 to microscopic examination in fluorescence, it was found to have no fewer than seven different paint layers. The bottom two were undercoats of the original work that van Meegeren had removed. The third, which was dark grey, may have been another such undercoat or a levelling layer applied by van Meegeren; the technicians could not establish which. The fourth, fifth and sixth layers, denoted as sub-layers by the Commission, were described as follows: 'Layer 2a, greyish, contained white lead, an unidentified pigment responsible for the greyish hue and artificial resin (bluish-white fluorescence). Layers 2b and 2c, whitish, also contained white lead and resin, and their fluorescences were respectively whitish and vivid white.'† The topmost layer was varnish.

It seems quite likely that either of these, if offered on the market, might well have won acceptance, and I imagine that van Meegeren must have thought of trying his luck. Instead he determined to be just that much more clever, thus showing his resolute

* Coremans, op. cit., page 38.
† From the official report, quoted by Coremans, ibid. page 18.

determination to produce nothing less than a highly important work of special historical interest and significance. For, in both, the composition and subject-matter were *precisely* those a run-of-the-mill forger might have chosen: they were *too much like* the accepted notion of a Vermeer.

In the unfinished *Woman Playing Music*, a seated girl is tuning a stringed instrument; a mirror reflects the back of her head, the floor tiles, and part of the still life on the table beside her—a music sheet and a bowl of fruit. There is a typical Vermeer light-source: an unscreened window on the left of the canvas. It is rather a pleasing work with many reminders of Vermeer: in particular, it has points of exact comparison with the *Music Lesson* (in Buckingham Palace)*—the mirror, its shadows, the reflected tiles, the window, the window-frames, the table covering. In *Woman Reading Music*, a girl is seated in profile at a desk: on the wall behind her is a large framed picture which Coremans identifies, erroneously, as the van Baburen *Procuress* that appears in two true Vermeers. He goes on to comment: 'The quality of this work is good; its composition is inspired partly by various real Vermeers and especially by the *Woman in Blue* in the Rijksmuseum.'† In fact it is much more than 'inspired' by it; the girl's face is an almost exact copy, even down to the hair ribbon, though van Meegeren added a pearl necklace and ear-rings; and she is wearing an almost identical dress. As in the original, which is widely held to represent Vermeer's wife, she appears moreover to be pregnant (compare plates 1 and 3).

Thus van Meegeren had painted two fakes whose subject matter and general appearance would be much more readily associated with Vermeer than those he would offer for sale. Yet, with the audacity of genius, he was to discard them in favour of the gigantic double bluff that was to be directly responsible, more than any other single factor, not only for acceptance but for eventual success at an unprecedented level. He reached the conscious decision that if he were to achieve his aim to the fullest, he would have to create a *new kind* of Vermeer, significantly different from any other painting in the master's accepted *œuvre*. Thus, firstly, his talent as a creative artist would be allowed more play—talent, it must be remembered, that he specially hoped to prove, if only to himself. Secondly, for the very reason that it would be absurdly

· * Plate 35.   † Coremans, op. cit., page 38.

improbable for a forger to turn out a false Vermeer that was reminiscent of no real one in subject matter or style, the possibility of it being thought a modern fake was less likely to be seriously considered. Thus the *Emmaus* was conceived.

3
The Emmaus

VAN MEEGEREN took his wife on a long-planned holiday, the first for four years, in the summer of 1936. Despite the researches which had increasingly occupied him since the move from The Hague, and which he now thought completed, he had continued with his portraiture and had in fact probably been earning more than at any period of his career, so for the first time in his life he had some money saved. This was necessary not only to pay for the holiday—they went to Berlin for the Olympic Games, a rather unexpected choice—but also because on his return he would be earning nothing whilst he painted the *Emmaus*. He was to put all else aside for the half-year it occupied him.

I have given my reasons for rejecting van Meegeren's statement that he sent his wife away for this whole period. Either he or de Augustinis must have been lying: the latter had no reason, whilst van Meegeren had every reason to do so. Moreover it is hard to imagine the middle-aged, undomesticated, disorganized van Meegeren living alone for months in the villa, performing the household chores and fending for himself, at any time—least of all when a work of such undoubted importance as the *Emmaus* was demanding so much of him. Whether his wife knew what he was doing is a matter for conjecture, but in view of the close relationship that existed between them it would be most remarkable if she didn't.

Van Meegeren's trial canvases had been in the manner of three different masters, but he must have come to realize that Jan Vermeer of Delft was now his perfect victim from every point of view. As perhaps the most highly esteemed of all his contemporaries, Vermeer presented the greatest challenge; he also offered the greatest rewards, financial or other, if he succeeded. He was already intimately acquainted with his work and technique. But there were more subtle reasons, of greater importance, for choosing him in preference to all others.

Vermeer was christened in Delft in 1632; his birth is unrecorded. When he died, at 43, he was completely unesteemed; it is therefore not surprising that very little is known of him. Over twenty canvases were left on his hands at his death and had to be sold quickly to pay his many debts; they fetched very little. Nor did his reputation soon improve. For two centuries his canvases could be more easily sold if falsely (or mistakenly) offered as the work of such better-known contemporaries as Terborgh, de Hoogh, or van Mieris. An eighteenth-century collector would have been most unhappy to learn that the supposed de Hoogh for which he had paid handsomely was the work of Vermeer, of whom he had never heard, yet now these positions are reversed; so much for the universality of artistic values, which simply does not exist. It was not until two hundred years had gone by that Vermeer was first seriously noticed—one could almost say discovered—by the French critic Thoré (writing under the pseudonym of Bürger) in 1866; almost solely as a result of his enthusiasm, Vermeer's work began slowly to be sought after, but even in 1882 one of his most beautiful pictures, the *Girl with Pearl Eardrops* (plate 36), was sold at public auction, almost unbelievably, for less than five shillings. Now that two centuries of non-recognition and false ascription had gone by, many of his canvases had simply disappeared (because not greatly valued) and with others it was necessary to decide, solely on the basis of intuitive judgments, whether they were Vermeers.

All this was greatly to van Meegeren's advantage. It largely accounts for the fact that so few works are today attributed with certainty to Vermeer. An exact figure cannot be given because the experts are much at variance: many canvases (such as the *Allegory of the Old Testament* and the *Girl with a Red Hat*) are accepted by some but spurned by others. Goldscheider accepts only thirty-seven;* even of these, half a dozen have been disputed. It is almost certain that Vermeer painted far more than thirty or forty canvases in over twenty years, though his business as an art dealer occupied much of his time, and it has therefore always been assumed that many unrecognized paintings of his must be in existence. If a family or museum has for two or three centuries owned an acknowledged Rembrandt, it will always have been prized, remembered and handed down as such. In the case of a Vermeer,

* In the Phaidon, *Vermeer* (London, 1958; revised edition 1967).

acquired perhaps in the mid-eighteenth century when he was quite unknown, with a doubtful or erroneous attribution, or with no attribution at all, it is very possible that no suspicion of its true authorship will have occurred to the owner: it is now firmly considered as 'school of de Hoogh', or 'by an unknown master', or the like, and there is no particular reason why he should ever stop to wonder if it is in fact a long-lost and greatly sought-after Vermeer. Signatures are not of great importance but the fact that Vermeer signed rather few of his works—not more than twenty-five of those accepted by Goldschneider—would make it less likely that they be recognized or noticed. Expert thought is therefore disposed to accept the discovery of a new Vermeer perhaps more readily than of any other comparable master.

Given all these circumstances and having therefore chosen Vermeer, van Meegeren next came to consider the very important question of the general and particular subject he would have Vermeer portray. It was here that he showed his genius. Vermeer is best known for his genre painting and portraiture: in fact, practically all his uncontested work falls within that category. *The Lace Maker*, *The Love Letter*, *The Milkmaid*—these are the typical Vermeer subjects. However, one biblical work is attributed to him, though some have held that it was painted by his namesake, Jan van der Meer of Utrecht: the *Christ with Martha and Mary* in the National Gallery, Edinburgh. This work was the cornerstone of van Meegeren's whole conspiracy. He knew that it had been largely through none other than Dr Bredius that the *Martha and Mary* (plate 8) was now widely accepted as being by Jan Vermeer of Delft, even though it is remarkably different in style as well as subject from any other work of his. Bredius first saw it in 1901 'in the shop window of a London art dealer', as he himself has recounted it, and 'recognized Vermeer in it'.* This was made more easy by the fact that the signature (*I. V. Meer*, but with the initials arranged in a different monogram from that used by van Meegeren) had just for the first time been mysteriously discovered after two and a half centuries. There was at once much argument and discussion, not only because the attribution was disputed, but also because, if it were a Vermeer, this would be of great and special significance to all the art historians: there was

* *Oud-Holland* (1938).

very little religious painting in Protestant Holland in the mid-seventeenth century, and the suggestion began to be put forward, based on nothing but the purest guesswork, by Bredius and others, that perhaps Vermeer had travelled as a young man to Italy, where he would have felt the influence of Caravaggio and his successors, and returned to paint a religious series of which the *Martha and Mary* would be the only known survivor. It would indeed have been most unlikely for him to have painted only one such work, and Coremans mentions the supposition of such theorists that other but completely hypothetical biblical Vermeers 'once adorned the premises of a secret religious society in the seventeenth century'.* A newly found canvas to lend strength to this hypothesis would be specially acceptable to those such as Bredius who had long predicated it.

Aware of this whole controversy, van Meegeren made the conscious and deliberate decision to profit from it: he would paint one of the 'lost' religious works that Bredius and his followers had always hoped to find. It would then be the natural next step to submit it for certification to Bredius himself. Since he planned that his forgery should be related to the Edinburgh canvas, van Meegeren would ensure that there would be important associations between it and his forgery. For example, it is almost the only supposed Vermeer in which the figures are nearly life-size; van Meegeren painted nearly life-size figures in the *Emmaus*. There were also to be enough similarities of composition and brushwork to make comparison certain, and this, as he foresaw and hoped, would encourage irrelevant discussion and controversy which would lead attention away from what should have been the main concern: whether the newly discovered canvas had been painted by Vermeer or was indeed an old work at all.

Thus the *Emmaus*, so far from being imitative—let alone a copy —of any canvas that is typical of Vermeer, was related to a work that may not be his at all, or, if it is, is quite unlike any other.

It has been said by some that there is a gap in Vermeer's life which this inferred religious phase could conveniently fill, but this is actually pure guesswork. Many attempts have been made to date his works but these, in most cases, are nothing more than conjecture. One only, the *Procuress*, bears an undisputed date, 1656; those painted on two others, the *Astronomer* (1658) and the

* Coremans, op. cit., page 34.

Geographer (1659), are almost certainly forgeries, as are the signature on the former and one of two found on the latter. Some may be assigned with a fair degree of certainty to his early years, some to his middle period, and some to the last declining phase of his short working life, but to assign a particular year is in most cases just a matter of opinion. A year in which a religious series might have occupied him, most probably early in his career (about 1656), could therefore be acceptably surmised by those who wished to do so, and these included Bredius.* The *Martha and Mary* is supposed to be a very early work; Goldscheider, indeed, describes it as being 'certainly the earliest',† dating it 'about 1654'. It is amusing to realize, however, that van Meegeren thought otherwise: he himself was to suggest that one of his *Last Suppers*, which was supposed to be more or less contemporaneous with the *Emmaus*, had been 'perhaps Vermeer's last work'.‡

Van Meegeren was hardly less clever in his choice of subject. The appearance of the risen Christ to two disciples at Emmaus has not been very frequently depicted despite its dramatic appeal and pathos, but Caravaggio painted three versions of it. By choosing this favourite subject of his, and making the composition somewhat reminiscent of the version he himself had probably seen in Rome, van Meegeren was to mesmerize to an even greater extent those who welcomed this apparent confirmation of their long-held intuitive belief that Vermeer, like van Meegeren, had travelled to Italy and been influenced, as he had been, by the same canvas.

Much preliminary work was necessary before van Meegeren could start painting. He first had to prepare for its unexpected new employment the authentic seventeenth-century canvas depicting the *Raising of Lazarus*, which he had already acquired. He is believed to have paid the equivalent of about £50 for it, which would have been a bargain at the price since it would suit him admirably: it was mounted on its original stretcher and had an intricate, uniform age-crackle. Van Meegeren must have bought several such old canvases, since he would have required them for experimental work as well as for the four unsold forgeries; the *Lazarus* would have been the best of them which he saved till he was ready to start work on the *Emmaus*.

* See his article in the *Burlington Magazine*, quoted below, pages 67–8.
† Goldscheider, op. cit., page 18.
‡ In his letter to Boon, see below, page 121.

It would now have been necessary to remove the canvas from its stretcher, which would be too fragile and precious to use during the long months of work, involving several bakings (three, or perhaps four). The canvas was attached to it by the original seventeenth-century tacks, and protected from them by leather squares, now greatly worn by age. He carefully removed them and put all aside for eventual re-use.

Now, from the left-hand side (as viewed from the front), he cut off his 50 centimetres of evidence. This would indeed have provided the conclusive proof he wanted, since the paint had not yet been removed and details of the *Lazarus* would therefore still have been visible; it would have been simple, from the exact correspondence of the fibres, to prove it an extension of the *Emmaus* canvas, and his claim to have painted the latter would have been quite beyond dispute. However, it was a risky course in more ways than one. He must have known that in all likelihood the *Emmaus* would be re-canvassed, and mounted on a new stretcher, in which case his evidence might become valueless. Both operations were in fact to be carried out, but by great good luck the old stretcher was lovingly preserved at the Boymans Museum and the old edges of the canvas were, unusually, retained in the backing process.

A further consideration is that it was established by Coremans and his colleagues (though this is of necessity still disputed by the Decoen school), that a careful inspection of the left edge of the *Emmaus* canvas gives indications that might well have given the show away. As the Commission propounded it, however skilfully van Meegeren might succeed in making the newly cut edge appear similar to the others, the fibres at the edge of a canvas, which begin by being more or less straight, acquire a slight but detectable waviness with the slow passage of time to a depth of 5 to 20 centimetres* all the way round, owing to the pull of the tacks or nails that attach it to the stretcher. It is in fact visible to the naked eye that those on the back of the *Emmaus* are straight along the left-hand edge but wavy along the others. This would not only suggest that van Meegeren was taking a considerable extra risk but also, very strongly, that he did paint the *Emmaus*. To controvert this, Decoen first puts forward a completely different account of how a canvas behaves: according to him, it is absolutely normal for waviness to appear in three but not four of the edges. 'M.

---

* As estimated by Coremans, op. cit., page 8.

Coremans, seeing that he is a chemist, has probably never mounted a canvas on a stretcher,' he writes with some disdain;* otherwise, it is suggested, he would know this. Strangely enough, the eminent members of the Commission had all thought otherwise. Decoen goes on to state in no uncertain terms that he possesses positive proof that the *Emmaus* canvas 'was never cut'. He does not, however, provide it.

As he is inclined to do, Decoen produces a written document which seems *prima facia* to put all beyond doubt. In this case it is a certificate signed by four eminent restorers (including Luitwieler, who had restored the *Emmaus*) and also by Meurice. It runs in translation as follows:

On December 15 1949, Mr Jean Decoen made an *exposé* before the following Dutch picture restorers: Mr H. G. Luitwieler, Mr van Grunsven, Mr H. J. Schrender, Mr C. J. Snoeyerbosch; and Mr Charles Meurice, Director of the Institut de Chimie at Brussels.

Mr Decoen's *exposé* was limited solely to showing without any equivocation that the *Emmaus* canvas has never been cut.

This point of view was accepted by the four restorers named. Mr Meurice recognised the exactness, from a chemical point of view, of the arguments used by Mr Decoen to support his demonstration.

As witnesses whereof, the four restorers, the chemist and Mr Decoen have signed this declaration.

This is an extraordinary document. Decoen reproduces it in facsimile.† Yet in his entire book, which goes into other much less important matters in detail, he does not present one acceptable grain of the evidence that convinced these five gentlemen on this vital point. In the text he mentions only that the cutting of the canvas, and the disguise of this mutilation including the removal of paint from the cut edge, 'is by no means an easy task to perform and an experienced man will easily see it'. Decoen forgets that the Commission members *did* see it—and accepted van Meegeren's version.

Decoen reproduces a pair of photographs‡ taken in 1937 showing the four edges of the *Emmaus* canvas. He states in the caption with something like triumph that all four may be seen to be 'in precisely the same condition' and adds: 'This is an absolute proof that this canvas has never been cut.' The suggestion is naïve; it would have been an obvious part of van Meegeren's plan to make the cut

* Decoen, op. cit., page 26.　　† ibid., plate 53.　　‡ ibid., plates 38-9.

edge appear as identical as possible to the three others, apart from the fact that its fibres would be straight.

In any case the stretcher fragment, found by the police at the Nice villa in 1946, provides absolutely incontrovertible evidence, as will be shown,* that the canvas was cut down. For this reason it is completely ignored by Decoen, who nowhere considers its inescapable implications.

Van Meegeren must have been aware that cutting down the canvas would involve some additional risk, but would have been quite prepared to take it, knowing well that a purchaser, in his enthusiasm and foolhardiness, gives no thought to such technical matters if an acknowledged expert, who also, in all probability, will never have considered them, has provided a certificate of 'undoubted authenticity'. However, in all the circumstances, it was a strange step to take. It would have been simpler and safer if (for example) he had taken photographs showing the work in production.

The dimensions of the *Emmaus* are $45\frac{1}{2}'' \times 50\frac{1}{4}''$. Those of the *Lazarus* must therefore have been about $45\frac{1}{2}'' \times 70''$, since the sawn-off stretcher fragment found by Wooning at the Nice villa implies that the strip of canvas removed had a width of some 50 centimetres (20''). These could have been quite acceptable if only aesthetic considerations had been involved, or at least van Meegeren would surely have preferred to accept them unless some special reason existed for doing otherwise, and it is hard to imagine one other than that given. This would be a certain indication that he was at this time planning to reveal himself as the author of the *Emmaus* or had at least convinced himself that this was his intention.

The cutting down of the stretcher was a more delicate operation. The work involved may be inferred from the known dimensions and method of construction of the *Emmaus* stretcher and from van Meegeren's relevant statement. As may be seen from the photograph (plate 12), its jointed frame is strengthened by four corner-braces, which come together to join it in pairs, more or less (but not exactly) midway along the frame's four arms. Van Meegeren was to say: 'In consequence of cutting down the canvas I had to shorten (with a saw) the old stretcher to the same extent, and so I also displaced to the right the corner-braces on the left-hand side of the stretcher.'

* Pages 164–5 below.

From this it may be supposed that the *Lazarus* stretcher was originally constructed as shown in the diagram below. Decoen postulates an alternative position for the corner-braces (indicated by the dotted lines), though this is less likely if one accepts van Meegeren's statement, since he made no mention of displacing the right-hand braces.

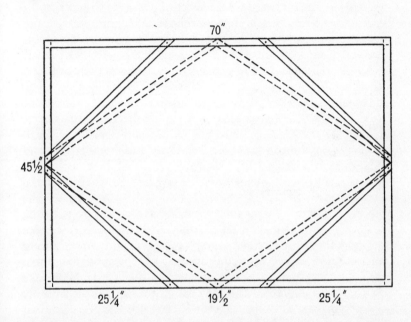

It will be seen that if the original design of the stretcher was as indicated, the right-hand braces would not have been moved at all. There would have been an original gap of some 50 centimetres between the points where the upper and lower braces met their respective horizontal arms, and it would have been logical for van Meegeren to reduce the latter by just that amount so that the braces would then meet neatly in the middle. This would involve a careful piece of carpentry: the left-hand braces could remain attached to the vertical arm, but the old tacks which held them to both horizontal arms would have to be removed, the latter shortened by 50 centimetres, re-shaped and re-attached to the vertical arm, and the braces then refastened to the horizontal arms, using the old nails. The alternative position suggested by Decoen would have been more difficult, involving the removal, shortening and repositioning of all four braces, but would of course have been feasible.

Having reconstructed the stretcher, van Meegeren put it aside to receive the *Emmaus* eventually. He next had to remove, if possible, all but the ground of the *Lazarus*. For this long and tedious task, he mounted it on a sheet of plywood to work in the manner suggested. It is known that in at least one area he ran into special difficulty: he could not completely remove one of the *Lazarus* heads, a woman wearing a headdress, because the old paint adhered with unusual persistence and a grave risk must have arisen of obliterating the crackle in it or of damaging the canvas. In the end he had to leave it largely visible; it is detectable in the radiographs of the *Emmaus* made a decade later, slightly above and to the left of the white jug on the table (plate 10). Van Meegeren also mentioned another small area where the paint proved irremoveable; this was white lead and he contrived to incorporate it with the table-cloth so that X-rays could not reveal it.

Now at last, after over four years of research and preparation, van Meegeren was ready to start painting. With some of his later forgeries, four or five undercoats were to be identified, comprising one or more layers from the original old painting and those applied by van Meegeren. The structure of the *Emmaus* was much less complex—indeed, it was the least elaborate of all: it has only two undercoats. The bottom one—all that was left of the *Lazarus* —was brownish; in the laboratory it was found to contain white lead and ochre. This had been covered by van Meegeren with a levelling layer, which was dark brown; its pigment and oil could not be identified but may have been burnt umber and oil of lilacs respectively. It can therefore be said that van Meegeren, having 'erased' *Lazarus* as completely as he could, applied a uniform, dark brown paint layer, to provide a level working surface. This contained phenolformaldehyde, and van Meegeren would have baked the canvas after applying it to bring through the crackle from the *Lazarus* ground. He could then start work on the composition proper.

It is hard to exaggerate the special difficulties that van Meegeren must now have found. I have tended to understate the artistic skill necessary because van Meegeren himself never doubted his

ability to paint cleverly enough for his work to be taken as
Vermeer's. Its importance must be recognized, however, above
all in the *Emmaus*, which is so much more successful than any
subsequent forgery. Indeed, whilst one significant fact about the
Emmaus is the remarkable skill and creative ability shown by van
Meegeren, the most important aspect of the others (especially the
last three) is that they deceived, despite being so unpleasing. The
fact that the *Emmaus* was a forgery, and conceived as such from the
start, detracts immeasurably from its value as a work of art, but it
is a fine picture and, by any standards, better than any other he had
painted in his own name or was to paint in the future. Such was
the power of his paranoiac desire for revenge which drove him to
more concentration, more resolution and a higher realm of
inspiration than he had ever previously known.

The greatest practical difficulty was that van Meegeren, in the
nature of things, had to work without models. This applied not
only to the figures (with the possible exception mentioned below)
but also, for the most part, to the still life. Over the years he was
to acquire many seventeenth-century props—jugs, pewter plates,
glasses and the like—to use as models in his forgeries; at the time
of painting the *Emmaus*, he is believed to have had in his possession
only the white jug that was to be found among his effects. Decoen
printed a photograph of this alongside a reproduction of the jug in
the *Emmaus*, commenting that the two had 'nothing in common',*
but this is simply not true. It may at once be seen that, although
the former has a somewhat longer neck, it is extremely similar; it
seems certain that van Meegeren did in fact use it to help him. The
jug in four later forgeries—the *Drinkers*, the *Cardplayers*, the *Footwashing* and *Isaac Blessing Jacob*—is on each occasion a more exact
but again not perfect copy.†

In planning his pictorial details, van Meegeren could have
obtained small assistance from the gospels. Luke tells the story,
alone of the evangelists. He reveals very little indeed about the two
disciples: only one of them, Cleopas, is even named, and he is
nowhere else mentioned in the Bible. He and his unknown companion failed to recognize Christ during a long encounter on the
road to Emmaus because 'their eyes were holden that they should

* Decoen, op. cit., plate 86, caption.
† A similar white jug also appears in several authentic Vermeers—e.g. the
Music Lesson (plate 35).

not know him', until at last 'as he sat at meat with them, he took bread, and blessed it, and brake, and gave to them. And their eyes were opened and they knew him; and he vanished out of their sight'.* Caravaggio always depicted the obvious dramatic moment when Christ is raising his hand to bless the bread—at the very instant, therefore, when his identity is revealed. Van Meegeren chose the same moment, or, to be quite precise, a second or two later or earlier, since Christ's forefinger is not extended.

His composition (plate 7) is simple to the point of austerity. The table is covered with a plain white cloth which could be almost described as skimpy. On it are set the wine-jug, two empty glasses and three pewter plates; on one of these are the two loaves that Christ is blessing. There is a typical Vermeer light-source, a window on the left, but it is excessively plainly drawn—no more than a light-coloured rectangle. The three seated figures are agreeably spaced round the table; a maidservant stands behind with one hand on the wine-jug.

There are many points of similarity to the relevant Caravaggio version: the full face of Christ, with downcast eyes, placed slightly to the left of centre; the left-hand disciple with his face turned to Christ and therefore not seen; the other (whom I take to be Cleopas) gazing at Christ in profile. There are also significant differences. One is that there are five figures in the Caravaggio: a manservant stands between Christ and Cleopas, gazing at Christ's raised hand, and a woman slightly in the background, also to the right. Another is that Caravaggio's figures are drawn with much more realism. One instantly believes in them: they are hard-working peasants with fine, lined faces whereas van Meegeren's have a remote, dreamy quality. Much more important, though this has not been generally noticed, is the fact that van Meegeren seems not to have understood what his picture was about. At this instant the risen Christ, after crucifixion and death, was being revealed as such to two adoring disciples. Their eyes, in Luke's phrase, were at that very moment being opened. In the Caravaggio, amazed recognition is striking Cleopas, who leans forward and clutches the table with his hands; the two arms of the other are stretched apart in wonder as the divine truth reaches him. Their astonishment is even more evident in the National Gallery

* Luke 7; 36-50.

version. There is *nothing* of this—the dramatic point of the incident—in the van Meegeren. Cleopas sits placidly, his left hand and forearm resting easily on the table (his right arm is not seen): the other disciple's attitude may be described only as wooden—he seems to be taking no special interest in the proceedings. There is no movement in van Meegeren's composition, whilst Caravaggio's abounds with it. One can only marvel at what Bredius was to write on this in his famous article 'A New Vermeer' in the *Burlington Magazine* (1937). After particularly drawing attention to the fact that 'Jesus is just about to break the bread at that moment when, as related in the New Testament, the eyes of the disciples were opened and they recognized Christ risen from the dead', he goes on to comment: 'The disciple seen in profile shows his silent adoration, *mingled with astonishment*, as he stares at Christ. In no other picture by the great master of Delft do we find such sentiment, *such a profound understanding of the Bible story*—a sentiment so nobly human, expressed through the medium of the highest art'.* It should first be remarked that it was curious of Bredius to suggest the *Emmaus* as Vermeer's most profound biblical composition, when only one other is known—and rather a doubtful one, at that. To write the words italicized seems completely incomprehensible. In fact van Meegeren missed the whole point. The dreamy face of Cleopas shows no astonishment at all. It can only be supposed that van Meegeren never looked up the story, and failed to understand the particular dramatic import of the moment he was depicting.

The face of his Cleopas, and his left forearm and hand, bear a strong resemblance to those of a well-known Vermeer, the *Astronomer*. This was probably intentional, to give the *Emmaus* some point of comparison with an authentic work. It is amusing to note that Decoen, holding the latter to be authentic, considers it superior to the *Astronomer* (which he mistakenly calls the *Geographer*) "in respect both of the draughtsmanship and of its distribution of light'. Also there is a strong similarity between this same head and that of Christ in the *Martha and Mary*†—a very clever touch. The face of the maidservant is supposed to be a pure product of van Meegeren's imagination. She and Christ both have the heavily lidded eyes which were almost a van Meegeren trademark,

* My italics. For the full text, see pages 67–8 below.
† Compare plates 7 and 8.

extremely noticeable in a number of his own paintings—for example *Mother and Child* (plate 22) and the near-pornographic *I Have Summoned up the Depths* (plate 21) to name only these—and to me are a very weak point in the painting.

Christ's robe is ultramarine, as is the undercloth on the table. Cleopas wears a yellow robe (mainly gamboge), the other disciple a grey one. The maidservant has a dark brown overgarment with a hood. The artist gave particular attention to the hands of Christ, which are beautifully executed, and also to the left hand of Cleopas. It has often been pointed out that his left arm is very carelessly indicated under the folds of the robe: in fact, it might be said that he appears to have *no* arm from the elbow to the shoulder. This makes it all the more remarkable that Decoen should consider this, too, as 'of better execution' than the very strong draughtmanship of the arm of the *Astronomer*.

The face of Jesus is of particular importance not only because it *is* the face of Jesus but also because it served as a model for Christ in all five subsequent 'Vermeers'. Unlike Caravaggio's, it is clean-shaven and decidedly effeminate. Van Meegeren said this was the one figure for which he dared to use a model. He told a story that he was alone at the villa one evening when a knock came at the door and he opened it to find himself 'looking into the eyes of Christ'. His unexpected visitor, when he recovered from his surprise, he found to be an Italian tramp on his way back to Italy (Roquebrune is within five miles of the border) after some months of work in France. He had come to the villa to beg. According to van Meegeren, he invited him in, weighed up the risk involved, and finally asked him to sit for him. The tramp stayed several days and was royally entertained by van Meegeren, though he 'would consume little but rye bread, garlick and wine'. Van Meegeren added some charming details. The tramp was greatly moved when he realized from the canvas that he was a model for Christ: he 'turned pale and crossed himself' and would call out in his sleep 'through fears of unworthiness'. Moreover he asked van Meegeren to pray for him lest Jesus be angered by the choice of a tramp as his model. Van Meegeren added that he did so and even gave the substance of his prayer. He said it was on these lines: 'God, if there be a God, please don't blame this vagabond for his participation in my work, for which I accept all responsibility. And, if you exist, please don't take it amiss that I've chosen a biblical

subject. No disrespect is intended; the choice is purely coinci-
dental'.*

Van Meegeren was an inveterate liar but I hope that this particular story is true and can think of no reason why he should have
invented it. The tramp, if *he* existed, would have thought that van
Meegeren was engaged on a painting no different from any other;
there would be no danger that he would ever visit the gallery
where it would one day hang as a Vermeer, or that a friend of his
should do so and recognize him. Van Meegeren is said to have sent
him on his way rejoicing, his pockets stuffed with banknotes.

It was probably in the early spring of 1937 that van Meegeren
put the final touches to the *Emmaus*. The next thing was the
signature. Van Meegeren must have given much consideration to
the question of whether he should sign Vermeer's name or not.
The signature is not really important evidence when authenticity
or attribution is considered. By signing it, besides, he would be
positively ascribing his own greatest masterpiece to another.
Moreover it would be a criminal act: when charges were brought
against van Meegeren, the principal offence alleged was that of
forging a signature. (Those who had bought the paintings might
sue for damages but in this only a civil action would be involved.)
And as a master of the double bluff it would not have been
surprising if van Meegeren had dared to present the *Emmaus*
unsigned; it can hardly be imagined that Bredius was so very
greatly influenced by the signature in granting his certificate and
he might well have thought his great discovery all the more clever
and remarkable, and therefore been the more willing to make it,
if there had been none to guide the flair, instinct and inborn
intuition that are the stock-in-trade of the great connoisseur.
Indeed he was to write: 'The beautiful signature . . . is not necessary to convince us that we have here a masterpiece—I am inclined
to say *the* masterpiece—of Johannes Vermeer of Delft.'†

However, van Meegeren must have decided that his work was
too completely unlike any universally accepted Vermeer to take
quite this risk. How then should he sign it? Four Vermeers have
only his initials, I.V.M. in monogram. Three are signed *I. V. Meer*
(the *V* and *M* forming a ligature) and three simply *Meer*: two of

* Quoted by M. Moiseiwitsch, *The Van Meegeren Mystery* (London, 1964),
page 129.
† *Burlington Magazine*, 1937.

the latter, including the *Martha and Mary*, have a small *v* underneath the *M*. One bears the fuller *I. Ver-Meer*. In all other cases,
there is the single word *Meer* with a capital *I* above the centre of
the *M*, thus forming the full initials in monogram (the *V* being
denoted by the central part of the *M*.) In five of these, the *r* has a
tail extending forward from its base (see plate 14).

Van Meegeren was always to sign the forgeries he sold (the de
Hooghs with the initials *P.D.H.* only); for all six Vermeers he
was to choose this most usual form. In three of them, but not in
the *Emmaus*, he gave the *r* its tail. When Vermeer did append a
signature, he gave it much care; Van Meegeren followed his
example and the faked signatures are, if one may say it, a credit
to him (plate 15). There is a curious point, however. Although the
chronology of Vermeer's known works is so much a matter of
conjecture, it is held that this particular form of signature was not
used by him till about 1662. He would then have used it almost
invariably (if he signed a canvas at all) for the remainder of his life.
This is a further indication that van Meegeren did not intend the
Emmaus to be taken for an early Vermeer, as it was; and yet he
must surely have intended that it should be associated (as, again, it
was) with the *Martha and Mary*.

At the trial van Meegeren was to insist that the painting of the
signatures was the most difficult task of all. What largely made
this so, he said, was that for technical reasons each had to be
achieved 'with one stroke of the brush'; there could be no breaking
off or going back: once he had begun it—after practising, one may
suppose, a hundred times—he had to complete it 'all in one
breath'. This certainly makes it sound the more difficult, but van
Meegeren was in fact employing something of a hyperbole, as he
was often wont to do. For the five letters never run together;
each, in every case, is wholly detached from the next. It can well
be imagined that each *letter* was completed with a single brush
stroke, but the whole word cannot have been.

There are several curious points in connection with the signature. Van Meegeren's initials are two-thirds identical with
Vermeer's. That seems strange enough. It is a pity he could not
claim that Han was a diminutive form of Johannes, rather than of
Henri, and then he would have had exactly the same initials. An
amusing legal question might then have arisen if he had signed the
Vermeers *I.V.M.* only: would it still have been forgery? This

leads one to notice the further coincidence that van Meegeren's son—and his second wife—both actually do possess Vermeer's initials. I might here mention that Jacques is a capable artist, and was one of his father's best pupils. Finally it is odd that even the names *v. Meer* and *v. Meegeren* should be so extremely similar—the abbreviation 'v' is used equally for either *van* or *ver*—with the letters of the former all appearing in the latter, and in the same order. (This was to lead a reporter at the trial to describe the fakes as 'Vermeergerens'.) If any of van Meegeren's own signatures are examined (even pre-1932) it will be seen that the double *ee* and the *r*—but not by any means the *M*—are strangely like the same letters in a Vermeer autograph. This may have been of help to him as he signed his best work away by the loving and careful inscription of the Delft master's usual signature—*Meer* with an *I* above it—in the top left-hand corner of the *Emmaus*, using a devil's brew of (most probably) lead white, yellow ochre, phenol-formaldehyde, lilac oil and benzene.

The canvas had already been subjected to one or more inter-mediate bakings as work progressed. Now, having at last com-pleted such a truly memorable work, it must have been with trepidation that he removed it from its temporary stretcher, tacked it to a sheet of plywood so that its whole surface would be equally exposed, and again approached the oven. That used for the *Emmaus* must have been large and elaborate, some $4\frac{1}{2}$ feet square and not less than 3 feet deep, probably of cast steel and insulated, with coils and elements built into the base. An external thermometer would have shown the temperature inside, which could be controlled by a thermostat. It seems likely that van Meegeren himself constructed this equipment, thus adding the trade of electrical engineer to those of chemist and painter. The completed *Emmaus* would have been slid face-up on its ply-wood backing into the cold oven along a ledge placed to receive it some eighteen inches above the base. Van Meegeren would then have closed the airtight door or doors, switched on, and waited till the internal temperature reached 105° Centigrade, at which figure the thermostat would hold it. He now had to wait two hours, and it is easy to imagine that they did not pass easily or slowly for him.

Just as, in baking a cake, it is supposed to be a mistake to open the oven door and see how it is going, so now it would have been wiser, in baking the *Emmaus*, to allow it to age unseen, since it would be equally important to avoid variations of temperature. None the less I believe van Meegeren may have slid out the canvas a couple of times to make sure that his whole work of the past six months, which he believed, quite rightly, to be his greatest masterpiece, was not going up in smoke or being irremediably damaged owing to some error in his chemistry. He must anyway have stayed beside the oven for the whole two hours to be sure that the thermostat maintained the desired temperature. When at last the time was up, he still cannot have been sure that all was well until he had removed the mounted canvas and taken it to the daylight. In particular the white lead, which he had used extensively, is liable to be discoloured, and there must have been a distinct risk that both tablecloth and wine jug would have yellowed. As we know, he found at once that no such disaster had occurred: the colours were quite unchanged. Equally, if not more important, the paint was perfectly dry, and van Meegeren would at once have seen that its surface had already spontaneously acquired a considerable part of the precious crackle from the undercoat. This may be inferred from the fact that the *Emmaus* crackle is accepted as the best he ever created—good enough for Decoen and others to hold it to be authentic.

Van Meegeren now took the *Emmaus* through the final stages already indicated which were invariable with all his forgeries. He first applied a light coat of varnish and allowed it to dry naturally; this would cause additional crackle to appear and the varnish itself would acquire the same pattern. Now would have been the time, if in this case it was necessary at all, for van Meegeren to induce more, by gently bending the canvas back and forth, by rolling it (paint uppermost) around a cylinder, or by pressing the back of the canvas with his skilful forger's thumb in those areas where enough had not developed. Other forgeries of his, in particular *Woman Playing Music*, give a very definite impression (with the great benefit of hindsight) of having been treated in one or more of these ways, but the *Emmaus* crackle is so excellent that van Meegeren may have induced all of it by means of the heating and varnish only. Next he had to face the very distressing operation, as it must certainly have been to him, of covering the entire visible surface—Christ, disciples and all—with a layer of Indian ink. Once this had dried naturally, he would have removed it,

The early trial forgery,
Woman Reading Music
(plate 1, left), is to be
compared with the
authentic Vermeer,
Woman in Blue
(plate 3, below).
The detail head of the
Adulteress (plate 2,
below left) is
reminiscent of both.

Three other trial forgeries,
Woman Playing Music,
after Vermeer (plate 4, right);
Portrait of a Man, after Terborgh
(plate 5, below left);
and *Woman Drinking,* after Hals
(plate 6, below right).

Plate 7. The *Christ at Emmaus*.

Christ with Martha and Mary, generally attributed to Vermeer (plate 8, above). For the importance of this work in influencing van Meegeren, see text, pages 39–40.

The sketch (plate 9, left) was made by van Meegeren after his confession to show the *Emmaus* superimposed on its underpainting (the *Raising of Lazarus*). He indicated the position of the head in the latter work (arrowed) which he had not been able to remove completely. A subsequent radiograph of the *Emmaus* (plate 10, below) shows the head in about the position indicated.

Plate 11 (above). The Villa
Primavera, Roquebrune,
where van Meegeren painted
the *Emmaus*.

Plate 12 (right). The
Emmaus stretcher, preserved
at the Boymans after
recanvassing.

Plate 13. Han van Meegeren.

The selection of authentic Vermeer signatures (plate 14, above) may be compared with one of van Meegeren's forged signatures—from the *Footwashing* (plate 15, below).

together with the varnish, first using soap and water, then alcohol
or turpentine. There was no danger of the solvent affecting the
paint, but he had to get rid of the varnish without disturbing such
all-important ink as had seeped through the crevices in its crackle,
and dried in the corresponding crevices in the paint itself, where it
might be mistaken for dust. If any ink had unintentionally reached
the paint surface, it could be removed with soap and water. He
next applied a careful coat of light brown varnish, which he again
allowed to dry naturally.

There was still work to be done. It would be most unusual if a
seventeenth-century painting were completely unharmed and
unrestored. Van Meegeren therefore intentionally damaged it and
then restored the damage. The former was all too easy; with a
palette knife, he completely removed the surface paint, and in some
cases the undercoats as well, from several small areas, and in one
place—at the base of the ring-finger of Christ's right hand—he
even made a small tear in the canvas. He then himself restored
these areas, using the technique known to him from his occasional
work in this field. He in fact did this rather badly, yet the restored
areas were by no means quickly noticed: it seems extraordinary
that Bredius should have described the work as 'without any
restoration, just as it left the painter's studio' in his *Burlington*
article. After the sale to the Boymans, the restorations were
thought so incompetent that they were removed and repainted by
Luitwieler, the best man in Rotterdam.

Now at last van Meegeren could remove the *Emmaus* from its
temporary backing and return it to the old stretcher that had
waited half-a-year for it, using the original tacks and the worn
leather squares to protect the canvas from them, all of which he
had carefully preserved. The last tack went home and the *Emmaus*
was completed.

The painting of the forgery was only half the battle. Success on
the unprecedented scale to be achieved by van Meegeren requires
not only great chemical and technical skills, besides artistic ability,
such as he had shown already, but also the nerve and knowledge,
and an understanding of the best psychological approach, to foist
his work on the market. This van Meegeren had now to undertake, and the evidence indicates that he was still to operate without
a guilty accessory. Thus he now entered on the final stage alone.

Until this point he had not finally committed himself. He could still have been open to the persuasion of his conscience that he was simply amusing himself, that he was no more than experimenting; he had as yet committed no illegal act. The signing of Vermeer's name had been a relative peccadillo. To go out now into the world, to take each successive step necessary to find an eventual buyer—this not only required new knowledge and skills but drove him for the first time to crime. Many will hold that this would have been so even if he still intended to reveal himself eventually as the author of the *Emmaus*.

His first necessity was to obtain a certificate from an acknowledged Vermeer expert that in his opinion it was authentic. Van Meegeren knew he would then be sure to make a sale. A few lonely voices might express doubts, but once certification had been obtained from a single honoured and respected figure in the world of Old Masters it was just about certain that most of his colleagues would agree with him. There were other reasons for choosing Bredius besides the most important one—that it was he who had 'discovered' the *Martha and Mary* in 1901, had insisted ever since that there must be other biblical Vermeers, and therefore might be expected to welcome a canvas that would confirm this long-held theory whilst adding to the credentials of his well-known but still disputed find. Dr Abraham Bredius was the most respected judge it were possible to approach. More an art historian than a critic, his word had been law in Holland for almost fifty years. He had already been associated with other remarkable discoveries; it is true that he had made one or two quite serious mistakes, but this was only human—it happens all too often to almost everyone—and they had soon been forgotten. A certificate from Bredius would carry more weight in the sale-room than perhaps anyone else's. By the same token, since a principal motive of van Meegeren's was the discrediting of the experts, he could aim no higher.

Bredius, moreover, was an old enemy. Van Meegeren had known and fought with him in Holland* and regarded him as one of those whose failure to appreciate his work had particularly contributed to his lack of recognition. It should finally be added that Bredius was now very old and extremely myopic; some have gone so far as to describe him as half-blind. He was in fact eighty-

* See below, page 99.

three, and living quietly in retirement, by coincidence within a few miles of Roquebrune at Monaco.

It was certain that he would remember van Meegeren, and in view of the antipathy that existed between them there could be no question of approaching him direct, or even of it coming to his knowledge that he was in any way involved. Van Meegeren had therefore to find an intermediary; he made his choice well. To put into effect the extremely cunning plan that had formed in his devious mind, he needed someone who was a fairly close friend, who was preferably well known, and whose integrity and public reputation were beyond question. Van Meegeren moved in bohemian circles and most of his friends and associates would have been in every way unsuitable. By luck there was one exception. He had been on fairly intimate terms in Holland with Dr G. A. Boon, a Member of Parliament and a much respected solicitor, whose active interest in the arts had accounted for their friendship. From every point of view, Boon was indeed a boon to van Meegeren, tailor-made for the unhappy role of stooge. He was now on vacation in Paris and it was for Paris that van Meegeren headed, with the *Emmaus* in a crate, on the *train bleu* from Roquebrune.

With his later forgeries, van Meegeren took increasingly less trouble to invent a story to explain their lack of provenance because he found this of hardly any importance. On this occasion, however, he had prepared an elaborate tale. It centred around a non-existent lady, whom he named as 'Mavroeke' and described as his mistress. Mavroeke is an uncommon name and it is not known how he came to choose it. According to his story, she was one of three last surviving members of an old Dutch family which had moved to Italy some decades previously from their ancestral home, a castle in Westland, Holland, taking with them a remarkable collection of (to be quite exact) 162 Old Masters, including work by such as Holbein, El Greco, Rembrandt and Hals, which had been handed down in the family since the seventeenth century. On her father's death, the collection had been divided between Mavroeke, her daughter, and a very old cousin named Germain. Mavroeke lived near Como, but paid frequent visits to the Côte; her daughter was in Strasbourg and Germain in the Midi.

Mavroeke—so the story ran—was planning to emigrate and had

asked him to sell some pictures for her on commission. On examining them, he had found one which he believed to be the work of Jan Vermeer. He had smuggled it out of Italy—the exportation of such works was strictly forbidden by the Fascists—and had it with him in Paris. He was now seeking certification; Dr Bredius was the obvious man to approach but he himself could not do so for the true reasons he provided. The canvas, if authentic, might fetch £100,000. Would Boon agree to approach Bredius on a commission basis? Apart from anything else, it might ensure the return to Holland from Fascist Italy of a great national treasure.

That was the first part of van Meegeren's complex plan and he must now move on to the second. Having given Boon sight of the possibility that he might be able to perform a patriotic act which would also put him in line for several thousand pounds, he had to point out that some untruth would be necessary. Not only must van Meegeren's name be left out of it, but also Mavroeke's; it must not become known, he explained, that the work had been smuggled from Italy. Van Meegeren coolly suggested that Boon should present himself as the legal adviser of the daughter and heir-at-law of a mythical French businessman, never named, who would recently have died; he would have been married to a Dutchwoman (also dead), who had brought with her as her dowry some forty years previously, from a castle in Westland to a castle in the Midi, a large number of oil paintings. His client had now fallen on hard times and had consulted him with a view to selling. The pictures had turned out to be of less interest than he had hoped, but then he had stumbled on the *Emmaus*, hidden away and forgotten. (This part of the story was to be much embroidered. Boon was to say he found the canvas in a large wardrobe in a seldom used back-bedroom; his client had accounted for this by saying that her father had always thought it 'ugly'—the French word used was *laid*. Such a tale was desirable to account for the fact that in several decades no visitor to the castle had seen this important masterpiece, prominently signed, and reported on its presence. It has its remarkable side because the *Emmaus* could hardly be thought ugly, whatever else one's opinion of it.) The more Boon had examined it, the more he had become convinced that it was in fact a Vermeer. His client had agreed to submit it for certification, but did not wish it to be known that circumstances were compelling her to dispose of family heirlooms and she could therefore not be identified.

Van Meegeren had thus concocted two different stories, though with points of similarity: one to persuade Boon to participate and one that he wished Boon to tell Bredius. It is interesting to consider why he thought this necessary—why he did not tell Boon the second story which he would ask him to pass on. The reason is simply that Boon had much standing as a Member of Parliament and respected solicitor, whilst van Meegeren was an unknown painter of dubious reputation. To get his reputable friend to work for him, he had to invent a very strong story (involving the need to dupe the Fascists) which would be extremely likely not only to convince Boon but to appeal to the democrat and patriot in him. It could not be told to Bredius and the world because it would seem unlikely that he would be ready to implicate Mavroeke, but the weaker account, suspect if presented by the likes of van Meegeren, would be strengthened to the point of acceptability if put forward by one of Boon's stature.

Van Meegeren was clearly asking his friend to take a risk. As Boon would have seen it, if Mavroeke were ever compelled, for example as a result of questioning by the Fascists after some other illegal act, to admit that she had owned this picture, or if its origin leaked out in any other way, it would become common knowledge that he had told Bredius a completely false story. Boon must have decided that his action would then be condoned because it was anti-Fascist. It was his bad luck that when the truth finally came to light, and his lie was revealed, there would be no such excuse to fall back on, but by then, for political reasons, he had long since vanished without trace and it was therefore of no importance to him.

It has been suggested by some that the unfortunate Boon was a party to the conspiracy to the extent of knowing that the *Emmaus* was a forgery. Coremans refers to him tactfully as 'Mr X' (though his identity is well known) and goes on to describe him as 'an old friend who . . . was open to financial persuasion'. He then comments: 'Whether Mr X knew that the picture was a forgery is of no immediate concern.'* I find this a highly remarkable statement; the question may not be of 'immediate' concern, whatever that may mean, but on its answer depends the degree of Boon's

* Coremans, op. cit., page 27.

involvement and Coremans never subsequently returns to it. When he says that Boon was 'open to financial persuasion' he may mean only that he was prepared—like Coremans himself or anyone else—to receive a commission for doing a job of work. I know of no evidence, and Coremans presents none, to support his innuendo that Boon was criminally implicated. He left Europe at the outbreak of war (perhaps he was a Jew) and was not seen again; he could not be found to give evidence at the trial, where his willingness to tell Bredius a fabricated story came in for some judicial criticism.

In view of the fact that Decoen maintains the *Emmaus* to be authentic, but has given no indication as to how van Meegeren was fortunate enough to obtain it beyond guessing wildly that he obtained it and the *Supper* from 'a church or some religious brotherhood', it is of interest to mention that de Augustinis, the *gérant* of the Domaine du Hameau, has a clear recollection that during this period (1936–7) van Meegeren did in fact receive at the Primavera a number of large crates which contained pictures and had come openly from Italy. There may therefore have been a 'Mavroeke' who—whether or not she was van Meegeren's mistress—was using him as an intermediary to dispose of works of art, and he may have merely altered actual circumstances by falsely including the *Emmaus* as one of them when telling his story to Boon. The exportation of minor works of art would have been permitted by the Fascists.

Van Meegeren showed the *Emmaus* to Boon, who was sufficiently impressed by it and by the story he had heard to agree to the part suggested. On 30 August 1937—for once it is possible to give an exact date—he wrote to Bredius giving such facts as he thought necessary, and Bredius was glad to welcome him a few days later in Monaco.

I cannot help feeling a little bit sorry for Bredius, who was now to fall headlong into the immensely skilful trap that van Meegeren had set for him. His whole professional life, now over and behind him, had been sincere, distinguished, academical; his reputation was secure. Now, in his retirement, came suddenly for certification what he was soon to consider the most important work of his entire career. It was in so many ways the masterpiece that he would have liked beyond all others to discover at this time that it must almost have seemed as though some benevolent deity had specially

conjured it to enlighten his old age. And it had indeed been
conjured for him—that he would be made to experience these
very feelings and react to them in this planned and hoped-for way.
He was to see this as an event that brilliantly crowned his life, and
so indeed it still seemed at his death. Yet today, because of it, he
is chiefly remembered as the great expert in the van Meegeren
case who made the most serious error because it was the first; by
accepting the *Emmaus* as a Vermeer, he was responsible for giving
the credence and esteem to van Meegeren's technique and style
that would so greatly facilitate him in presenting the whole subsequent series that Bredius could in the end be made a scapegoat
by all his colleagues. No crown to his life but ridicule after death.

Bredius has himself left an account of his immediate emotions
on seeing the *Emmaus*. It was brought to him by Boon from Paris,
still in its crate, and opened in his presence. Writing soon afterwards of this moment,* Bredius recalled his feelings when he
first saw the *Christ with Martha and Mary* to emphasize that he was
moved by even greater emotion 'as soon as the crate was opened
that contained the *Emmaus*'. It must therefore be taken that he was
at once greatly impressed, though this must have been an emotional and superficial judgment. He asked Boon to leave the
canvas with him and spent two days examining it alone.

Everything now depended on this 'half-blind' old man, yet his
decision, as is almost always the case, could be based solely on a
purely subjective opinion, formed by using his remarkable flair
and instinct. As with Bredius now, no tests are normally called for
in the laboratory: no radiographs, no microchemistry, no macroscopy, no microscopy. It may well be that nothing is known of
provenance beyond a vague, nameless, unverifiable, and quite
untrue story of the kind told by Boon, beyond which he could
know absolutely nothing. Yet on just such a personal opinion as
Bredius was now forming depended—and still depends—the
question of whether a work of art, safely certificated, is to hang
through the centuries in a major gallery or wealthy man's home
after making six figures in the saleroom, or is to be ignored and
forgotten. (It must be remembered that if van Meegeren had died
unconfessed the *Emmaus* would still be in the Boymans, still the
pride of the collection.) If Bredius had even expressed doubt, van
Meegeren would have been back at the beginning. There would

* *Oud-Holland* (1938).

have been no appeal; the art world is a small world, the news would have quickly got round, and the *Emmaus* would have become 'fishy'—to use the trade word.

Bredius would have examined visually the back of the canvas and the stretcher, and noticed with satisfaction that they were certainly original. But it would of course have been the composition—its subject-matter, its brushwork, its technique—that mostly occupied him. It is known that he was specially impressed by the *pointillés* 'in the bread and elsewhere' which he was to describe as being 'as good as a signature'; indeed he was to add that 'as soon as I saw them, I no longer had any doubts',* though this must have been an exaggeration. One by one, he found and nibbled each successive crumb of bait that van Meegeren had laid for him: the religious theme, Caravaggio's subject, the almost life-size figures, the disciple who recalled the astronomer and the *Martha and Mary* Christ, the admirable signature. Van Meegeren had included so many features that would be of profound interest to Bredius if the work were a Vermeer that he may soon have become more interested in their implications than in the question of authenticity, which he would begin to take for granted. Bredius would at once have seen that the colours were right—none could mistake Vermeer's ultramarine and gamboge—and that the crackle looked authentic.

Boon remained in the neighbourhood, though not, it may be supposed, with van Meegeren in nearby Roquebrune. After forty-eight hours he was recalled by Bredius, who expressed enthusiasm and asked for the work to be photographed. This was arranged and 'shortly afterwards he wrote and signed a certificate of guarantee on the back of the print to testify that it was genuine'.†
A translation runs as follows:

This glorious work of Vermeer, the great Vermeer of Delft, has emerged—thank God!—from the darkness where it lay for many years, undefiled‡ and just as it left the artist's studio. Its subject is almost

---

* Ibid.
† Coremans, op. cit., page 30.
‡ *Ongerept*—a curious, old-fashioned word to use in this context, but the certificate is all expressed in rather old-fashioned, flowery language. *Ongerept* would more usually be employed to describe, for example, a virgin (=untouched), or snow that has just fallen and not yet been disturbed. The inference is that the *Emmaus* had not been restored—or rather that Bredius failed to notice the restorations.

unique in his *œuvre*; a depth of feeling springs from it such as is found in no other work of his. I found it hard to contain my emotions when this masterpiece was first shown to me and many will feel the same who have the privilege of beholding it. Composition, expression, colour— all combine to form an unity of the highest art, the highest beauty.

Bredius, September 1937.

And thus the world lay at van Meegeren's feet.

4
The Changed Aim

THE importance of this unequivocal certificate cannot be over-emphasized, nor the fact that it was based on nothing more than the intuition of one old man, without laboratory testing. It may be marvelled that this was enough to ensure with almost complete certainty not only the general acceptance of the fake, but its sale at a high figure. But such is usually the case; there may be those, as was indeed to happen here, who form a different opinion and therefore refrain from bidding, but the continuance of the market in Old Masters depends almost entirely on the acceptance of instinctive opinions as indisputable facts by the vast majority of those involved in the trade, because often there is simply no other way of establishing authenticity.

Proof of this unhappy fact is by no means hard to find, and hardly a month goes by without an example coming to light. It is instructive, for instance, to consider the supposed Antonello, *Dead Christ Supported by an Angel*, which was discovered in 1965 by the Prado, and was later described by a director of the Museum to be 'as valuable as any painting in existence; there simply is no market price for it—it's priceless'.* The facts are that this rather small work (30″ × 20″), painted on wood, was brought to the Prado by a young student who asked if it might be saleable. He said it belonged to his father, whose mother had bought it in Irun in 1881 from 'an unknown native of Galicia'. It needed cleaning so badly that not much could be said with certainty but the museum's experts formed the opinion that it was a work of the fifteenth-century Venetian school and therefore might be extremely valuable, though they did not tell the student this. They implied that it might be of interest. At this point the student said his father did not wish to sell; a Prado official replied 'casually'—as the New York *Times* reported—that if he ever changed his mind the museum might be willing to buy it.

* New York *Times*, 13 January 1967.

It should be here noted that there was thought nothing immoral in the museum's quite clear attitude, which other factors were to underline, that the young man should be given no idea whatever of the painting's possible value. The museum's interest could have been expressed in this 'casual' way only for such a reason. The student returned two years later and offered to sell the work; the Prado's board of trustees was assembled to inspect it and the purchase was made within a week for an undisclosed but insignificant sum. On this matter a spokesman replied to questioners with almost unbelievable *naïveté*. Asked if it would be improper to enquire the price, he replied in the affirmative, adding: 'The board is composed of elderly gentlemen who simply do not discuss money.' These elderly gentlemen, however, had acquired a painting which may be worth close on a million pounds for a very small handful of pesetas. When the Prado's restorers began cleaning it, 'they discovered that it was a heretofore unknown Antonello. The painting turned out to be in astonishingly good condition.' On the question of its authorship, it was said simply: 'There could be no doubt that it was an Antonello. One knew right away.'

Such a statement, however, in fact reveals the necessary and inescapable weakness of the system because in fact, however sure 'one' may be, there can be no proof whatsoever that such a personal opinion, based purely on conjecture, is in fact true. Bredius, every bit as skilled and esteemed as the experts at the Prado, felt there could be 'no doubt' that the *Emmaus* was a Vermeer and indeed staked (and lost) his reputation on it; he may not have known 'right away', but it is to be noted that the Prado in fact took a week to decide, though they were getting the work for next to nothing. That the *Emmaus* turned out to be a valueless van Meegeren was bad luck, posthumously, for Bredius, because one of the facts that will always console and reassure such an expert is that even though he may never hope to prove beyond doubt that his attribution is correct, it will be equally impossible— or so it may be assumed—for any other expert to prove that it is wrong. Others may express a contrary opinion but he has only to stick to his guns; if the Prado officials state positively and firmly that their discovery is an Antonello, and exhibit it as such, then it becomes an Antonello, because no expert opinion can matter more to them than their own. It can surely never happen again that the forger himself will proudly claim authorship, and adduce the very proof that was so totally and necessarily absent in arriving at the first opinion.

Just as a forgery may be taken for an Old Master, so an extremely valuable Old Master may be taken for a forgery, or for a work of no importance. The recent case of the Rubens has already been mentioned. Another good example is the Rembrandt self-portrait (1643), which, as is now known, had been stolen (together with a Terborgh and a Tischbein) from the Grand Ducal Museum, Weimar, in 1922. This highly important canvas, which is certainly worth up to half a million pounds, came into the possession of a German-born plumber from Dayton, Ohio, one Leo Ernst, who said he picked it up for 'next to nothing' from an unnamed sailor aboard an unnamed ship in 1934. When his wife accidentally found the canvases stuffed carelessly inside a trunk in the attic, he told her: 'They're nothing, just some junk I got gypped on.'* It happened that Mrs Ernst had attended art school in Dayton and believed they could be of value: she went the rounds of dealers in New York but all declared with splendid unanimity that they were 'worthless fakes or copies'. It was only in 1966, when the Ernsts after years of research found a newspaper account of the 1922 theft, in which the stolen paintings were described in detail, that the same experts were compelled to change their minds and to acclaim the works with equal unanimity as being certainly authentic. If the plumber from Dayton had not chanced upon a faded news-clipping, proof instead of guesswork, the Rembrandt would still not be a Rembrandt.

The false *Emmaus* found much less difficulty than the true Rembrandt self-portrait, but more than the Antonello, in securing general acceptance.

The name of van Meegeren was never once mentioned in any of the negotiations leading to its sale; these were set in motion and conducted by Boon. It was he who now returned to Paris and deposited it for safe keeping at the Crédit Lyonnais. Van Meegeren may have accompanied him; he and his wife are known to have paid a visit to Amsterdam at this time (October 1937) and would have travelled by way of Paris, but he kept completely in the background.

Here his arrogance received what must have been a terrible and

* As reported in *Time*, 20 January 1967.

most unexpected blow. The impression exists widely that as soon as Bredius had given the forgery his enthusiastic certificate it was universally accepted and buyers came forward eagerly to bid for it. The truth is far otherwise. Enthusiasm for the *Emmaus*, when it was a question of paying hard cash for it, was much less great than van Meegeren had hoped or is now generally supposed. The shattering evidence of this—and it is indisputable—lies in the cable sent by a representative of Duveen's to his principals in New York after seeing the picture in Paris. Formal negotiations had to await the publication of the article by Bredius in the November issue of the *Burlington Magazine*—he had insisted that he himself should have the honour of announcing his discovery (as it had now become) to the world—but meanwhile one or two potential buyers were allowed into the secret, and Duveen's man was one of them. He saw the *Emmaus* on 4 October and cabled as follows:

SEEN TODAY AT BANK LARGE VERMEER ABOUT FOUR FEET BY THREE
CHRISTS SUPPER AT EMMAUS SUPPOSED BELONG PRIVATE FAMILY
CERTIFIED BY BREDIUS WHO WRITING ARTICLE BURLINGTON MAGAZINE
NOVEMBER STOP PRICE POUNDS NINETY THOUSAND STOP
PICTURE ROTTEN FAKE.

It would soon be forgotten, in the wild enthusiasm a few months later for the new Vermeer at the Boymans, that one true expert had disdainfully stigmatized it, without doubts or qualifications, not merely as a fake but as a rotten one. Naturally the news got round and this did nothing to help; other potential buyers saw the *Emmaus* in Paris but no sale was made.

The appearance of the Bredius article indeed caused great interest, as had been confidently expected, but the inferior quality of the accompanying reproduction did nothing to help van Meegeren. A French commentator, Georges Isalo, writing in *Beaux Arts* six months later, was to report: '*La réproduction . . . ne donnait pas une interpretation exacte du tableau. Aussitôt des chuchote-ments: Ce n'est pas un Vermeer! C'est un faux!*'

Bredius wrote as follows: 'It is a wonderful moment in the life of a lover of art when he finds himself suddenly confronted with a hitherto unknown painting by a great master, untouched, on the original canvas and without any restoration, just as it left the painter's studio! Neither the beautiful signature "I. V. Meer" (I.V.M. in monogram), not the *pointillé* on the bread, which

Christ is blessing, is necessary to convince us that we have here a masterpiece—I am inclined to say *the* masterpiece—of Johannes Vermeer of Delft, and moreover one of his largest works, quite different from all his other paintings and yet every inch a Vermeer. The subject is *Christ and the Disciples at Emmaus* and the colours are magnificent—and characteristic: Christ in a splendid blue; the disciple on the left, whose face is barely visible, in a fine grey; the other disciple on the left* in yellow—the yellow of the famous Vermeer at Dresden,† but subdued, so that it remains in perfect harmony with the other colours. The servant is clad in dark brown and dark grey; her expression is wonderful. Expression, indeed, is the most marvellous quality of this unique picture. Outstanding is the head of Christ, serene and sad as He thinks of all the suffering which He, the Son of God, had to pass through in His life on earth, yet full of goodness. There is something in this head which reminds me of the well-known study in the Brera Gallery at Milan, formerly held to be a sketch by Leonardo for the Christ of the *Last Supper.* Jesus is just about to break the bread at that moment, when, as related in the New Testament, the eyes of the Disciples were opened and they recognized Christ risen from the dead and seated before them. The disciple on the left‡ seen in profile shows his silent adoration, mingled with astonishment, as he stares at Christ.

'In no other picture by the great master of Delft do we find such sentiment, such a profound understanding of the Bible story—a sentiment so nobly human, expressed through the medium of the highest art.

'As to the period in which Vermeer painted this masterpiece, I believe it belongs to his earlier phase—about the same time (perhaps a little later) as the well-known *Christ in the House of Martha and Mary* at Edinburgh.

'The reproduction can only give a very inadequate idea of the splendid luminous effect of the rare combination of colours of this magnificent painting by one of the greatest artists of the Dutch School.'

Mention has already been made of certain aspects of this document; it remains only to call attention to the extraordinary fact

---

* He means 'on the right'.
† The *Lady Reading a Letter at an Open Window.*
‡ Again he means 'on the right'.

that Bredius *twice* described the right-hand disciple as the left-hand disciple and indeed, in the first reference, gives the impression that both disciples are to the left of the picture. For a man who must have studied the work with great and loving attention, it seems incredible that he should make such an elementary error about a basic feature of the composition (and hardly less so that it should not have been noticed and put right by a sub-editor on the magazine staff). Perhaps the most charitable explanation is that Bredius had reached a more extreme stage of dotage than van Meegeren had believed and to some extent relied upon.

In considering the opposition to the *Emmaus* that certainly did exist at this time in some quarters, it must be remembered that it had been planned by van Meegeren as a highly controversial work, quite unlike any universally accepted Vermeer. He did this not only because, if his work were accepted, it would be a greater achievement than if he had chosen a typical Vermeer subject and style, but also in the hope that the critics and art historians, in their arguments as to its significance and implications, might lose sight of the question of whether it was an old painting at all. Nonetheless it has to be said, and it is of no small significance, that he achieved success much less quickly and less easily than he had hoped.

These setbacks turned out to be only temporary, however, though they might have proved fatal if so positive a certificate had not been provided by so respected an authority as Bredius. Boon approached leading figures in the Dutch art world and impressed upon them that such a great national treasure should return to its homeland. The most important of those interested were Dr D. Hannema, the Director of the Boymans, who had recently organized a major Vermeer exhibition there, and Mr D. A. Hoogendijk, Holland's leading and most respected dealer, whose name is to reappear again and again in the story. The latter approached known public benefactors, and one of them, Mr W. van der Vorm, a very wealthy industrialist who was later to buy on his own account, on Hoogendijk's advice, a false Vermeer (*Isaac Blessing Jacob*) as well as a false de Hoogh (*Interior with Cardplayers*), agreed to pay the greater part of the asking price, which had by now descended to 520,000 guilders. The balance was put up by the Rembrandt Society, as agreed unanimously by the society's board, and by two or three private individuals, including

Bredius himself. The *Emmaus* was made over to the Boymans before the end of December.

The price was the equivalent of about £58,000 at the existing exchange rate. Even allowing for the fact that Boon would have started by asking a good bit more than he would have been ready to take if necessary, it is significant that he had eventually to accept less than two-thirds of the figure quoted in the Duveen cable.

It is an astonishing fact that Hoogendijk was to be involved in the sale of not only the *Emmaus* but at least four of the seven other forgeries sold. In fact of all the false Vermeers, only the *Adulteress* (which was to have a very special sale history) may be said definitely to have been sold without Hoogendijk's knowledge, if not without his active participation. To many this has indicated that he must have been a party to the conspiracy, but there is absolutely no evidence to confirm this and no charges were ever brought against him as an accessory. The belief perhaps springs from a failure to understand the working of the saleroom world. This world is extremely small, especially within the borders of one small country (and, owing to the war, the later forgeries could not be offered outside Holland): everyone knows what everyone else is doing, and Hoogendijk would certainly have heard anyway when works as important as the later 'Vermeers' reached the market, and would almost certainly have seen them, so there could be no additional risk to van Meegeren in seeking him out each time if he used different intermediaries who on no occasion revealed his involvement. Indeed Hoogendijk might well have thought it strange, and initiated enquiries that might have had embarrassing results, if he found that Vermeers similar to those he was widely known to have handled had come on the market without an approach being made to him. He was the obvious person to consult if one wished to dispose of *any* important work in Holland, especially if it were a supposed Old Master. Moreover it was to happen that one of the forgeries, the *Head of Christ*, was still on his hands at the time of van Meegeren's confession; it was clearly a study for the central figure in the *Last Supper* and as such, whilst the latter was accepted as an undoubted Vermeer, was of great interest and importance and could easily have found a buyer. It can hardly be believed that Hoogendijk would have retained it for four years, and allowed it to be found on his premises, if he knew it to be a forgery.

Before the *Emmaus* could be exhibited at the Boymans, it had to
be cleaned, restored and framed. The work was entrusted to
Luitwieler, the *doyen* of Rotterdam restorers. He decided it should
be 'backed'; this delicate operation involves the removal of the
old canvas and the substitution of a new one. The picture is taken
from its stretcher and pasted, face downward, on a sheet of heavy
paper. Shred by shred, the old canvas is carefully picked away; the
paper helps the paint to cling together while there is no canvas at
all. A new one is then glued firmly on the back. When a painting
is backed, the entire old canvas including the unpainted edges is
usually removed. By chance, Luitwieler did not find this necessary
or desirable. He was able to incorporate the old edges with the new
canvas by cutting both, so that the latter fitted exactly inside the
former. This was extremely lucky, because, unknown to him, he
was leaving intact vital evidence: the straight fibres at the left-
hand edge of the canvas. The old stretcher, equally luckily, was to
be preserved at the Boymans.

Luitwieler, having removed first the varnish and then van
Meegeren's amateurish restorations, himself restored the painting
and applied new varnish. The canvas was mounted on a modern
stretcher; a handsome frame was provided and at last the *Emmaus*
was ready for the world.

There had indeed been dissenting voices when it had been a
question of finding a buyer who was prepared to put up a small
fortune in hard cash and who therefore wished to be as certain as
humanly possible—which in all conscience is not certain at all—
that he was getting the real thing. Once the *Emmaus* was on show,
and therefore had the backing and guarantee not only of Bredius
but also by implication of the Rembrandt Society and of the
Boymans itself, almost all doubts were swept aside. The horrid
Duveen cable was forgotten. In fact, after those distressing early
setbacks, it became every bit as great a success as van Meegeren at
the height of his paranoia could ever have expected. It would not
have been enough for him to have created a work that had been
accepted and sold as a run-of-the-mill Vermeer. It had to be
generally recognized, as it now was, as a masterpiece of very
special significance, and to receive all but universal enthusiasm.
Any who held a contrary opinion, who were always to maintain
afterwards that they failed to share the general delight, with almost
no exception kept remarkably quiet now, though even here it is

possible to cite Miss Margaretta Salinger, a senior research fellow at the Metropolitan Museum, New York, who reported in 1938 that she believed the *Emmaus* was a forgery. This is of particular interest because her opinion was not helped by any scientific examination—the *Emmaus* was submitted to none until 1945—but on purely visual appraisal: it was her 'immediate conclusion on seeing the picture that it was not a Vermeer'.

It must, however, be emphasized that in this case laboratory tests might well have been ineffective. It is virtually certain that no trace of the artificial resin would have been identified, since chemists found it impossible to agree that its presence was positively indicated even when they knew much later what substances they were seeking and could use specific tests which would not now have occurred to them. The pigments were all authentic. The cut canvas might very well have been missed because there would be no possible reason to look for it and its significance— which Decoen in any case denies—might not have been appreciated. A radiograph would have revealed evidence, if carefully studied, of an underpainting—the small head from the *Lazarus*—in one small area, but this would have been acceptable. The crackle would have stood up to the test of infra-red or X-ray photographs.

Where the experts now led, the public followed like lambs. Van Meegeren, after his confession, enjoyed telling how he himself paid a visit to the Boymans in early 1938 to see their new Vermeer, which was attracting the largest crowds the museum had ever known. It was hung in the position of greatest honour with a special carpet in front of it and a rope barrier to prevent the throngs from approaching too closely. Van Meegeren used to recount how he patiently made his way through them to get a good look at his picture. When he had at last reached the front, and thoroughly savoured the moment, he leant forward across the rope barrier to examine it more closely, in particular those areas that had been cleaned and re-restored. At once a uniformed attendant sternly motioned him back.

It would be remembered later that van Meegeren more than once expressed his opinion at about this time that the new Vermeer was a forgery and that he himself could produce one every bit as good. The wonderful irony pleased him when the latter claim was violently disputed. When his collocutors disputed the former, he would listen attentively and then play the part of his own devil's advocate, arguing against them and stating in turn the various reasons for holding a contrary view: there are no biblical Vermeers, there have been no scientific tests, the brushwork or composition are inferior, and so on. Having thus enjoyed hearing affirmations to the contrary, he would sometimes put on a show of being convinced, of coming round to the others' point of view, of agreeing that it might after all be a Vermeer.

By the springtime, van Meegeren's success could have hardly been more complete. The leading Vermeer expert had given his work an unconditional certificate; it had been sold for a very large sum to one of the leading museums of his homeland; the discovery of 'the greatest Vermeer' had received worldwide publicity; it had been described as 'the art find of the century' and intemperately extolled in print by many of those he considered his prime enemies. His whole purpose, he was to maintain, had been to prove these incompetent and to compel acknowledgement that he, van Meegeren, so long despised by them, was a great creative artist. The time had therefore now at last come when he should have assembled his evidence—the cut canvas, the sawn-off stretcher arms, the chemicals and pigments—and proved to the world that he had painted the *Emmaus*. But van Meegeren, when at last this moment came, stayed as quiet as a mouse.

It is unreasonable to infer from this one fact, however important it may be, that the original motive never in fact existed but was invented by the forger to give his achievement a more laudable object than mere financial gain. As has been mentioned, his retention of the evidence is an extremely strong indication that he intended to claim authorship. Had he done so it would have proved him a far greater man; from no quarter could he have been censured and his whole achievement might have been legal as well as admirable. The explanation of his silence, much more probably, is that it was now already too late, already too difficult to go through with his plan, owing to his weakness and profligacy in the months since the sale. A fatal danger had always lain, if he had only recognized it, in the fact that this interval had necessarily to elapse before he could publicly claim the *Emmaus* as his own. It was not enough that it had been certificated and sold. He had to wait for its public exhibition, for the critiques, for the acclaim, until the world had been deceived. Meanwhile, with money in the bank, he possessed the illusion of wealth; with each act of extravagance it would be harder to repay until soon it became impossible.

There is a tendency to think of a man as having a fixed character, and as driven by motives that are the considered product, rational or irrational, of complex introspection and prolonged internal debate. In fact there are few such men; van Meegeren, certainly, was not one of them. A man often acts on impulse; his motives may change or be altered, or may not be clearly known even to himself. If he has strength of will or character, he may sit down from time to time to consider where he is heading in life, to set himself targets, and may then possess the singlemindedness and determination to reach or at least approach them. This, however, is in fact rare; most men go along from day to day without much consideration, allowing themselves to be affected and deflected by fortuitous and often extraneous circumstances, which easily divert them from ends they have set themselves. Although van Meegeren may indeed have been obsessed by a desire for revenge which had driven him with greater power than any previous impulse in life, and had consequently achieved a work of more intrinsic merit than any previous canvas, his inherent and inescapable weaknesses now took charge again and caused him to be diverted in precisely such a manner.

I do not imagine that he ever reached a conscious, deliberate decision to stay silent, on the considered grounds that he had, after all, proved himself (if only *to* himself) which he now came to think sufficient; and the world could wait to recognize him— either till his death or to some shadowy, undefined and in fact impossible future date. (He would say after his confession that he had resolved to leave a testament, with evidence appended, to prove after his death that he had painted the *Emmaus*. The fact remains that he never did compose any such document and it seems most unlikely that he would have done so in the two years of life remaining to him.) I think it far more likely that he was diverted from what had been a true and laudable purpose by purely superficial influences, that he gave in to irrelevant temptations which, though of no importance, would be hard for a man of his natural hedonism to resist, and never realized the disastrous implications of his irresponsible actions until it was too late.

Van Meegeren was in Holland when the *Emmaus* sale went

through in the last days of 1937. At today's values, the Rembrandt Society handed over the equivalent of almost £200,000. Van Meegeren received about two-thirds of this; the tidy balance, after payment of expenses, was shared by Boon and Hoogendijk. Van Meegeren had never before handled money on anything remotely approaching this scale, and it might be suggested that he could hardly be expected to hand back such a sum. But if he had really thought about it, and if he had been a man of more strength and integrity, he must surely have seen that greater advantages, not all of them material, might be expected to accrue by doing so than might at once superficially appear. Firstly he would have the moral satisfaction of knowing that he had committed no criminal act—or no criminal act, at least, that he could not later put right. He would have the personal pleasure of observing the public downfall of his enemies as he had planned, whilst at the same time being able to claim that his work had been judged the equal of Vermeer's. Even on the money side, there would have been very important recompenses. He would at once have been famous; his paintings—past and future—would be of very much greater value (as was in fact to happen after his confession); and moreover the *Emmaus* itself would presumably have reverted to him. At the height of the controversy it could well have fetched a high price as a notorious canvas which also had considerable artistic merit; as the owner of the copyright, he could have obtained further very worthwhile sums from the sale of reproduction rights to magazines and newspapers, not to mention the rights in his first-person account of how and why he had painted it. From what is known of him, however, it seems likely that he never seriously considered these and other implications—or not, at any rate, until it was too late.

It was when Boon handed him his cheque that he stood at the very crossroads. Who can be surprised that he paid it in, to give himself something for out-of-pocket expenses, when now for the first time he had access to tens of thousands after living from hand to mouth for almost all his life? It was not, I believe, that he now became corrupted by money as has been suggested; nothing so serious was necessary. Having money, he at once began to spend it. After as little as a week or two of the reckless extravagance to which he had always been subject if a windfall came his way (but never as reckless as now with such a fortune in the bank), the immediate claiming of authorship, if not yet impossible, would soon have presented financial problems that would be very hard to face.

In principle, he may have been heading for Roquebrune to lead a quiet life in the sun, to read and savour the reviews, to wait until he judged the moment right to return to Amsterdam for his long-planned day of glory. It didn't work out that way. He went shopping before he left Holland, and he also had something to celebrate; a couple of thousand guilders would have seemed of no importance. The very existence of that money in the bank must indeed have provided a perfect illusion of wealth, making it virtually impossible to accept that every thousand spent would have somehow to be repaid. The thousands multiplied, thoughtlessly, uncaringly. His route homeward was through Paris, where it was natural to break the journey, to spend a night: in fact he stayed the better part of a week, largely owing to his encounter, which could well have been predicted, with a cabaret girl, a Swede, in a *boîte* off the Champs Elysées. Having money, he spent it—with increasing ardour as it seemed more each day to have been earned, to belong to him by right. *Petits cadeaux* (soon very far from *petits*) for his companion and her friends; compensating, equal gifts to take home with him for Jo, all in a haze of champagne. It may already have been too late before he even reached Roquebrune.

Thus the abandonment of his grand design, conceived with such inspiration and wholly praiseworthy, and put into effect till now with such obsessive skill and determination, may have resulted from mere weakness and extravagance in less than a month of riotous living, which slipped away so swiftly and gave him nothing of value in return. A fatal weakness had prevented him all his adult life from achieving the true greatness that was otherwise, perhaps, within his potential. Now, after its submergence for five years in the swirling waters of his desire for justification and revenge, it re-emerged at precisely the moment when both were at last at his finger-tips and by driving him to foolishness put both beyond his grasp.

If it were not already too late, if too much cash had not already run through his pockets even before he reached Roquebrune, it certainly had soon after his return. It was as though the little artist, who had almost always been penniless till then, was compelled to show the world he had made good, had achieved wealth and was every man's equal. He must have forgotten that by doing so he was preferring a spurious and valueless esteem to a true professional and artistic triumph. Van Meegeren invented two different stories to account for his sudden wealth, which he could not help making evident whenever he entered a bar or restaurant, took his wife shopping in Nice or Monte Carlo, or visited the casino where he had never played more recklessly. To his wife, if she were ignorant of the truth, he is supposed to have told precisely the half-true story, the intermingling of fact and fantasy, that was entirely typical of him. Whatever else she knew, she must certainly have been aware that large works of art had been arriving from Italy at the Villa Primavera; he had never attempted to conceal this, as is obvious from the fact already mentioned that de Augustinis, the *gérant*, still after thirty years clearly remembers their arrival. These were in fact canvases of no major importance, bought from an unknown Italian source for resale in France—a speculative transaction of the kind in which van Meegeren did from time to time involve himself. He would have told his wife that amongst these he had found the *Emmaus*; from this point, he could have told the true story. It was all a great piece of luck: amongst the job lot of canvases purchased, one had turned out to be by Jan Vermeer of Delft. He had told a similar story to Boon; and his wife would at once have accepted, as Boon had done, that it must not be told to the world, since the exportation of such a major work might involve the vendor in serious trouble with the Fascist authorities in Italy, even if it were maintained that he (or she) had been unaware of its value and importance, as would have been implicit in the story. What then to say? He had prevailed upon Boon to retail an invented account of the *Emmaus'* provenance, but this had been for the express purpose of not revealing his name and would not do at all to account for his new-found affluence. A third invention was necessary.

The one he chose was simple to the point of bathos. It was that he had won first prize in the *Loterie Nationale*—in which, as his friends and neighbours would certainly have known, he used to take a ticket almost every week. This story was in fact less safe than he may have thought or than may at first appear. It would indeed be accepted by his neighbours and acquaintances who would have no reason to doubt it. If one is lucky enough to win a prize, it may be collected without publicity or fuss at any bank in France. However, it is such an obvious way of explaining sudden wealth that in certain cases, if there are other grounds for suspicion, it may lead to a discreet enquiry on the part of the local police. A minor prize may be claimed without formality—it is paid in cash and no receipt is necessary. The *gros lot* is so large that it has to be paid by cheque and a written record therefore always exists. It has happened in a few extreme cases that the police have required sight of such evidence.

Van Meegeren was known to the Roquebrune police—it will be remembered that he had been briefly (and quite mistakenly) suspected in a murder case—but there is no known reason why any such investigation should here have been initiated. He was thought of as a law-abiding citizen. He may well have had eccentric ways, he would get drunk from time to time, he would shout a good bit when he became involved in passionate public arguments, but such idiosyncratic behaviour may be expected of an artist. By the local police as by the local residents, van Meegeren's invention was at once fully accepted. No questions were asked. He became overnight that much-envied and sympathetic figure, the little man who had nothing previously and now has a vast first prize, like a bank clerk or factory worker who has scooped the treble chance.

And yet what a comedown! If money were all, he had indeed lost nothing—had rather gained. But van Meegeren presented himself as an idealist, as an intellectual, intent upon proving a serious point of view and his own genius. If the world could not be told the truth, he was merely proving facts to himself alone—facts, moreover, in which he already believed so passionately that they themselves had been a major spur. This should have been his time of triumph, for which he had worked and planned so long, with such obsessive passion, to which all had been subordinate. When the moment came, he could share it with nobody, was forced to confine the knowledge of achievement to his own burning soul. He passed up the opportunity of intellectual justification, or moral and professional integrity, of artistic recognition, choosing to appear as one who had rather achieved a purely material success by an action that necessarily, and above all others, involved no merit at all: the purchase by the purest luck of the right little meaningless slip of paper.

5
Backgrounds

EVEN if van Meegeren had never intended at any level of consciousness to claim authorship of the *Emmaus* either now or later, which is possible but most unlikely, it would certainly still be true that a driving motive from the beginning had been to prove himself beyond doubt a master, and to show those to be incompetent who failed to recognize him, even if he could share the knowledge with no-one. It is arguable that he could in fact achieve neither end, despite the success of the *Emmaus*, since on the one hand its creation—whilst showing genius in such fields as chemistry, technique and psychology—had nothing to do with his ability as an artist, and on the other its very excellence as a forgery would give critics and experts a valid excuse for deception. This, however, if true, would only confirm that van Meegeren, like most of us, was often impelled by irrational motives. Had this been the only defect in his character, it might not be necessary to probe any more deeply. If he had indeed been a great artist, if for years he had been painting brilliantly and had failed to achieve recognition solely owing to the malice or total lack of perception of all or almost all his contemporaries, then no further explanation might be sought for his determination to set things right by painting the *Emmaus*. But if one considers his previous career objectively, it is hard to believe that such was indeed the case. For a decade before the move to Roquebrune, his painting had been increasingly mediocre—all too often no better than fourth-rate. Apart from the fact that he was still painting in the outdated traditionalist style of the seventeenth and eighteenth centuries, which would already have been against him, his work was often superficial, his inspiration dull, his drive lacking, his creativity small. It has thus appeared already that his belief in himself as a master, as an ignored genius, was in fact neurotic. The same neuroses would equally have impelled him to take for granted (as he did) such acclaim as he received and to resent with force all adverse judgments, however trivial. The critics had given him generous praise when he was young, his talent strong; since then he may be thought to have received almost exactly as much acclaim as he deserved. It has thus appeared, however hard it may always be for a man of his ambition to admit to being a failure, that his resentment of them, a part of his *folie de grandeur*, was pathological. Symptoms of the same mental disorder may be seen in his chronic inability to concentrate and persevere, in his experimentation with all known media, and in his tendency to leave canvases unfinished, all of which had prevented him from achieving his full potential as a painter in his own right. It is now necessary to consider the causes behind the motives; if the latter were neurotic, whence did the neuroses spring and what made them develop as they did?

If the known facts of his childhood are explored, they reveal a classical example of those 'struggles of the developing infant to assert his personality against his environment' that Adler held to be responsible for all neuroses, which would develop in adolescence and early manhood along equally classical lines.

He was one of those who is born with or soon acquires a strong artistic talent and desire, despite being a member of an uncomprehending bourgeois family. Moreover there was to be implanted and grow in him, from as far back as he could remember, a wish to overcome his feelings of personal inadequacy, arising from his small stature and physical frailty as well as from the open hostility of a highly conventional father to his sensitive, highly strung son, by attaining a position of strength and power through recognition and acclaim in a chosen field.

He had been born in 1889, in Deventer, the home of Terborgh, who was now its most loved son. The town stands on the River Ijssel in the inland, eastern province of Overijssel: it is slow-moving and beautiful with fine churches and many elegant buildings dating from Terborgh's days and earlier. His father, Henricus, a schoolmaster, was unimaginative, stern, and a strict disciplinarian. He taught English and History in the Deventer teacher's training college, had written several textbooks and had degrees from Delft University in English and Mathematics, but his reputation was more for his strictly ordered life, and the discipline he instilled in his family and pupils, than for academic distinction. He was forty before he married. His wife, Augusta, bore him five children: Han was the middle one, the second son. He would recall that they were not permitted to speak in their father's presence unless he first addressed them. The few treats he allowed them were unoriginal and standardized. Every Sunday they proceeded to Mass in a crocodile, headed by father and mother.

It may have been to his mother that Han van Meegeren owed his creative impulses. Augusta was delicate and sensitive, fifteen years younger than her husband, and is known to have been artistically inclined till her marriage put an end to it. Han certainly had her delicacy, alone of all the children, and was always much the smallest for his age. His father took to referring to him as 'Little Han'—Han being already a diminutive form of Henri— and this, it seemed to him, more with regret than affection. Han began to draw profusely when he was eight or nine years old, perhaps already to compensate for his physical shortcomings. Soon it involved him passionately: he made pictures of his dreams, as he was to recall in later life, and 'invented a world where I was king and my subjects were lions'. Dismayed by this evidence of an artistic tendency in a member of his family, the schoolmaster habitually tore up his young son's drawings, forbade his wife to encourage him, and lacked the perception to understand why this drove him to draw more than ever.

Wishing to protest but not yet able to defy his father openly, he found an outlet by attacking authoritarian symbols. He was to delight in telling his own children of two particular escapades, of which he must therefore be supposed to have felt special pride, and it may hardly have been a coincidence that these were directed not just against authority, but against symbols of Church and State, its two primal founts. It was the State's turn first. Having noticed one morning that the key had been left in the front door of the police station, he quietly closed the door, locked it, and threw the key into a canal. Then he hid to watch the police climbing out with indignity through the windows; there was no duplicate key and they had to break the door down. God came next: he and Herman, his elder brother, stole all the wine one evening from their uncle's church—he was priest in the next parish—and happily got drunk on it. The loss was not discovered till just before Mass next morning. Herman, destined for the priesthood at his father's insistence, had felt some misgiving but Han had talked him into it.

In passing off his *Emmaus* as a Vermeer, he was in fact doing just the same thing on an immensely larger scale: an attack of daring and ingenuity against accepted conventional standards, which he himself despised, to attain what he could feel to be a position of power against them.

On entering High School, Han came under the protective influence of Bartus Korteling, a dedicated artist and teacher from whom he now received his first lessons in drawing and painting. Korteling was to become a lifelong friend. Although he remained little known as a painter, he had a real knowledge of methods and technique; he gave Han the early training in care and meticulous brushwork which would always stand him in good stead. His young son, Wim, was Han's age and soon his best friend. Korteling soon become more than a master to him; he took to going home with him after school, to watch him at work in the studio and to pick up what tips he could. Korteling recognized his talent, gave him special attention and answered all his questions, thus becoming the father he had needed and never had.

Henricus continued his opposition even when Han started to win prizes, and it became clear that he was Korteling's outstanding pupil. He was the kind of man who would find it hard to understand why they had to teach art in school anyway, who believed that artistic talent was of no advantage at all in any acceptable profession—rather the reverse, since it provided evidence of waywardness and instability. The thought of Han becoming an artist would have so appalled him that it probably never occurred to him. Noticing inevitably that he was less and less at home, he resented his relationship with Korteling and attempted to reassert his influence. He continued to destroy Han's work if given any pretext.

Han grew in achievement under Korteling's protection. Though still of small stature and frail, he soon became determined not to be thought a weakling. As a grown man, he would proudly show a scar on his forehead which he had earned when fighting, he would say, in the front High School ranks against their rivals, the Commercial School; the wound had been inflicted by a well-aimed lump of coal from an opponent's catapult. But he came to learn from Korteling that the body is subject to the mind, and that intellect could more than compensate, when it came to ruling lions, for lack of physical strength. Once he became convinced of this, be began to be driven violently to intense intellectual effort by his growing desire for success and justification. Soon he was reading and absorbing all the books he could find. Of his own accord he attended evening classes, discovered a bent for mathematics and learned poetry easily at the second reading.

There can be no doubt that Korteling's liberal and enlightened influence was of essential value to Han during his difficult adolescence. He was totally out of sympathy with his unimaginative father, who valued nothing that he valued, and who for his part must have wondered why his son should be so far from his desires—dreamy, undisciplined, feckless, and possessed of this artistic passion which he found useless and incomprehensible. Perhaps the schoolmaster was right. Perhaps Han would have led a happier life, perhaps a more productive life, if there had never grown in him this one unquenchable passion. Perhaps would Shelley too. But, since it existed, it needed acceptance and nurture; to oppose it as his father did was to build up resentments and conflicts which were to unbalance his character and gravely weaken his confidence.

Too often such instability is facilely attributed to a supposed broken home or warring parents. This may frequently be so, but neither was present here. Han was one of a large, united family. His brothers and sisters (apart from Herman, who died young) were to lead conventional settled lives. His parents, so far as is known, had a contented, stable relationship: Augusta, by nature timid and submissive, was ready to accept—indeed probably welcomed—the domination and discipline which came naturally to her husband. If a child of theirs grew up as insecure as Han, it is the first step to attribute it to the incompatability between him and his father. The second is to ask why the incompatability existed—why, to be more specific, such strong artistic impulses, which largely caused the conflict between them, should have been present in him at all, and in him alone of the children.

Unfortunately no answer can be given because not enough is known of his antecedents or of his boyhood. An artist does not spring from nowhere. The influence of heredity may often be exaggerated, as for example when an artist father gets an artistic son, since this may in fact be rather due to the artistic background of his childhood. But its importance is shown all the same when a child is brought up by an unrelated foster-father from its first days, through the death, departure or indifference of its own, yet still begins to show his characteristics, though these be totally absent in the adoptive parent. Han's artistic talent and proclivity may have been inherited from an antecedent—perhaps Augusta's father—but this would be the merest guesswork since nothing whatever is known of him. It could equally well have been implanted by some fortuitous and unrecorded meeting or event— a visit to a gallery or a single chance encounter with someone in the world of art who had it in him to inspire admiration; in Deventer, neither would have been unlikely. At his highly impressionable age—it will be remembered that he was eight or nine when he began to draw profusely—one such event might have been enough to start him, and his father's unreasonable opposition (itself neurotic) would then have greatly stimulated what might otherwise have been no more than a passing fancy.

It is unlikely that Han would have ever become an artist without Korteling's encouragement and support. Yet these came with such strength that they may have been largely responsible for his eventual failure to reach maturity and make a name for himself. Korteling was a man of liberal principles, but as an artist belonged immoveably to the old school: he had no time for 'the moderns', as he would have described the Impressionists and Post-Impressionists who were then coming to the fore. It was through this father-substitute, with all the respect he commanded, that Han already learned to emulate, beyond all others, the great Dutch masters of the Golden Age. Throughout his life, this early-instilled admiration was never once to falter; the grown van Meegeren, *l'homme fait, mais mal fait* (as it is not unfair to describe him), was to remain a traditionalist, despite superficial indications to the contrary, just as Korteling had been.

When he was eighteen, he was sent to Delft to study architecture at the Institute of Technology. The schoolmaster had been compelled to recognize that the erratic Han, alone of all his children, might be clever enough to follow him to Delft, and had agreed to his sitting the entrance provided he would do his best to complete the course, if admitted, in five years instead of the usual six. Architecture had been chosen, not without reluctance on both sides, as a compromise offering a profession just within the bounds of what Henricus thought respectable—he would have preferred him to become a schoolmaster like himself, or a priest like Herman—and yet within which Han's artistic talents, which his father now had to recognize, might perhaps be of some use. He had removed him from High School two years earlier, acknowledging that a boy who had already reached the top form would get inadequate preparation there. He passed his entrance without trouble after eighteen months' cramming with a private tutor at home.

At Delft, which he enjoyed more than any other period of his life, Han's stature developed and his independence grew. He was much affected by an incident when at home on vacation after his first year. Herman, always the closest to him of his brothers and sisters, ran away from the seminary where he was completing his training for the priesthood and turned up at Deventer to implore his father to remove him. He had at least realized that he had no vocation. The bishop arrived a few hours later in person and Henricus sent Herman back with him. Han realized that he, too, was being compelled by his father, just as Herman was, to follow an undesired profession and resolved to escape with more success than his brother. He gave less time to architecture than to painting, and to studying art on his own; many of his vacations he spent with Bartus Korteling.

It is significant that the technical side of painting was already of special interest to him. Korteling used to make up his own paints; despising the practice, now almost invariable, of buying paint in a tube, ready-made and synthetic, he manufactured his own in the manner of those Golden Age masters who were at the same time his gods. He was also inclined to experiment with his media, again preferring the natural to the synthetic. Van Meegeren had watched him at such work from the days of his first visits and regarded it as a normal part of the creative process; he knew his methods well and lovingly followed his example. The importance to him later of his knowledge and experience in this special, unusual field will be obvious.

On a fine summer evening in 1911, when he was just twenty-two and in his fourth year, he met a very pretty art student at the rowing club. Her name was Anna de Voogt, and she was of mixed blood: her mother was Sumatran and a Moslem, her father a government official serving in the East Indies. Their marriage had been opposed by the local prince who had seen Anna's mother as a bride for his son; it lasted five years. After the divorce, her father moved on to Java; her mother soon married the princeling and had never been seen again. Anna had come to Holland with her Dutch grandmother, with whom she now lived in nearby Rijswijk. Han had little experience of girls—he was shy, much withdrawn and lacking in self-confidence—but a romance blossomed with Anna, and before long she was pregnant. His father, though greatly disturbed by its improvidence, was in no position to oppose their union, though he insisted that Anna should first become a Catholic. To this she agreed as being a matter of no importance and they were married in the late spring of 1912. There was no hope of running to an independent *ménage* and they accordingly moved in with Anna's grandmother in Rijswijk.

The young van Meegeren had thus contracted precisely the kind of marriage that might have been expected from one of his instability. Not yet twenty-three, he had chosen a bride whose parents' marriage had never really existed and whose life had been without any true parental influence. She no longer remembered her mother; she saw her father extremely seldom on his occasional, unpredictable returns from the Far East. With no money of their own, they were dependent on the unchanged meagre allowance from Henricus, which was supposed to cease as soon as he sat his finals, and on the kindness of Anna's grandmother who had, however, little money to spare. Thus he was to ensure that he went out into the world more disorganized, insecure and resentful than ever.

He had now entered what should have been his final year at Delft. Encouraged by Anna, who recognized his talent, he now already hoped to become a professional artist if he could, but thought it wise to complete his architectural studies to buy time before having to support himself, his wife and their expected child as a young and unknown painter. Rijswijk, now a suburb of The Hague, was in those days a pleasant country town midway between the capital and Delft; he used to cycle the seven miles to and from his classes. His academic studies were not helped by having a pregnant wife as well as his painting to occupy him.

The first troubles came that winter. Everything happened at once. The baby was due in November, his finals the following month. At precisely the same time, work was occupying him that probably mattered more to him than either. A gold medal was awarded every five years for the best painting submitted by a student. The Institute of Technology in Vermeer's home town had a large and active art school; its gold medal brought great prestige to the winner. Van Meegeren fully realized that he would be setting up as a professional painter—that very month, if things went as planned—without any relevant diploma or degree, and knew how much even minor success would mean in securing commissions. He decided on a water colour and began work in the autumn on his first sketches. In choice of subject, he was at the same time clever and exceedingly ambitious (as he was also to be with his forgeries): he decided on an interior of the St Laurens Church in Rotterdam—clever because his architectural knowledge would stand him in good stead, ambitious because of its very great complexity. The work necessitated numerous visits to Rotterdam, some fifteen miles from Rijswijk—it seems curious that he could find no subject to challenge him nearer home, for example in Delft itself—at a time when his wife was far advanced in pregnancy and when he should in any case have been working hard for his finals. When he failed them, his father agreed to *lend* him the money for another year at the Institute, but demanded repayment, with interest, by instalments out of his earnings over the next ten years. Van Meegeren agreed; he was again buying time.

It may be that his work for the prize had distracted him from his architectural studies; he did not allow the arrival of his son to divert him from the St Laurens painting as it neared completion. It is a remarkably fine work, clearly showing inspiration and confidence; as almost always with a van Meegeren, the technique was impeccable. It walked away with the medal—a remarkable achievement for probably the only competitor who was not a full-time art student. It is of no little significance that the finished work was almost pure seventeenth century, a fact that not only already shows his unwillingness to develop the principles implanted in him by Korteling, but would also indicate the favour shown by professional judges in Vermeer's citadel for the traditional Dutch style in preference to that of a modern school.

Van Meegeren had previously sold some half dozen canvases for next to nothing. The St Laurens watercolour fetched almost £100—an exceedingly high price for an unknown young painter in 1913. Moreover he found as the Institute's gold medallist that he could sell other works more easily and at enhanced prices. He received this reassurance just when it was needed (reassurance, as it would always be, was already most necessary to him) and it increased his self-confidence to the point where he could finally decide to abandon any thought of ever becoming an architect. To his father's impotent fury, he refused even to sit his finals when December came again.

However, he was not to remain long without a degree. He knew it would give him status in his chosen vocation, and tangible evidence of his skill, and the always-needed reassurance, if he could obtain an art degree even though he could have no opportunity to study for it specifically. Relying solely on the knowledge he possessed already, he enrolled briefly in The Hague Academy of Art for the sole purpose of sitting their examinations; he passed them, though it is on record that he was classed 'unsatisfactory' in portraiture. He received his degree on 4 August 1914, the day England declared war on Germany. He was twenty-five and his future shone with promise.

So long as his work as an artist was well rewarded, van Meegeren seems to have been able to live down the effects of his disturbed childhood and lead a stable, productive life. Yet it may well have been this initial success, which was in one way so necessary to him, that led him through personal weaknesses—another product of that childhood—to complacency, an inability to change his methods and develop as a creative artist in the context of his times, so that his high promise was never fully realized. When recognition and acclaim began consequently to diminish, it may have been the feelings of insecurity, implanted in him through his early environment and always in the background, that caused him to react with a neurotic hatred of his detractors, most of his fellow artists and finally the whole established art world, instead of with a desire to mend his shortcomings.

The impetus of van Meegeren's talent carried him successfully through the first six or eight years after obtaining his degree and setting himself up as an artist. He was soon offered a professorship at the Academy; this flattered him and he was tempted to accept it since he would have gained a position in life as well as financial security, but it would have left little time for his own work, which he considered all-important, and he turned down the offer. At the end of the year, the young man who worked as assistant to

Professor Gips, a senior teacher at Delft, was mobilized, and the professor invited young van Meegeren to replace him. This was more to his liking, since it involved less work and would take him back to Delft; he accepted on a temporary basis.

He and his family, including grandmother, had moved that summer from Rijswijk to Scheveningen, a pleasant seaside town not far from the capital. He now decided that he and Anna could set up on their own and they took a flat in Delft. Life, however, was difficult. His assistant's salary was eight pounds a month; he had expected at least to double this by working for himself, but though he did succeed in selling some paintings they fetched extremely low prices and he had to cover the cost of paints and canvases. Delft proved expensive and Anna was soon pregnant again. At this critical time an event occurred of great interest and significance in the light of later history. For his prize watercolour, van Meegeren had received some twenty or thirty times more than for any subsequent work. With bills to pay and no money in his pocket—he had pawned the gold medal—he proceeded, secretly, to start work on a copy of it. When his wife discovered this and questioned him on his intentions, he began by stating the naïve proposition that if the original had fetched £100 there was no reason why a duplicate should fetch less. Anna, whose high principles are unquestioned, would never for a moment have swallowed this, and after further questioning van Meegeren told her the truth. He planned to pass it off as the original. He had a particular buyer in mind—a foreign collector who would soon be leaving Delft so the risk would be negligible—and he planned to say that he had previously sold a copy and himself kept the original. He justified this blatant dishonesty by just the kind of argument that he would employ with his forgeries, which it so clearly foreshadows: he was deceiving nobody, the work was necessarily as good as the buyer believed it to be, the aesthetic joy of beholding it was the only criterion of value and its true history was irrelevant so long as the client was satisfied. It may thus be seen that van Meegeren, at the age of twenty-five, not only had convinced himself, or pretended to have convinced himself, of the truth of certain value-judgments which were convenient but in fact not seriously tenable (thus revealing a grave defect in his intellectual integrity), but also would already have been capable, if left to himself, of a probably criminal act in no way comparable to the boyhood prank of stealing sacramental wine. The same intellectual fault, having greatly widened and grown, was to propel his thoughts in the direction of forgery, just as the same moral defect would encourage its commission.

Anna would have none of it. She insisted that the true story be told, and on this basis a sale was in fact made. The duplicate fetched £4. Though this was predictable, it served only to stimulate—may even have initiated—van Meegeren's resentment, so vital to his story, of the principles governing the value of all works of art, especially his own.

Nonetheless, he made progress rapidly: within a few months he had his first work exhibited at a gallery in The Hague, and this led an art dealer, one van der Wilk, to commission four pictures a month from him at a monthly salary of £6. Van der Wilk would also pay for his paints and canvases. The arrangement continued until his first one-man show, which occurred in Delft next year (1916). This had been arranged largely through Anna's initiative: she had persuaded her relatives and their well-to-do friends to put up the money to finance it and to come along in force. Van Meegeren laboured long to fill the hall. Versatile to a fault, he had no set style, no set medium, no favourite subject. He painted in watercolours and oils; he drew in pencil, pen and ink, charcoal. His wife in her boudoir, his young son asleep—with cathedral interiors, the countryside and bathers on the beach, these were among his subjects.

His work was well received critically and attracted local attention; the fact that he sold all his paintings was not solely due to the relatives. The following year he moved with his growing family to The Hague where, as Coremans has said, he quickly achieved success, 'chiefly in high social circles where the ease and mastery with which he executed his drawings, watercolours and portraits was appreciated'.* Soon he was giving lessons, for rather fancy fees, to a small, admiring group of well-to-do young amateurs who came each week to the studio he had rented in another part of the city. They were usually more remarkable for their position in Hague society than for artistic talent and ambition; it was also noticeable that they were usually girls, and very often pretty ones.

It was during one of these lessons that van Meegeren produced his best-known 'original', if so it may be termed to distinguish it

* Coremans, op. cit., page 24.

from his forgeries. This was his famous *Deer*, which is said to have been more frequently reproduced than any other drawing or painting in Holland. It happens that its popularity was largely due to the artistically irrelevant fact that the animal belonged to Princess Juliana; van Meegeren had somehow or other arranged for it to be brought each week from the Royal Palace to his studio as a model for his pupils. At each visit, van Meegeren made several sketches, between correcting those of his young ladies; after six months of this, one of them teased him that he should know it well enough to draw it in ten minutes. He at once took up the challenge and accomplished the work in nine. His rapid masterpiece pleased him; he was already engaging in commercial work from time to time and at once saw it as a Christmas card or calendar. The publisher to whom he showed it, however, was unimpressed until van Meegeren mentioned that the deer was Juliana's. Van Meegeren found confirmation of his belief that aesthetic considerations were of relatively minor importance when the publisher's indifference changed promptly, if predictably, to enthusiasm—with complete justification, as has since been proved.

By now (1917) van Meegeren was on more than intimate terms with the accomplished and sophisticated woman who was soon to become his mistress and, eventually, his second wife. There had been irony in their meeting, since it had occurred as a result of his one-man show the previous year, which Anna had been largely responsible for organizing and promoting. Johanna Oerlemans, a fairly well-known actress, was married to a leading art critic, Dr Karel de Boer; there had been a flutter of excitement in the van Meegeren home when he and Jo called after the show. He had been much impressed and now wished to publish an interview with van Meegeren. The latter was more interested in his wife than his interview, and asked if he might paint her. The portrait took an unconscionably long time, and Jo de Boer was soon an important part of Han van Meegeren's life.

He was entering the long period of easy-going promiscuity that led to his divorce in 1923 and that was to continue for six years after it until at last he remarried. His bedfellows were to come and go in remarkable variety; with Jo alone did he maintain a continuing if interrupted relationship. His constant search for new conquests may be thought further evidence of his need for reassurance and of emotional immaturity. It may not have been altogether a coincidence that he preferred as his leading mistress the wife of an eminent critic. He was already beginning to regard the critics as enemies—though he was receiving no little attention from them—through his ever-present tendency to take all praise for granted, as merely a statement of fact, whilst always remembering the smallest adverse judgment and deeply resenting it. Seducing a critic's wife must have been a special satisfaction though it did him no good professionally; he was not thought to have shown his appreciation to de Boer for a laudatory article in a very appropriate manner.

Though unpredictable and moody, van Meegeren had very considerable charm and had quickly become involved in the social life of The Hague, where he soon achieved the popularity and social acceptance that was necessary to his nature. He spent less and less time at home and seldom took his wife with him to the many parties and social-intellectual gatherings to which he was invited. He was elected a member of the Haagsche Kunstring (the Art Circle of The Hague), a select band of the city's writers and painters, who met each week in the Ridderzaal for discussion and the exchange of ideas, and it was noticed that he less often brought his wife with him than Jo, or one of his models or pupils. Anna was quickly losing him.

He still had no set style, no set medium, no favourite subject. He was extremely prolific, though a temperamental weakness was beginning to appear: he would tire of a work before completing it and leave the canvas unfinished. In fact his attitude to painting was becoming very comparable with his attitude towards women, and both may have been symptoms of the same sickness. However, his second show, in 1921, was no less successful than his first. Again all his pictures were sold. It is of interest that all were biblical—and impeccably traditionalist—less because it indicates that he was sometimes capable of some degree of specialization than because his forged Vermeers were also all drawn from the Bible. Indeed one of those now exhibited was a portrayal of the young Christ teaching in the temple which he was to choose as the subject of his demonstrative 'Vermeer' painted before official witnesses in 1945.

This liking for religious subjects is unexpected, since van Meegeren had by now to all intents and purposes abandoned the

Catholic faith, which may have been largely because religion had
been hammered into him throughout his childhood; he had been
forced to learn much of the Bible by heart and had attended Mass
every Sunday for fifteen years. He was again rebelling against
father. Disillusionment also came through the death of his brother
Herman before his ordination. Van Meegeren convinced himself,
rightly or wrongly, that his brother's fatal illness had been due to
neglect and ignorance at the seminary; he never forgave the
Church and never afterwards thought of himself as a believer.
Nevertheless he was still irrationally fascinated by the mysticism
of religion, by its very unknown nature. He replaced his lost faith
with no other except perhaps a defiant belief in himself. It is
perhaps not over-fanciful to suggest that he saw his Christs as
self-portraits; he would certainly have had little difficulty in
identifying with the deity.

On a nature and personality such as van Meegeren's, early
success had two main effects. Fairly well-off, and surrounded by
admirers, who were, however, more distinguished socially than
intellectually, he began to lead a debauched life which led to a
falling off in the quality of his work. At the same time his acceptance and success appeared to him—it may be thought mistakenly
—to justify his adherence to the old-fashioned principles instilled
in him by Korteling and long nourished by the atmosphere of
Delft. He would perhaps have stood a better chance if life had
removed him from the town of his student days—to Amsterdam,
perhaps, if Paris or Florence were too much to hope for—from
the danger of there becoming a 'perpetual student' to which
indeed he half-succumbed. Yet why should he have returned to
Delft unless he *wanted* the illusion of security to be obtained from
going back to the known environment of studenthood, which
would itself imply an unwillingness to develop, to mature?

So whilst the world of art was being convulsed and revolu-
tionized by the progressive movements of the twenties, as it had
already been by those of the previous half-century, van Meegeren
remained an out-and-out reactionary: he was still in the Golden
Age. This had been enough to win him his medal and degree, to
be highly admired in a young man at the threshold of his career,
and to bring him this measure of fashionable success, but it should
have been no more than a firm foundation on which his mature
work would be built. Instead, deceived by facile praise, he was

content to stay where he was—under the safe protection of his father-figure, Korteling.

It has often been suggested that van Meegeren's contempt of the critics and his determination to discredit them arose from his belief that they were venal as well as ignorant. It has been said that they would publish a favourable notice only if they were paid, that van Meegeren incurred their enmity by refusing to comply and by disclosing the practice publicly. There seems to be some truth in this; some certainly were no better than they should have been, and their circle in Holland at the time was far from being enlightened or inspired. But if van Meegeren's hatred were pathological, such exaggeration of their dishonesty is just what might be expected of him if, through his failure to mature, he deserved little more acclaim—if any—than he received. In these circumstances a man of his nature, who could see criticism where none existed, dislike where there might even be deference, would be far more likely to attack his detractors than be influenced by their strictures.

The nine years between van Meegeren's first divorce in 1923 and his move to Roquebrune with his second wife in 1932 were in every way the least satisfactory of his life. On the one hand he was leading a disordered life of promiscuity and drink—he had not yet taken to drugs—which was a symptom of his instability and resentment; on the other, his professional achievement was seriously diminished, partly as a result of leading that kind of life (but which caused which?) and partly through a need for money at a much higher level than he could earn by painting in strict accordance with his principles and desires, to finance the extravagance that had become a part of his nature. This led him increasingly to portraiture and to indiscriminate commercial work—the easy way out.

Already his paintings and drawings had been used from time to time in reproduction for Christmas cards and calendars; his *Deer* is the best-known example. Such commercialism involved no lowering of standards. But now he turned more and more to posters and advertising, for which he found no difficulty in obtaining lucrative commissions. Posters can be minor works of art—one had only to think of Lautrec—but van Meegeren's had no such pretensions: they were for the most part thoroughly bad work, riddled with the second-rateness that was always close to the surface in him, revealing the contempt that he felt for himself in

The false de Hoogh,
Interior with Drinkers
(plate 16, above), has
much in common with the
authentic *Cardplayers* in
Buckingham Palace
(plate 17, left).

Plate 18. The false de Hoogh, *Interior with Cardplayers*.

The *Head of Christ* (plate 26, above) is almost identical to the detail head of Christ in the subsequent *Last Supper* (plate 27, below).

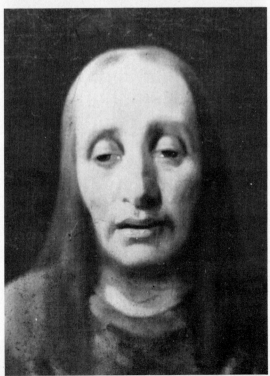

The head of the woman in van Meegeren's *Mother and Child* (plate 22, above) may be compared with the detail head of a disciple from his second *Last Supper* (plate 23, right), completed some years earlier.

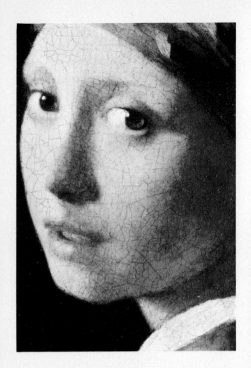

Plate 24. This detail from Vermeer's *Girl with Pearl Eardrops* may be compared with the head of St. John (on Christ's left) in the *Last Supper* (right).

Plate 25. The "second" *Last Supper*, sold to van Beuningen for 1,600,000 guilders.

Plate 21. Van Meegeren at his worst: the near-pornographic
I Have Summoned up the Depths.

Two typical van Meegeren
portraits: his *Portrait of Jo*
(his wife), (plate 19, above),
and a near-potboiler in
traditionalist style,
Portrait of Schuh
(plate 20, below).

perpetrating them. Van Meegeren distinguished in his own mind between this commercialism and his diminishing serious work, regarding them as two separate areas of endeavour with nothing but a paint-brush in common. But the former did much to harm his artistic reputation; the critics and his fellow-artists often took it, not surprisingly, as evidence of his increasing lack of integrity and inspiration.

The field of portraiture was one for which his particular talents and artistic principles eminently suited him, even though it had been thought his shortest suit when he took his degree at The Hague. A man who commissions a portrait is looking for a likeness—or frequently, though he may not know or admit it, for a tactful, more flattering version. In portraiture the traditionalist may come into his own; and here, in these in-between years, van Meegeren built up a considerable reputation. He would paint in the grand manner, in the style of a Rembrandt or a Hals. His technique was impeccable and he would achieve likenesses that seemed instantly to epitomize, to express the essence of his sitters—despite or even because of the tactful 'improvements' he was happy to incorporate. The result would be precisely the painting—the immediately recognizable but wartless portrait of his wife, the delicately romanticized version of his daughter—that an industralist or leader of society would wish to have over his fireplace.

For work of this kind, van Meegeren was soon commanding a fee of 40 or 50 guineas, and occasionally up to 100 guineas, a very worthwhile figure in those days. It is indicative of his success that during this period he was offered—or said he was offered—a contract to spend a year in the United States with all expenses paid; he was to paint a portrait a week at his maximum fee and would thus have returned with £5,000 in his pocket. He is supposed to have turned down the offer because such intensity appalled him and would have forced him to abandon his 'real' work—his painting of subjects because they pleased him, because they were significant to him—for an unbroken year at this critical time of life (he was now in his late thirties). It should be noticed that for van Meegeren, as for most artists, his portraiture did not come within this category. He regarded it, like his posters, as no expression of genius, but a way of making money that he found undemanding and at the same time brought social if not critical success. His portraits and posters were potboilers; there is little wrong with that, but soon they were occupying far too much of his time. Having made a killing by flattering a millionaire or pleasing a perfumery, he would embark on a month of licence instead of allowing his fee to finance a stable period of creativity. Like seeks out like. Van Meegeren's closest friends at this time were the painter Theo van Wijngaarden and a journalist named Jan Ubink. Apart from their shared enjoyment of a riotous, undisciplined life and total disrespect for accepted standards and conventions, these three had other striking similarities in their convictions and histories which must have cemented, if they did not cause, their friendship. All believed in the greatness of the past, in the superficiality of most modern work in the fields of art and literature. All three, moreover, had been compelled, through their inability to make a decent living if they followed their chosen vocations and stayed within the ambit of their principles, to undertake work for which their talents and knowledge would in a way qualify them, but which diverted them increasingly from their true purposes. In addition—though this they may not have realized—it was perniciously eroding their true gifts and ability, especially in the cases of van Meegeren and Ubink.

Just as van Meegeren had turned largely to portraiture and commercial work, so Ubink had been compelled by lack of financial success to turn to popular journalism from poetry and literature. He still turned out a book or sonnet from time to time, but his day-to-day employment was in the office of a Hague newspaper and his serious writing must have been less good as well as less frequent than it would have been if his style and way of thinking had not been subject to this influence. Van Wijngaarden's case was different: his love of the Old Masters had led him, besides seeking to emulate them, into the associated fields of dealing in pictures and restoring them—work that would have been less demoralizing than Ubink's but now occupied too much of his time. When he painted, he painted as van Meegeren did, in strictly traditional style.

This disrespectful trinity, these three *hommes manqués* who had dissipated their genius as they diluted it, were agreed together that their material failure was due to the world's ignorance—the belief long held by van Meegeren which was to be a major impulse in driving him to forgery. He had not yet reached that stage as a means of excusing his failure; instead, in 1926, he proposed that the three of them should band together professionally and bring out a monthly journal which would spread their beliefs, propagate their ideals and demolish their detractors. *De Kemphaan* (meaning in English *The Gamecock*) was opposed to almost everything. Its revelations of venality were all but actionable. It attacked every major painter since Delacroix. Each issue came solely from their three barbed pens, though to disguise this they wrote under many different names. It wasn't a success. Ubink's professionalism, and his contacts in publishing, helped them to bring out ten or a dozen numbers, very seldom on time, but the public's lack of interest in the principles they sought to express had already been shown by the lack of acclaim for work that those same principles had inspired. It never sold outside The Hague, was soon losing more than they could afford, and collapsed after a year.

Meanwhile van Wijngaarden's interest and success in the peripheral artistic fields of dealing and restoring had led van Meegeren into them. Van Wijngaarden had always possessed a happy knack for spotting an old canvas in a junk-shop or forgotten attic and re-selling it at a profit after cleaning and restoring it. His friend's capacity had fascinated van Meegeren and he had taken to going round second-hand furniture shops and tatty galleries in The Hague on the look-out for bargains; he found he had a flair and was lucky from the start. Soon the two friends joined forces to exploit their skills. Van Wijngaarden had many curious contacts, in Holland and elsewhere; if he heard of valuable paintings that might be going cheaply in Italy or England, the two of them would take themselves off there, appraise them themselves and import them into Holland. When it came to restoring, van Meegeren found that his profound knowledge of method and technique stood him in good stead. This was particularly so if the canvas belonged to the seventeenth- or early eighteenth-century, of which period he had such very special knowledge. And this was not merely theoretical; since he had always made most of his own paints himself, often using the same raw materials as his beloved Old Masters besides painting in their manner, he had much practical experience which came in useful now.

Van Meegeren had shown an early tendency to lack moral integrity in the sale of works of art through the episode of the duplicate watercolour that he was intending to sell as his original prize work. It seems likely that dishonesty of a comparable order was sometimes involved when he began dealing in old paintings. Yet can it be called dishonesty? It would rather appear to be the normal accepted practice to use almost any means to make a profit on a sale. The dividing line between right and wrong is in any case shadowy. If a dealer chances upon a painting which he believes might be, let us say, a Breughel, he is hardly likely to tell its owner his opinion. He would decry its merit, play down its value, attribute it to a minor contemporary—in short, do all he could to get it for next to nothing. This, it seems, is not dishonest at all. For it is not only fly-by-night operators who work thus; even some Prado directors, so far from thinking it a duty to give the owner any idea, before or after its sale, of the potential immeasurable value of his supposed Antonello, on the contrary kept him as far as possible in ignorance—and subsequently announced the fact with something akin to pride. They had got a splendid bargain and that was all that mattered. And if it seems perfectly acceptable to cheat a vendor up to a point, it is similarly a frequent practice to deceive a buyer—and the point to which this may acceptably be taken is a matter of little more than personal opinion. Van Meegeren was already moving towards or even beyond such a point in his dealings at this time. As he gained in skill as a restorer, it became easier and more of a temptation to 'improve' in his studio a work that he had picked up cheaply and hoped to sell as—let us say—a Terborgh to the gullible Mr X. (And who knows? It might even *be* a Terborgh.) To clean the picture would be perfectly unobjectionable. To touch up the colours would be a normal part of restoring—but just how much touching up is permissible? From this it is a relatively short step to touching up the signature, and thence—is it any more reprehensible and, if so, why?—to adding a signature where none existed, as has been so frequently done through the centuries.

The ultimate step of painting the whole picture was coming perceptibly closer.

Its advent must have been hastened by·a significant event, and its no less significant corollary, that occurred at this time (1928). As van Wijngaarden told it, he had by luck picked up a canvas—a portrait of a cavalier—which he believed might be a Hals. No satisfactory account of its provenance was ever to be given. It was badly in need of cleaning and restoration; as was his practice, he carried out this work before offering it for certification or sale.

Because it was potentially a valuable canvas, he did the work with exceptional care, and used certain unusual solvents and oils with which he and van Meegeren had been experimenting with favourable results. Van Meegeren knew from the beginning of his friend's lucky find, may even have had a stake in it, and almost certainly assisted with the restoration.

The work was submitted for certification to the extremely eminent art historian and critic, Dr Hofstede de Groot, who liked it, certified it as an undoubted Hals, and himself arranged its sale to a private buyer at a very high price. It was a great triumph for van Wijngaarden—his most successful coup.

It was now that Bredius first entered van Meegeren's scene. Already in his seventies, his complete authority was undisputed in Holland. He saw the canvas soon afterwards and denounced it as a forgery despite his colleague's certificate. His main ground was technical: the softness of the paint in some areas. Van Wijngaarden had specifically told de Groot to expect this; it would certainly be expected in the paint used by him in restoration but he had made a point of mentioning that the special solvents employed might have had the effect of softening areas of the old paint too. De Groot had accepted this but Bredius would not do so.

A bitter battle ensued with many hard words, in which van Meegeren was much to the fore in support of his old friend, but the word of Bredius was law and his opinion prevailed. The purchase money had to be returned, van Wijngaarden was left with an unsaleable canvas on his hands, and his coup had evaporated.

In the light of subsequent events, it was an extraordinary occurrence. Hals was to be one of the masters chosen as a victim a few years later by van Meegeren (though the canvas, *Woman Drinking*, signed *F. H.*, was one of those never offered for sale); the hardness of his paint was to be a main problem; and Bredius was to turn up again, though this time to authenticate a fake as a Vermeer instead of denouncing as a forgery what may have been a Hals. But much more was to come.

Van Wijngaarden was in a state of fury. He and van Meegeren saw the event as the fullest confirmation of their passionate belief that great experts such as Bredius and de Groot—one or other of whom must have been totally wrong—knew nothing about their business, were incapable of artistic appreciation, and were influenced by considerations about which they were very often grossly ill-informed. The fact that they wielded immense power, since the value of a highly important canvas might depend solely on their beliefs, made this all the more ludicrous. And if they made a serious mistake, it seemed in no way to lessen their reputation; if de Groot had in fact been wrong, nobody thought the worse of him. The ignorance of the experts had long been used by both of them, rationally or otherwise, to explain and justify their lack of success as artists. Now it had also snatched away from van Wijngaarden the five-figure fruits of his find. He was determined to get his own back and quite simply decided to paint himself a Rembrandt.

It must be emphasized that he did this *only* as an immense practical joke to take revenge on Bredius. It could never have been any part of his intention to put the canvas on the market. He took no trouble with the technical side: he employed synthetic pigments and allowed the paint to dry naturally. But a great expert works largely from that splendid intuition of his; he likes from time to time to give a virtuoso performance by instantly recognizing the 'unmistakable' work of a master. That is precisely what happened as soon as Bredius saw the joke picture painted by van Wijngaarden. The latter, since it *was* a joke, had given Bredius an invented account of the picture's provenance such as, if it had been true, would have gone far towards proving its authenticity, and this Bredius would have had no reason to doubt. As far as he could have known, it would be perfectly simple to check it before his judgment became public (and since van Wijngaarden would have been aware of this, it would never have occurred to Bredius that the whole thing might have been invented). Thus he fell fair and square into the trap. After one superficial glance he pronounced the work a Rembrandt, adding with a smile that it would make up to van Wijngaarden for the Hals. This it certainly did, though not at all as Bredius expected: the artist approached with his palette knife and ripped the canvas to pieces before the doctor's eyes.

It was a pleasant *coup de théâtre*, but some aspects of its importance should not be overrated. This particular forgery could never have reached the sale-room, since even a moment's superficial technical inspection would at once have given the show away: for example, any ordinary solvent would at once have dissolved the paint. Bredius must have been taking it for granted, in his desire to show off his flair for instantly recognizing a work of genius, that such inspection, when carried out later, would give a satisfactory result; if it didn't, he knew he could excuse himself. If it did and yet his opinion was disputed, he need only stick to his guns; it could be nothing more than his word against the rest, and he knew himself to be supreme, his reputation unshakeable, his authority unchallenged. It was only in such unprecedented circumstances as now existed—and as were to exist again, with such infinitely more serious implications, with van Meegeren in 1945—that his fallibility could be indisputably revealed, since in both cases this would be the positive desire of the forger, instead of his major fear, as is otherwise always the case.

Other aspects are of much significance. The supposition cannot be avoided that his friend's success brought van Meegeren one further step towards the *Emmaus*. And even on the basis of such facts as have been related, it is clear that his devious nature and increasing lack of scruples were involving him in back-door activities of a kind that had nothing to do with the vocation that he claimed for himself as a talented serious artist. The doubtful Hals and the joke Rembrandt are the only two dubious canvases in which he is known to have been involved, and in these only indirectly, at this stage; the Rembrandt must indeed have been nothing more than a joke, but it is hard to avoid feelings of suspicion about the Hals—the special chemicals used in restoration, the softness of the paint, the unexplained provenance—when viewed in the light of subsequent events.

Moreover the Rembrandt episode, which soon became common knowledge and with which his name was closely associated, made a lasting enemy of Bredius—a fact that contributed to his choice by van Meegeren as the expert to whom the *Emmaus* should first be sent—and served to increase the antipathy which was certainly felt towards him, and which he heartily reciprocated, by the Establishment in general. There can be no doubt that this antipathy had long existed. On the one hand van Meegeren had now, for a decade, chosen the latter's ignorance and prejudice as the one possible pretext to which his lack of recognition could be imputed—and this he had done loudly: in *De Kemphaan*, in public controversy, in impassioned argument. On the other hand the Establishment, hardly surprisingly, had resented such imputations and regarded him as a nuisance, as a noisy braggart with too high an opinion of himself. His long affair with de Boer's wife had hardly helped him; now came his involvement in the trick to deceive old Bredius, the *doyen* of their world, and open warfare was declared.

After the divorce in 1923, Anna had moved with the two young children to Paris. Life had been far from easy for her—van Meegeren had been predictably unreliable in supporting her—and she had had to go out to work; now that he was much more comfortably off through his portraiture and commercial work, and also through dealing, he was able to do more for them. At the same time, he began to see rather more of the children. He was in Paris fairly often and would make a point of looking them up. His son, Jacques, who was now in his teens, was showing talent as an artist; Inez was two years younger and already very pretty, with long dark hair and wide, soulful eyes. It was now that Anna established contact with her mother, who had never left Sumatra. She had not seen her since early childhood and in fact her father had told her she was dead. Anna became seized with a desire to meet and know her mother. Van Meegeren at first opposed this; a sympathy had grown between him and his talented, insecure, artistic son, and he enjoyed being seen around the cafés with his pretty daughter. He feared that if they went off to Sumatra he might never hear of them again. In the end, however, he relented and in a single handsome gesture paid Anna twelve months' allowance in advance. She departed with Jacques and Inez in 1929; they were away a couple of years.

It was soon after she left that van Meegeren finally got round to marrying Jo de Boer. She had now been his off-and-on mistress for over thirteen years, and for much of this time they had been living as man and wife. De Boer had divorced her several years previously, but van Meegeren would have found it hard to abandon promiscuity, had been too unsettled (and, it may be thought, emotionally immature) to commit himself to a single, supposedly permanent relationship, and had fought shy of marriage. Having reached forty, he now probably came to realize that, if he were ever to find any stability through remarriage, it could not conceivably be to any other than the accomplished, scheming, ambitious and beautiful woman, who believed in him and had waited through his infidelities.

Van Meegeren's remarriage was the final disappointment to his father, the perpetual schoolmaster. As a devout Catholic, he refused to recognize it. He had been distressed by the divorce—till then van Meegeren and Anna had gone dutifully from time to time for an uneasy visit—and had seen little of his son in the intervening years; he now disowned him. It mattered little to van Meegeren; he was used to being disowned.

Marriage, though it did nothing more than legalize a *ménage* that had long existed already, does seem to have brought some increased stability to his life, especially after the coming move to Roquebrune. Apart from other accomplishments, Johanna had a cool head for figures and the organized mind of a businesswoman; she kept track of his finances and bargained over his commissions. Moreover she ran their easy-going home, now brought at last within orthodox conventions but unchanged in its bohemian character, with originality, economy and tolerance. Van Meegeren would still sleep with his models from time to time, or disappear on a drinking bout which might last several days with Jan or Theo, but she would be happy to turn a blind wifely eye. She appears to have been one of the very few, beside her husband himself, who really believed him to be a great and inspired painter—a genius, even—whose immortal talent would one day be fully recognized and bring them fame and fortune. Till then she must be patient, attend to his whims, spur him to work and feed his animal needs.

Nobody else in The Hague, outside their own little band of friends, shared their opinion of him. It is true that an artist can be made or broken by the critics and gallery owners, equally true that they are subject to unpredictable whims and inconsequential thought: they will take up one particular painter, build his reputation and give his work a fashionable demand, though half a dozen others might equally have been chosen. It is not unknown for them to be venal, and van Meegeren must be admired for his continuing unwillingness ever to pay for a notice, for his courage in exposing venality as he had done in *De Kemphaan*. This did not make him friends. The critics did not like van Meegeren as a man; his hostility to them as being ignorant as well as corrupt, which became increasingly of paranoiac order, drove him to excesses of vituperation which could not easily be forgiven. It is of greater significance that they may have been fully justified in not liking him as an artist, let their opinion be based on subjective or objective grounds, on personal or professional considerations. A wide, garish vein of second- or third-rateness had run through all his work for over a decade. It had developed a lurid, morbid quality; at times it was near-pornographic; there was much that was banal about his choice of subject and its treatment. It was as though he had cheapened himself by his increasing engagement in purely commercial activity. He tended besides to be romantic, even senti-mental, which are both dirty words. All this was within the frame-work of a style and outlook that was still basically traditional: he still sought a photographic representation, an aim that went out of fashion before the invention of the camera, that no critic con-sidered a virtue. They took pleasure in deriding him, and still do: he has been described, for instance, by one well-known judge as 'a bad artist, whose pictures of dainty roebucks sniffing almond-blossom, and of Paderewski-style pianists receiving inspiration from the ghost of Liszt, had failed to win critical acclaim'.* It was only his technique that was at all times admirable; this was to be of value—indeed it was indispensable—when it came to painting Vermeers, as it had been in the field of photographic portraiture, but was enough to lift him from being nothing more than a very ordinary and somewhat debased craftsman in all other and more important fields.

The van Meegerens thought otherwise. The years immediately preceding their departure from Holland 'never to return' were marked by increasing, impotent fury against his detractors, by his unavailing abuse of those who refused to accord him the glory he certainly craved but cannot seriously be thought to have deserved. The entire world was against him; it was all a sinister conspiracy; he would somehow wreak his revenge. Such, only too obviously, are the classical symptoms of advancing paranoia; they were seething within him when he and Jo departed for Roquebrune in 1932.

* David Carritt, writing in the *Evening Standard*, 2 February 1961.

6
Two Last Suppers

WITHIN a few months of the *Emmaus* sale, van Meegeren was at work on another forgery.

It is hard to give dates, since van Meegeren, as was his custom to cause general confusion, often gave different and incompatible accounts of the chronology. It may have been now—that is, in 1938—that he painted one of the experimental canvases already mentioned, such as the Hals or the Terborgh, which were never offered for sale, but the balance of probability is that his next was the false Pieter de Hoogh, *Interior with Drinkers* (plate 16), which may have been completed before he moved to Nice that summer, though it was not sold till over a year later.

This is a less important canvas—it was to fetch only 220,000 guilders, which is considerably less than half the *Emmaus* figure— and it had none of the latter's brilliance or originality. In painting the *Emmaus*, he had gone out of his way to choose a subject and style that were untypical of Vermeer and would by no means shout his name as soon as it was seen. His forged de Hooghs—this one and the *Interior with Cardplayers* (plate 18), probably painted in 1939—are, on the other hand, exceedingly conventional, and indeed bear close resemblances to known works of that master. Van Meegeren's *Cardplayers* was to have many points in common with the undoubted de Hoogh, *Dutch Interior*, which is in the Metropolitan, New York: the window on the left of the canvas, its open wooden shutter, the wooden rafters, the map on the wall, the table—all these are so alike and so similarly positioned that they are nearly copies. Moreover the same girl, wearing the same dress, who is standing at the left of the table in the New York picture, appears in the forgery seated at the right of the table. To make a difference, van Meegeren was to paint an open doorway on the right of the canvas framing a maidservant at work in the background with a window beyond her—altogether typical of de

Hoogh. The tiled floor is almost identical to that of the authentic *Cardplayers* in Buckingham Palace (plate 17).

It is the latter canvas that served largely as van Meegeren's inspiration, if so it may be called, for his *Drinkers* ($31\frac{1}{2}''$ × $27\frac{1}{4}''$, signed *P.D.H. 1658*). The open door, the doorway, the windows, the table, the cushioned bench, the wall, the shadow on the wall— these are all in almost the identical positions and again closely copied. In both works a maidservant is again seen (though in a different attitude) through the open door in the background; in both there are four figures at the table. In the de Hoogh, two men and a woman are seated with a man standing on the right; in the van Meegeren, two men and a woman are seated with a woman standing on the left. On the wall above them is a large map of the world; the authentic seventeenth-century map which van Meegeren had acquired to use as a model for it was to be found later in his Nice studio.

There are two curious points. One is that the girl in the *Drinkers* appears to be performing some kind of conjuring trick. She is holding her wine glass as it could never possibly be held, pre- cariously balanced on the half-clenched fingers of her raised right hand; the very tip of her thumb is just barely touching it. Small wonder that she is observing the glass with an enigmatic smile. The second is that the wine-jug is extremely similar to that used in the *Emmaus*, though rather more elongated; this time it had been accurately drawn from the seventeenth-century jug that had been bought as a prop by van Meegeren and was also found at his studio. This is not all. The same wine-jug—and on these occasions it is almost exactly the same—also appears not only in the false *Cardplayers* but in two other false Vermeers: *Isaac Blessing Jacob* and the *Footwashing*. Admittedly it was a Delft jug of a design that was common there in the mid-seventeenth century and appears in several true Vermeers, but it seems remarkable that he took the risk of using it in five of his eight sold forgeries. It became a trademark.

Van Meegeren displayed extraordinary skill on the technical side, even for him, in the *Drinkers*. The paint structure was more complex than in any other of his forgeries: there were six separate paint layers (the *Emmaus* has only three). The bottommost of these, which was found to contain ochre and oil, was the original ground of the authentic seventeenth-century work, about which nothing is known, the rest of which had been removed by van Meegeren in the manner already described. Next came a greyish layer, consisting of chalk and glue; then one of darker grey with an oil base. The three topmost layers, which were grey, white and grey-white respectively, all contained phenolformaldehyde.* Having carefully left the authentic crackle in the original brownish ground, van Meegeren persuaded it to reappear, at least for the most part, in each succeeding paint-layer applied.

Decoen's book includes an illustration† that shows the surface crackle admirably. It is a full-page 'detail' covering one small area —the wine-jug and goblet. Under it he has written: 'The increased size of the crackle immediately reveals that it is faked. All the various substances show the same crackle.'‡ The book is full of untenable and often self-contradictory remarks, and in this case he actually goes on to say in the very next sentence: 'It should however be observed that certain genuine paintings may, throughout the whole of their surface, exhibit crackle of the same character.' It is very easy to be wise after the event; the fact is that the canvas was seen by several great experts before and after its sale, who must have been aware that nothing whatsoever was known of its previous history. This, as before, would have made careful examination desirable, yet to none did the induced crackle reveal it as a fake at any time, let alone 'immediately'.

At least a year was to go by before this forgery was sold. Fewer details are known than in the case of the *Emmaus*, and the reason for this time-lag is not among them. Van Meegeren again used Boon, telling him that it too was from Mavroeke's collection and had been smuggled out of Italy. Boon was to approach a well-known dealer in Holland, P. de Boer (no relation to Karel), who was later to be involved in the disposal of the *Footwashing*, the last of the false Vermeers. De Boer found a buyer in Mr D. G. van Beuningen, the extremely wealthy Rotterdam ship-owner, who was also to purchase the *Head of Christ* and the *Last Supper* (though he sold back the former to help pay for the latter). The *Emmaus* was to be the only van Meegeren forgery ever publicly exhibited; one of the others, the *Footwashing*, was bought by the

* From the report of the Commission, quoted by Coremans, op. cit., page 19.
† ibid. plate 131.
‡ He means that the crackle pattern remains much the same, irrespective of the pigments used in each part of the surface area shown.

Dutch State but never hung, and the rest went to private buyers. Van Beuningen was a true patron of the arts who built up the finest collection of Old Masters in Holland and left much of it to museums and galleries. Many such buyers lean heavily on the advice of a well-known dealer such as de Boer. It should not be imagined that he was in any way less careful or scrupulous than his colleagues, nor indeed that it is necessarily safer to buy from a large, established auction house than from a well-known respected dealer. The purchase by van Beuningen of this canvas—not as a major masterpiece on the scale of the *Emmaus*, nor even of the subsequent, inferior 'Vermeers', but none the less as an important work which involved a very considerable investment (£24,000 in 1939)—may be seen as being no more foolhardy, no more ill-advised, no more risky than in a high proportion of all such sales. But if such a picture is a forgery, it is virtually certain that this will never come to light; indeed the fact that it was for many years in van Beuningen's well-known collection will add weight to its acceptability. It is in no-one's interest to denounce it. The *Drinkers* would almost certainly still be a de Hoogh but for the circumstance that in this case the forger, as had never happened before and is unlikely to happen again, was eventually to claim it proudly as his own and was able to prove the full truth of his claim. This was such bad luck for van Beuningen, so totally unpredictable, that is has hardly discouraged others.

Whilst the *Drinkers* was waiting to be sold, much of importance was happening.

In the summer of 1938, some six months after the *Emmaus* sale, the van Meegerens terminated the Primavera lease and moved from Roquebrune to Nice. This provides clear evidence that van Meegeren had by now discarded any intention of publicly claiming the *Emmaus* as his own, at least in his lifetime, because he now bought outright a large and magnificent mansion. It was in a *quartier* that had once been highly fashionable and still had residues of greatness: les Arènes de Cimiez owes its name to the two splendid arenas which are the most impressive of its extensive Roman remains, though they are somewhat dominated by the enormous Hotel Regina, so called in wistful memory of Queen Victoria's frequent patronage. Cimiez is high above the centre of the city, already in the foothills of the Alpes Maritimes. It has many fine villas, looking out to the sea across the lights of Nice, but few more splendid than the Villa Estate, which van Meegeren now chose as his permanent future home. (It is a curious coincidence that *estate* should mean summer, as *primavera* means spring: he was moving from spring to summer in three different ways.) The marble villa, which was to become a kind of pleasure-dome, was set in its own grounds, with a vineyard, rock-pools, well-kept rose-gardens, olive trees. It had a dozen bedrooms and, on the ground floor, five large reception rooms, so designed that they all caught the sunshine and looked out to the south and west towards the sea. A separate wing contained a gallery, a music room, and what had previously been a library; this was now to be the studio (and laboratory). The newly affluent couple set about furnishing their palace with taste and luxury; its walls were hung with original van Meegerens, exquisitely framed. Then they invited their friends and most of their neighbours for a series of house-warmings which are still remembered.

By the time they had done, more than half the *Emmaus* money must already have been spent. Van Meegeren had obtained the Estate relatively cheaply—the exact figure is not known—because it was so large and expensive to run that the agents had come to regard it as something of a white elephant. It cannot have gone for a song, however, and van Meegeren had given his wife a completely free rein in furnishing and decorating it. He would not have worried; he would have had enough left to cover expenses at their new exalted level for a year or more, and by then he could count on the *Drinkers* having been sold. It cannot therefore have been purely a desire for money that led him back to forgery as soon as they had settled down. More probably he had by now become utterly fascinated by work that challenged and obsessed him more completely than any previously—and at which, moreover, he had reached a high pinnacle of success. He had new refinements to consider, new and more sophisticated equipment to assemble and try out, new theories to explore.

He is believed to have painted at least two fakes during their year in Nice. The first is of no great interest: it was the second de Hoogh, the *Cardplayers*, which has already been described.* The other, however, is of outstanding importance, and highly controversial, with unexpected implications no less significant, in sum,

* Although this is known to have been completed at Nice, it was not sold till 1941. See below, page 139.

than those of the *Emmaus*. The evidence regarding it, which is complex and conflicting as well as being of unusual fascination, must be examined in some detail.

One of the rather few facts that may be stated with absolute certainty is that van Meegeren wrote a letter to Dr Boon* informing him that he had found a large canvas—he gives the dimensions as '±1·50 × 2·70m.', that is, about 5 by 9 feet—depicting the *Last Supper* and signed by Vermeer. Even the date of this letter is open to argument: Decoen, who reproduces it in full,† states in the caption that it was written 'prior to 1939' but in the body of the book (page 41) that it is 'dated 1939'—an inconsistency that is unhappily typical of him. By glancing at the reproduction one can at once see that the latter statement is inaccurate: the letter—written in Dutch except for the words 'What to do?' in English—is dated simply 'Monday night, July 2nd'. It might be imagined that this would allow the year to be calculated, but unfortunately this is not so: 2 July did not fall on a Monday in any year between 1934 and 1945, both of which are impossible. All the indications point to the year having been 1939, when 2 July fell on a Sunday, and to van Meegeren having written that date in mistake for 3 July (or 'Monday night' instead of 'Sunday night')—a quite understandable slip. In any case it is indisputable that the letter was written before van Meegeren's return to Holland later that year, when Boon was to disappear.

It is also indisputable that van Beuningen paid 1,600,000 guilders in April 1941—the then equivalent of about £160,000 or of some £400,000 today—for a large canvas, signed *I. V. Meer* and depicting the *Last Supper* (plate 25), which had come to him from the omnipresent Hoogendijk, who had had it from a house agent named Strijbis, who had had it from van Meegeren. (Strijbis was to assume Boon's mantle after the latter's disappearance; four of the forgeries were to pass through his hands.) When this canvas—which Decoen and certain others still today maintain to be a true Vermeer—was subjected to radiography, for the first time ever, after van Meegeren's confession, it was found that areas of an underpainting were extremely clearly visible: a hunting scene with dogs and horsemen (plate 29). Beneath the figure of Christ, a spaniel is sniffing a partridge. This seemed curious at the time because van Meegeren had said that the canvas in question had

---

* Quoted in full below, page 121.   † Decoen, op. cit., plates 27 and 28.

previously depicted two children in an ornate carriage drawn by a
goat—and in fact drew a pencil sketch of the original work as he
remembered it, which bears a signed caption in his own handwriting: 'Underpainting of the Last Supper'.

Unlikely as it may seem, the proved existence of this underpainting was not taken by anyone as proving in itself that the
Supper was a forgery. It is true that traces of underpaintings have
been detected under one or two Vermeers, or supposed Vermeers,
and these are still accepted by many judges as genuine. The present
case is of a different order: the great experts, who were to decide
much later, on other grounds, that the painting was inauthentic,
found it absolutely acceptable that Vermeer, when setting out to
create what would certainly have been an extremely important
work to him, and a biblical one at that, was content to use a
second-hand canvas and paint his *Last Supper* over a group of jolly
hunters painted by someone else. (No-one could pretend, from
what could be seen of it, that the hunting scene, too, had been
painted by Vermeer.)

In 1948—more than three years after van Meegeren's confession
and eight months after his death—an event occurred that was so
remarkable, so convenient and at the same time (in certain ways)
so suspicious that Decoen has refused to accept it as anything other
than a dishonest fabrication—indeed, a criminal conspiracy—on
the part of Dr Coremans and his followers. The situation had long
since developed in which Decoen was proclaiming with the active
(and interested) support of van Beuningen and others, that the
Coremans Commission had reached a false conclusion in accepting
van Meegeren's claim to have painted the *Emmaus* and the *Supper*.
Their thesis was that he had somehow acquired these two authentic
Vermeers, had used them to inspire his forgeries, and had finally
claimed that they too were his work, thus gaining much greater
admiration and esteem than if he were thought the author of the
later works only, which by common consent were very much less
accomplished. Decoen was strongly implying that Coremans and
his supporters now had a vested interest in maintaining the correctness of the Commission's finding—that all eight were fakes—and
were prepared to go to any lengths to do so. Now, on 27 September 1948, Coremans received from his eminent colleague, Dr A.
van Schendel, Curator of the Rijksmuseum, what he describes as
'a most important document which he [van Schendel] had

discovered in the art market of his city [Amsterdam]'.* It was a photograph of a picture which Douwes Brothers, the Amsterdam dealers, now stated they had sold to van Meegeren in May 1940 for 1,000 guilders (about £100). It represented a hunting scene and was the work of Hondius, a minor Dutch painter of the seventeenth century. On comparing the photograph with the areas of the underpainting that are visible in the radiographs of the *Supper*, it was found that they were to all intents and purposes identical.†

The discovery of this photograph at first seemed certain to silence Decoen for ever. He would later try to indicate, by superimposing a negative of the Hondius (which he mistakenly called a positive) on a positive of the radiograph (which he mistakenly called a negative), that the two do not perfectly coincide.‡ But exact coincidence would not in any case be expected, since the Hondius would have been partially obliterated by van Meegeren, and in any case would not completely appear in the X-ray. Where they do differ, it is always because very slightly more white is visible in the radiograph, and this is just what would be expected, because white lead is less penetrated by X-rays than any other paint. Suspicion would only arise if it happened the other way round; in the circumstances, the two coincide to a remarkable extent. However, there were indeed some curious aspects of the find. Van Meegeren's incompatible statement about the underpainting could be explained by his bad memory—or by his everpresent tendency to invent in order to confuse. But it was on the record that he had informed the police in the course of his interrogation that for one of his later forgeries, unidentified, he had used a canvas bought 'around May 1940 from the dealer Douwes for about 1,000 guilders', which bore a painting by Hondius representing 'a hunting scene with horses, dogs and hunters resting'. With this very important line to follow, it seemed incredible that neither the police, nor any member of the Coremans Commission, nor anyone else (for example, the press), had located this highly important photographic evidence till so long after the trial.

There was, however, a far more serious snag. The Douwes'

---

* Coremans, op. cit., page 39, footnote.
† Compare plates 28 and 29.
‡ Decoen, op. cit., plate 161; and see his text, pages 48–9.

records showed beyond doubt that the Hondius had been sold on 29 May 1940. Decoen fastened on this as a terrier fastens on a rabbit: if his *Last Supper* had been painted over a canvas bought by van Meegeren in May 1940, how could he have given a detailed description of it* at least nine months previously?

A battle of great bitterness broke out, with Coremans and his followers (who were very much in the majority) ranged against the Decoen faction. Coremans asserted blandly that there must have been two *Suppers*: one, never sold, painted at Nice in 1939–40 over the goat-cart, and another, van Beuningen's, painted in Holland over the hunting scene in 1940–1. Decoen, predictably, would not wear this; he took the line that the whole thing was a frame-up. Coremans and his followers, needing incontrovertible evidence that would at last put the matter beyond all doubt, had committed an act of the most despicable cunning and dishonesty: they had engineered the painting of a picture by none knows whom—a forged Hondius, no less—in which those parts of the underpainting visible in the *Supper* radiographs would be exactly reproduced. This would then have been photographed and destroyed. They would then have prevailed upon the respected Douwes Brothers to pretend that the photograph—on the back of which are certain particulars in a form and handwriting that would presumably be known to them—had been in their files since 1940. It is an interesting fact that although Decoen frequently made such derogatory allegations in writing against the personal integrity of Coremans, the latter at no time initiated any legal action to clear his name.

The one weak point in the Coremans thesis was that the predicated 'first' *Last Supper* had vanished without trace. Van Meegeren was dead; he had never mentioned the existence of such a work, let alone its location, and for all anyone knew it might well have been sold, probably through Boon, in 1939 or soon after, and be now reposing proudly in a private collection anywhere in the world. But now occurred a most remarkable event. In September 1949—a year after the discovery of the Hondius photograph—Coremans decided, on what must have been the purest hunch, that he would pay a visit to the long-abandoned Villa Estate in Nice. He has said that he did so in the principal hope of at last finding the famous strip of canvas said by van Meegeren

* See translation of his letter to Boon, page 121, below.

to have been cut from the *Lazarus* before the painting of the *Emmaus*.

A decade had gone by since the van Meegerens' departure and for much of this time the villa had been empty. They had indeed left behind many possessions—and much incriminating evidence, including, it will be remembered, four unsold forgeries—but the Dutch police had been through the entire villa with a fine tooth-comb in 1945–6 in their search for evidence, and it seemed highly unlikely that they would have missed anything of significance for Coremans to discover. The diligence shown by Inspector Wooning had been greatly praised at the trial. However, after several days of fruitless search, 'the miracle occurred'—to use Coremans' own words. He described the event as follows at a special conference in Brussels soon afterwards:

During the whole morning and part of an afternoon on September 26, I turned over and over the objects lying in the two basement kitchens and in the corridor leading to them. It was here that most of van Meegeren's paraphernalia had been stored by the gardener after his departure. When I was beginning to despair, all at once the miracle occurred and there appeared to my eyes two sheets of plywood stuck together, measuring no less than 146 × 267 cms [$57\frac{1}{2}''$ × $105\frac{1}{4}''$]. On separating them I found—not the piece of canvas that I was seeking—but another version of the *Last Supper*.

This he had brought back to Brussels and now triumphantly exhibited to his amazed audience.

Decoen and his followers at once reacted predictably. They did not hesitate to allege publicly and openly that this vital evidence—precisely what Coremans needed, his *deus ex machina*—was nothing but one more product of his apparently bottomless duplicity. As the Hondius had been, they said, this too was a forgery recently commissioned by Coremans to provide the evidence he needed to make his thesis incontrovertible. There are indeed some highly suspicious aspects. How could it have happened that these two huge plywood sheets, over eight feet long, had not been found four years earlier by Wooning and his men? Or by Coremans himself earlier in his search? Why should he have expected them—with a surface area of forty-one square feet—to contain a strip of canvas one-seventh of that size? And why would van Meegeren have abandoned in his villa a canvas which he had described to Boon as being 'much larger and more beautiful than the *Emmaus*' and which he must therefore have expected to sell for an extremely high figure?

There is a further consideration. Van Beuningen was to go on record as saying—and such a statement cannot be simply ignored—that in 1949 the news had reached him that a new *Last Supper* was being fabricated, to the specification of Dr Coremans, and on his orders, which the wicked fellow was intending to plant in the Nice villa. He went so far as to say that he knew who was painting it, though he never named him (or informed the police). Instead he sent Decoen there a few days before Coremans was expected. Decoen says he reached the villa on 22 September and was able to 'visit' the basement—he does not say he searched it—on two separate occasions before the arrival four days later of Coremans. He would have gained entry with the assistance of the gardener. He did not find the two great sheets of plywood.

There is one more curious point. If Coremans was expected then, and if it was believed that he intended to bring with him a perfectly enormous fake which he would then pretend to have found there, it would have been extremely easy to arrange surveillance of the villa—or of Coremans—and catch him red-handed as he entered. If it was not wished to bring in the police, private detectives could have been employed, or any newspaper would have gladly co-operated if let into the secret.

Moreover I can offer evidence from my own personal experience which tends to confirm the Coremans version. I first met Jacques van Meegeren, the forger's son, early in 1949 (before the alleged commissioning of the fake). He then told me as a fact that his father had painted one other Vermeer, which had never yet been found but was hidden—somewhere—'between two sheets of plywood'. He said his father had begun to tell him of it the day before he died, when he was already in hospital and *in extremis*; before he could whisper the details, a nurse entered and said the visit must end. I suppose Decoen would say that the same story had come to the ears of Coremans, who would then have adapted it to give credibility to his plan, but in fact Coremans never made such use of it, and to me this evidence gives added reason for siding with him.

There is one final thought. In his pre-war letter to Boon, which Decoen fully accepts as authentic, and indeed uses as evidence in his favour, van Meegeren goes out of his way to emphasize that the *Supper* of which he was writing had not been restored. The phrase he uses is a strange one—literally translated it means 'straight from the mother'—but it is quite clear that he means to imply that it had not been tampered with. Yet Decoen admits that the van Beuningen canvas had been *much* restored (and supposes that van Meegeren did the restoring). He writes: 'Like all bad restorers, he [van Meegeren] enlarged considerably on what would have been strictly necessary to repair, and altered the character of the work. He did not hesitate to repaint the background entirely and to affix a forged signature of Vermeer.'* Van Meegeren would have known that such restorations would be immediately noticeable to the expert and would have been most unlikely to describe such a work as 'fresh from the mother'—a strong indication that he was not referring to the *Supper* bought by van Beuningen. It is significant that Decoen quotes where it suits him from the Boon letter but leaves out the phrase that would greatly weaken his argument.

There is a final consideration, of no small importance. Coremans, beyond any doubt, held a position of honour and undoubted integrity in his own particular field. Decoen, on many occasions, has publicly attributed actions and motives to him in connection with this canvas, and on other matters as well, necessarily implying that he was guilty of behaviour at once totally dishonest and totally unscrupulous. Yet on no occasion did he find it desirable to take legal action to clear his name. Each must therefore form his own conclusion on the basis of allegations not verified judicially.

On balance I must prefer the Coremans version, which is also the official version, to that of van Beuningen and Decoen. If the latter were right, van Meegeren would somehow have acquired, in 1939 or earlier, a genuine Vermeer *Last Supper* (the one sold eventually to van Beuningen). This major biblical composition would have been painted by Vermeer over someone else's earlier painting of a still visible hunting scene; it would have been to this work that van Meegeren was referring in his famous letter to Boon. But this is already unlikely to the point of incredibility because van Meegeren specified dimensions of '± 1·50 × 2·70m.'. These are extremely close to those of the canvas supposedly found by Coremans (1·46 × 2·67m.) but unacceptably different from those of the van Beuningen canvas (1·74 × 2·44m.). And despite

* Decoen, op. cit., page 14.

the authenticity and special importance as a Vermeer that Decoen attributes to it, it would not have been for almost two years—perhaps longer—that van Meegeren sought a buyer for it. During this time he would have kept it hidden and showed it to nobody. The general belief is as held by Coremans, that van Meegeren painted both the *Suppers*: one in Nice in 1938-9, which was never sold, and the other—similar in composition but in every way more accomplished—after his return to Holland. Decoen, on the other hand, maintains that van Meegeren never painted a *Last Supper* at all: of the two canvases in question, one would be a genuine Vermeer and the other a forgery painted by an unknown hand after van Meegeren's death with the connivance of Coremans or even to his orders. This I find impossible to credit. It must also be taken into account that Decoen had a material motive for proving authentic the *Supper* owned by van Beuningen, since the latter was supporting him, whilst Coremans, whose integrity had always been unquestioned, would have had practically nothing to gain by perpetrating the two separate criminal acts so blithely attributed to him by Decoen—certainly not enough to justify the terrible risk of his handiwork being discovered. Coremans had given it as his opinion that the van Beuningen *Last Supper*, as well as the *Emmaus*, were forgeries; this conclusion, and the evidence that led to it, were already accepted almost universally. Only the van Beuningen set, with their strong vested interest, held out in opposition. Coremans would have had no good reason for sticking to his guns if any later evidence made him doubtful. In any case, I cannot believe that Coremans would conceivably have put his whole career, his entire reputation, in such fearful and unnecessary jeopardy simply in order to prove wrong a small, discredited and strongly biased faction. I am therefore taking it that the Coremans thesis is correct.

In the course of the investigations carried out by Coremans after van Meegeren's trial and death, he located in Paris a firm of dealers from whom van Meegeren had bought a large canvas by Govert Flinck on 11 October 1938. The firm still held a copy of van Meegeren's receipt, which included a detailed description of the canvas, and also a good photograph of it. Flinck, a contemporary of Vermeer, is by no means unknown, and van Meegeren is shown to have paid 15,000 francs for it (about £125 then). Its significance lies in the fact that it portrays two children in an ornate chariot drawn by a goat.

It is reasonably similar to the van Meegeren sketch. The latter, it's true, has only two figures—the children in the chariot—whilst the Flinck had no fewer than eleven, including five assorted cherubs playing on the clouds, but it would be an acceptable explanation that van Meegeren sketched only the protagonists. It was therefore assumed that the Flinck canvas must have been used for the unsold forgery found in Nice by Coremans; van Meegeren, intentionally or not, had simply confused his *Suppers*.

There was no necessity for their inference, since he was a compulsive liar and might well have used the canvas for some other quite different purpose, but it as is likely as not to be true. There are, as usual, several curious facts. The Flinck was $80'' \times 87''$; the first *Last Supper* (as the Nice canvas may now be described) was $57\frac{1}{2}'' \times 105\frac{1}{4}''$. It would therefore have been necessary for van Meegeren to cut up the Flinck and reassemble it, by sewing two parts of it together again, as suggested in the diagram below,* in order to have a canvas of the proportions required. Coremans finds this acceptable; to Decoen it is inconceivable. The latter, firstly, cannot accept that van Meegeren 'could be so vile of soul and possess so little respect for a work of art that he could have wilfully destroyed a beautiful work, in good condition, by a master so universally admired as Govert Flinck, while any other canvas would have served precisely the same purpose and he could have found as many as he required for a few hundred francs'.† This I find in part naïve, in part untrue. By no means 'any other canvas'—not even any other Dutch seventeenth-century canvas, as he presumably means—would have served van Meegeren's purpose: he required one that was large ̄ and in good condition and, most important, that had an undoubtedly authentic, well-defined and conspicuous crackle-pattern. If the Flinck possessed these characteristics, it is ridiculous to suggest that van Meegeren would have been discouraged by the price, a mere bagatelle to him. As to the destruction of a beautiful work of art, it is not true that Flinck was or is 'universally admired'—if he were, why should such a large, well-executed work of his fetch so relatively little? It is in any case very naïve to imagine that van Meegeren, having acquired at the right price a canvas that perfectly suited

* See page 120.   † Decoen, op. cit., page 57.

him from a technical point of view, would have hesitated to
'destroy' it, any more than he hesitated with the *Lazarus*.

The difference in dimensions is, however, remarkable. The
cutting and sewing of the canvas, and the disguising of the newly
cut edges, would have been arduous and difficult; however well it
was done, moreover, it could still evoke suspicion. Here was van
Meegeren in possession of a fine undamaged canvas; it might be
thought that he would have accepted its dimensions, which happen
to be of almost identical proportions to those of the *Emmaus*. If it
were his special desire that the *Supper* should be more elongated
—that its width should in fact be nearly twice its height, making
it suitable, perhaps, for use above an altar—some might imagine
that he could have acquired without too much trouble some
other old work that approached the required dimensions without needing such basic alteration. The fact is, however, that it
is by no means easy to get hold of *any* large seventeenth-century
canvas at about that price.

There is another consideration. According to Decoen, the 'first'
Last Supper was fabricated in 1949 to the precise specifications of
wicked Dr Coremans. It was Coremans, too, who unearthed the
evidence of the Flinck sale. If it were as incredible as Decoen
would have us suppose that van Meegeren should have cut up and
reassembled the Flinck canvas in the manner suggested, why
should Coremans ever have proposed it? He was no fool and the
Flinck was in no way a necessary fact of his thesis. Finally it is a
relevant fact that the Flinck has in fact disappeared from human
ken. It was not found among van Meegeren's effects; if he bought
it as a speculation and sold it to a private buyer, the latter has never
come forward. It can hardly have been used for any other of the
forgeries because all were very much smaller.

It therefore has to be taken as most probable that van Meegeren,
having bought the Flinck for 15,000 francs, when on a visit to
Paris in October 1938 (which would have been ten months after
the *Emmaus* sale, shortly before the completion of the *Drinkers*, but
probably before he began work on the *Cardplayers*), did subsequently use it to provide the canvas and ground for the first of his
two *Last Suppers*. He would first have removed the goat, the
chariot, the children, the cherubs with their mandolins hovering
overhead, and then any undercoats down to the ground itself. In so
doing, as with the *Lazarus*, he would have taken particular pains to

preserve such crackle as already existed in the latter. He would next have cut the canvas into three parts, as indicated in the sketch. (Dimensions have been adjusted from those given above to allow for an unpainted edge of an arbitrary two inches or so.) Section B would be discarded; Section A, which could have been cut to the precise length required, would have been narrowed by three or four inches before being turned on end and sewn to Section C in

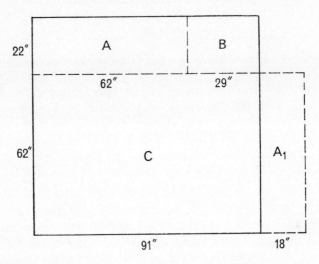

position A_1. Christ was thus destined to materialize just above the goat.

The forgery, though far superior aesthetically to such later daubs as the *Adulteress* and the *Footwashing*, does not approach the same class as the *Emmaus* and is markedly inferior to the 'second' *Supper*, although the composition, portraiture and arrangement of figures are extremely similar in both—in some areas very nearly identical. The faces of the two Christs are very much the same, and reminiscent of the *Emmaus* Christ, though with eyes less lowered. His right hand, in both *Suppers*, rests on the bread; in both, his left hand is partly covered by that of an effeminate St John, who in both cases is largely based on Vermeer's undoubted *Girl with Pearl Eardrops** in the Mauritshuis. In fact he and Christ look rather like man and wife. The other apostles, too, are similarly grouped in both paintings and with only one exception—the saint

* Plates 24 and 36.

on the extreme right who is young and clean-shaven in the first
Supper, old and bearded in the second—could have been drawn
from the same models. Two apostles, seated opposite Christ, have
their backs to the viewer: the left-hand one is greatly reminiscent
of the left-hand disciple in the *Emmaus*. An enormous goblet, over
a foot high, stands before Christ; it is extremely similar to that
found afterwards among van Meegeren's effects.

It may be noted that one apostle—the second from the left—is
absurdly like the mother in van Meegeren's unpleasing drawing,
Mother and Child (plate 22). This is of no importance; the latter
was not painted till towards the end of the war. This same saint,
however, is still, to me, a very weak point: he has heavily hooded
eyes—as, to a smaller extent, have two of the others, not to
mention Christ—which are unrealistic, quite untypical of Vermeer, and at the same time almost a trademark of van Meegeren.

If the first *Supper* was painted over the Flinck, which is known
to have been purchased in October 1938, it would necessarily
follow, as already seems almost certain, that it was in 1939 that van
Meegeren wrote Boon the letter dated 'Monday night, 2 July'—
either *on* the Monday, which was in fact 3 July, or the previous
evening. He wrote as follows:

*Amice.**
I'm in a crazy artistic mood—otherwise I would give out to you like
hell.
First, something else!!
Last Monday, Mavroeke stood suddenly before us, bearing letters
from her daughter, of which one was most important to us. She wrote
that Mavroeke's cousin, Germain, who lives at his castle in the Midi,
wanted to see her as he is nearly finished through cancer (86 years);
Mavroeke is one of his heirs. The daughter wrote that she had seen a
photograph of the *Emmaus* and wanted to sell from her own collection
(as I think I told you before). But she remembered having seen at
Germain's, whose collection had the same provenance as the pictures
that her father brought with him when he married, a similar biblical
painting, but much bigger and with far more saints. On Tuesday, I
went to the place with Mavroeke: we spent two days searching—found
no saints—only pictures from later periods—until on Saturday one of
the servants told us that there were some rolled-up canvases in an attic.

---

*This form of address indicates 'colleague' more than 'friend'. It would be
used by any professional man (or art dealer, or painter) in writing to another
with whom he had business dealings, whether or not a close friendship existed.

There we discovered together a painting which is the finest and most important ever made. It is a Last Supper painted by—Johannes, much bigger and more beautiful than the Rotterdam picture [i.e. the *Emmaus*]. It is stirring in its composition, venerable and dramatic, more sublime than all his other paintings. It is perhaps his last work and is signed—on an open spot on the table. ± 2·70 × 1·50m.

After rolling it up, we walked into the mountains like a couple of idiots. What to do?

A canvas of at least two [here a word has been deleted and not replaced]. It seems to me nearly impossible to sell it, though it is perfect as a new-born babe*, not recanvassed, undamaged, without frame or stretcher. I much regretted having to roll it up again after long deliberation.

Imagine a Christ of impressive sorrow, gazing with half-closed eyes over a wine-goblet; a Saint John of fine melancholy, a Peter—no, it is impossible to describe it—this symphony of the most beautiful character, such as *never* was painted before, by Leonardo, by Rembrandt, by Velasquez, by any other master who painted the Last Supper.

Because van Meegeren never publicly mentioned the existence of this picture, and because Boon left Europe soon after the outbreak of war and was never heard of again, nothing is known of what action he may have taken on receiving this letter. All that may be said with certainty is that the van Meegerens left Nice for Holland some six weeks later; and—unless Coremans was guilty of the grave deceit imputed to him by Decoen, which I do not believe—left the canvas behind with many other of their possessions. It is not known if in those six weeks it was shown to an expert or buyer, but it seems unlikely. The war overtook van Meegeren.

For something over a year, he and his wife had been living a riotous life at the Estate. If one credits his own statement, he had £15,000 left when he returned to Holland, all that remained of his share—probably about £55,000—of the £87,000 (at then exchange rates) paid for the two forgeries sold. Even if he had spent two-thirds of the vanished £40,000 on buying the villa and furnishing it, he and Jo would have been spending at an average of £700 a month since the *Emmaus* sale. This seems almost impossible when it is remembered that the cost of living was less than one-third of today's, but they entertained on the most lavish scale imaginable; both enjoyed all the good things of life, and certain of

* Literally, 'fresh from the mother'.

the bad, and would have seen no reason to stint themselves. Van Meegeren had tended since student days to drink heavily, a tendency that had increased, and now there was nothing to stop him. It may have been during this period that he began taking morphia, which was to end by demoralizing him in the last years of his life.

But now the summer was ending. It was 29 July when van Meegeren left for Holland with his wife at short notice. It seems almost certain that they intended to return, that they were going on a visit (possibly in connection with the *Supper*), since they took few of their possessions and made no arrangements for letting or selling the villa, which was to stand empty apart from a housekeeper until used as a billet by the Italian army after the fall of France. Certainly they would have been worried by international events, but these alone would hardly have moved them to return to Holland yet. It seems more probable that they found themselves there by accident when war broke out and thought it prudent to stay.

Van Meegeren's career as a forger was now only starting.

7
The War Years

BETWEEN the outbreak of war and June 1943—that is, in less than four years—van Meegeren was to paint and sell five forgeries, four of them major ones and all 'Vermeers', besides finding a buyer for his second false de Hoogh, which he must have brought with him from Nice. The total paid for them was 6,300,000 guilders: from 1940 there was no official pound–florin exchange rate, but the sterling equivalent was about £630,000 then, or between two and three times that figure today. It was thus to be his most prolific and most lucrative period.

However, the most significant fact about it was that van Meegeren's standards, both technical and aesthetic, steadily deteriorated (as did his moral standards), yet he had increasingly less trouble in finding buyers and sold his wares at ever higher prices.

The first of this series, the *Head of Christ* (plate 26), bought by van Beuningen in early 1941 but later sold back to Hoogendijk, was nothing more than a sketch for the central figure of his subsequent *Last Supper*.* It was also much smaller than any other of his forgeries (19″ × 12″) and even though it fetched an absurdly high price—475,000 guilders, slightly less than the *Emmaus*—it is not in the same class as the last four. The first of these, the second *Last Supper*, is a very fine work, a great improvement on the Nice canvas, and of sufficient competence, as is known, for Decoen and his followers to persist to this day that it is in fact a Vermeer. The next, *Isaac Blessing Jacob* (plate 30), begun in 1941 and sold next year to van der Vorm, shows a very great falling-off—in composition, execution, scope—and this tendency was to continue with the *Adulteress* (plate 32), painted in 1941–2, which ended up with Goering. The last forgery, the *Footwashing* (plate 31), painted

---

* Some hold it was painted before the return to Holland, in which case it would presumably have preceded the first *Supper*, but 1940 is the more likely date from such evidence as is available.

a year later, is the worst of all, and it almost passes comprehension that it should have found a buyer at all, let alone the Netherlands State at the outrageous price of 1,300,000 guilders, or some £320,000 in today's money.

If one examines the series, it may be seen that van Meegeren was in fact reverting to type. He painted less and less in the manner of Vermeer—whose own works seem to have been forgotten, amazing as it may seem, by those who appraised, dealt in and bought the forgeries—and more and more in the manner of van Meegeren. This will at once be recognized if his first forgery, the *Emmaus*, is compared with his last, the *Footwashing*. It is understandable that the former was accepted—as a curious Vermeer, an unusual Vermeer, but a Vermeer all the same—but the latter is almost pure van Meegeren. And because even the *Emmaus* was designed to be reminiscent of a canvas—the *Martha and Mary*—that is by no means typical of Vermeer and may not have been painted by him, van Meegeren was moving further and further away—not from Vermeer—but from his own forgery which had itself been compared with a doubtful canvas; no undisputed Vermeer bears any resemblance to it in subject or composition. It is hardly an exaggeration to say that van Meegeren was now forging van Meegeren.

On the technical side also, as will be shown, there was a progressive decline: he seldom bothered to remove very much of the underpainting, took much less trouble over crackle, and with the *Adulteress* made the bloomer of using cobalt. It made not the slightest difference.

What seems to have happened for van Meegeren's part is that he simply found it unnecessary to take the extreme pains, technically and aesthetically, that he had assumed would be essential when first he turned to forgery. He had then taken it for granted that each work, particularly when no provenance could be offered, would be subject to the most careful technical scrutiny, or at the very least to elementary testing in such obvious fields as microchemistry and radiography. He was to find that this never happened, that the forgeries were never examined technically at all. To give a perfect example, Dr A. M. de Wild, a member of the Coremans Commission who had been involved in the *Footwashing* sale, was asked at the trial why no tests revealed its inauthenticity. He replied: 'Because the art dealer, de Boer, refused twice to allow radiographs to be taken of the van Meegerens in his keeping. [These included the *Footwashing*.] Such a test would have certainly shown that the paintings were not genuine.' This extraordinary statement reveals, to begin with, that those who bought the *Footwashing* on behalf of the Netherlands State were in no way discouraged, although they 'didn't like it', from paying a huge price by the *prima facie* highly suspicious fact that the dealer had twice refused—and why did he refuse?—their reasonable request to X-ray it. More important, it shows that having acquired the paintings, and therefore being completely free to do whatever they liked with it, they apparently did not carry out the elementary test that they had unsuccessfully asked de Boer to allow them. Had they done so, they must immediately have laid bare the completely un-Vermeerlike *Horse and Rider* that van Meegeren had hardly bothered to remove from under it (plate 34). Yet the canvas had been in their possession for almost two years at the time of his confession. Van Meegeren's talent and powers were in any case diminishing, since his approach to old age (he was now in his middle fifties) was much accelerated by his debauched life. He would have seen no reason for knocking himself out to produce a forgery of the very high order of the *Emmaus* when he found that any work of his, if painted more or less after the *Emmaus*, on seventeenth-century canvas and artificially aged, and bearing a fine signature (with which alone his loving care and skill never grew less), would be acceptable as a Vermeer and fetch a ludicrously high price.

There could no longer be any pretence that a principal motive was to prove even to himself that he was a great creative artist. There was nothing great and next-to-nothing creative about works such as the *Footwashing*. But if the brilliance of the *Emmaus* gave Bredius and others a fair excuse for their deception, if its very excellence had thwarted van Meegeren's other supposed purpose of proving them fools, the same cannot be said of the later ones. Perversely, it may have been only through his rapid descent to forgeries that were precisely as careless and slapdash, as lacking in inspiration and originality (but also as technically competent) as his own work had usually been, that he would finally succeed in discrediting those who had been fully justified in refusing him the recognition he desired. Rather than any genius of his, as he himself would have had the world believe, it was the deficiency in his talent and character—the same deficiency that had made their opinion of him justifiable—that was now responsible for their downfall, since they were still to be deceived when it now emerged again to lower the standard of his fakes.

As van Meegeren moved on from one forgery to the next, they judged each new work by comparison with those that had preceded it. As much was admitted by Hoogendijk at the trial. When asked how he could account for his acceptance as a Vermeer of *Isaac Blessing Jacob*, he replied: 'It's difficult to explain. It is unbelievable that it fooled me. But we all slid downwards—from the *Emmaus* to *Isaac*, from *Isaac* to the *Footwashing*; a psychologist could explain this better than I can.' (Hoogendijk had sold the canvas that he was now decrying to the unhappy van der Vorm for a little matter of 1,270,000 guilders; it takes more than a psychologist to explain why, as they all slid downwards, which indeed they did, the prices extracted from clients slid ever upwards.) The same tendency may also be seen at once if one considers the *Footwashing*, to take the obvious example, in awful isolation. If this had been the first or even the second forgery perpetrated by van Meegeren, if those that preceded it had never existed to influence the critical beholder and offer a basis for comparison, it is impossible to imagine for an instant that it would have stood the remotest chance of being taken for the work of Jan Vermeer of Delft.

Even in wartime. For it is true that conditions under the Occupation, which began some seven months before the first of the last six forgeries was sold, do something but not very much to excuse some of those deceived. By no means do they begin to exonerate them as they themselves have sought to claim. In fact, it worked both ways. The most important effect was indeed the ever-present fear of confiscation or compulsory purchase by the occupying Nazis. This would have been particularly strong in the case of a work by a national master as highly esteemed as Vermeer, which gave van Meegeren and his agents a perfect pretext for insisting as they did that each sale be conducted in deep secrecy. Thus this plethora of new Vermeers, which would increase the total attributed to him by about one-seventh over a six-year period, would not become known to the art world at large. On the other hand quite a few individuals who cannot have been criminally implicated—most of those, it may be thought, at the heart of artistic affairs in Holland—must have seen all or many of these canvases, or would at least have known about them: the prime example is Hoogendijk. Similarly, from van Meegeren's point of view, he could offer his wares only to the relatively very few potential buyers in his homeland, who all knew each other's activities. In peacetime he could have slipped one on the market in Washington, one in London, one in Rome. An attempt has been made, by those who seek to excuse, to mention as relevant that those implicated had only the Vermeers in Holland with which to make comparisons. This really cannot succeed: it cannot seriously be suggested that a director of Sotheby's, let us say, if today concerned to determine if a Botticelli is authentic, would be very likely to fly off to Florence to see it beside the *Birth of Venus*. In any case, none of the forgeries remotely resembles any known Vermeer anywhere. The war and the Occupation had many important effects, but by no means all of them worked in van Meegeren's favour.

He himself would readily agree, as he could not escape doing, that his standards fell off greatly in the war years. He was to admit as much in these words:*

As for the later forgeries, first of all I neither conceived them nor carried them out with the same care. (What was the use? They sold just as well!) Secondly, once I had admitted the true story about the *Emmaus*, only a little time would be required for the recognition [as my work] of the others, of which, incidentally, I am not so proud.

It seems probable, though it is curious, that neither he nor his wife returned to Nice in the course of the nine months between the outbreak of war and the fall of France, when the journey—till then feasible—would have become impossible, to collect or safeguard some at least of the important belongings that they had left behind there. It can be said with certainty that these included the four unsold trial forgeries, since these were to be found there by the Netherlands police in 1945, and also, unless Coremans is a most unscrupulous villain, the 'first' *Last Supper*, which van Meegeren must have believed, to judge from his letter to Boon, to be readily saleable for a higher price than the *Emmaus*. Van

* In a conversation with Coremans, quoted by the latter, op. cit., page 33.

Meegeren did arrange for two canvases which cannot be positively identified to be sent from Nice to Paris in October 1939, and contrived to get them to Holland two years later. Their movement for other reasons must soon be considered in detail; here it need only be mentioned that, although it is thus shown that it was possible to arrange such a transfer, van Meegeren did not bother to move any of the important and incriminating canvases mentioned. He may have feared taking them through the customs; if so, it might be thought that he would have arranged their transfer to a bank, or at least to a depository, rather than leaving them in the basement of the villa. And there was the all-important evidence—the famous strip of canvas and the fragments of the stretcher—to prove he had painted the *Emmaus*; the exportation of these would have presented no problem. The police could never find the canvas strip—a fact which some have taken as indicating its non-existence—and only one of the two stretcher fragments, but such disappearance is precisely what might be expected if objects of no apparent value or importance are left lying around for several years in an abandoned villa. If only to ensure their preservation, it would surely have been prudent to make a trip, when van Meegeren could also have stored or brought back to Holland many possessions of intrinsic value which had been left behind and which it would have seemed improvident not to rescue from a country now at war. But perhaps he had by now abandoned any intention of voluntary confession.

However, van Meegeren was not prescient: he could not have known that France would fall, that his own country would be occupied. He may have seen no urgency in making such a trip, have several times postponed it, and then been caught by the *Blitzkrieg*. Even after it, however, communications were less impossible than might be imagined. Decoen reproduces three documents which show this;* they are of very considerable interest, though not for the reasons he states. His attempt to prove van Beuningen's *Supper* authentic would clearly be greatly assisted if he could show with certainty that it had been painted before 29 May 1940, the day on which van Meegeren is said by Coremans to have purchased the Hondius (as I believe he did). This would be proof positive that the whole Hondius story was a complete fabrication, the Hondius itself a bare-faced forgery, procured by Coremans

* Decoen, op. cit., plates 167–9.

with the active connivance of Douwes Brothers. To this end, he was to write as follows:

Much time and effort might have been saved if I could have obtained all the documents which I have now collected . . . That of June 6 1950 itself alone would have been sufficient to prove that the whole Hondius affair had been entirely faked. In fact, this document enables one to prove irrefutably how the *Last Supper* arrived in Holland.

Dispatched from Nice by van Meegeren, it reached Messrs Tailleur, Fils and Company, of 91 Rue du Cherche-Midi, Paris, on October 6 1939; it was contained in a case which measured 261 × 190 cms. [102¾" × 75"]. The consignment consisted of a further three cases, one of which also contained a picture, whilst the others contained various objects of porcelain and earthenware. They remained in the Tailleur warehouse until May 22 1941. They were taken away by a German army lorry and conveyed to Holland; they were received in the early days of June at Hilversum by Messrs van Meegeren and Strijbis. The latter took charge of the large case of 261 × 190 centimetres, had it placed on the train, and himself took a seat in the same luggage van in which he accompanied it to Amsterdam.

There a van Gend and Loos lorry took it over; still accompanied by Strijbis, it was conveyed to the antiquary, Mr Hoogendijk of that city. Immediately after its arrival at the latter's house, the case was opened. On removing the French newspapers which completely covered the picture, the *Last Supper* appeared for the first time in the full light of day to the eyes of Messrs Hoogendijk and Strijbis. A few days later it was purchased by Mr van Beuningen.

Here then we see established in a positive manner, without any possible doubt, by means of information of a totally different nature from mine, that the whole of this story of the forged Vermeer [i.e. the first *Last Supper*] was intentionally contrived so as to have the two pictures which he had never painted attributed to van Meegeren.*

Underneath his reproduction of the document dated 6 June 1950, Decoen states with splendid simplicity: 'This document proves that the [van Beuningen] *Last Supper* was dispatched from Nice before 6 October 1939.'†

These statements must be taken apart and their completely misleading nature revealed. It is not very difficult to do so, and indeed it is hard to imagine how Decoen can have hoped that anyone would accept them. It is only necessary to read through the three brief documents presented. The one dated 6 June

* ibid. page 50.   † ibid. plate 167, caption.

1950 is a certificate from Tailleur Fils, a Paris removals firm which is still extant in the Rue du Cherche-Midi. It runs in translation as follows:

By this document we certify that we received four crates from Mr van Meegeren at Nice,* two of which contained one picture each, of the following dimensions: 261 × 190 and 155 × 95 cms. The two others contained porcelain and earthenware. These four crates were taken away by a German lorry on May 22 1941 for transfer to Holland.

And that is *absolutely all.*

Decoen also reproduces a copy of a signed receipt issued to van Meegeren by Tailleur on 6 October 1939. It reads: 'Received today from Nice two crates containing pictures (270 × 190 and 160 × 100 centimetres) and two crates of various objects. To await the client's orders for forwarding.' At the bottom has been written in German: 'Taken away, May 22nd 1941.' The only other relevant document reproduced by Decoen shows a standard dispatch docket issued by Tailleur and bearing the same date, in which the dimensions given are the same as those in the 1950 certificate.

It will thus be seen that these three slips of paper, which Decoen describes as 'important vouchers', provide *absolutely none* of the 'irrefutable' evidence claimed of them. They give no single word of information, as in his text he would have us believe, as to what happened to the crates after their mysterious collection by the Germans; that whole story, which he certainly implies to have been extracted from a reproduced document, is in fact nowhere mentioned in it and he gives no other source whatever for his alleged facts. Much more important, however, is the fact that, so far from offering the smallest evidence that the larger of the two pictures involved in this transfer was van Beuningen's *Last Supper*, these documents tend rather to indicate that it cannot possibly have been.

The question turns on whether the two sets of dimensions given are those of the crates or of the canvases inside them. If *any* refer to the pictures, then van Beuningen's *Supper*, which is 174 × 244 centimetres, is immediately ruled out. And this in fact seems on balance most probable, though unfortunately the wording in each

* For reasons given below, I do not take it from this phrase that van Meegeren himself went to Nice to supervise the transfer.

case is too ambiguous for this to be quite certain. Tailleur have informed me that the employee who received the crates in 1939 is (not very surprisingly) now no longer with them, but in their opinion the figures on the receipt would give the external dimensions of the crates, whilst those on the dispatch docket and on their 1950 certificate *would be those of the pictures*. They add: 'We presume that the employee who received them [in Paris] took down the pictures' dimensions which were perhaps written on the crates.' The canvases were packed by Tailleur at the Nice villa and such details would very probably have been noted. It is significant that in the case of the two other crates no dimensions are given— they did not contain pictures.

It may have been noticed that there is at least one discrepancy in the figures: the 1939 docket and the 1950 certificate give 261 × 190 and 155 × 95, whilst the 1939 receipt gives 270 × 190 and 160 × 100. If, as I hold to be the case, the former figures refer to the pictures inside and the latter figures to the crates, the measurement of 190 centimetres, which appears in all three documents, would be an error in the 1939 docket, copied by Tailleur when they made out their certificate in 1950. This is in fact more acceptable than that three measurements were wrongly taken, as would be necessary to accord with Decoen's view (since all three sets should then be identical). If my interpretation is correct, and it is also Tailleur's, it would at once destroy Decoen's proposal, stated by him as a fact, that the 'second' *Supper* was one of those in the consignment, for which in any case he offers no acceptable evidence of any kind whatever.

It is a minor matter that van Beuningen is stated by Coremans* to have bought the *Supper* in April 1941, a month before the German lorry supposedly left Paris, since the month given could have been an error. At the time he wrote the book, Decoen's precious vouchers had not yet been found and it would have been of no special significance.

From the 1950 certificate it might at first appear that van Meegeren himself went to the villa at the time since it is stated that the crates were '*en provenance de M. van Meegeren à Nice*'. However, this certificate was drawn up by Tailleur, at the request of Decoen, on the sole basis of the two 1939 documents which then reposed in their files. One of these, the dispatch docket,

---

* Coremans, op. cit., page 29.

describes the *destinataire* as '*Mr* van Meegeren (Hollande)*' with
the further information: '*provenance Nice (colis livrés par S.R.)*';†
the other, addressed simply *Mr van Meegeren* with no address,
begins: '*Reçu ce jour en provenance de Nice . . .*'. It may therefore
be seen that they provide no evidence that he ever left Holland.

Van Meegeren and his wife had taken rooms in an hotel when
they reached Amsterdam. After the outbreak of war, when they
decided to stay in Holland for the duration, he began looking
round for a house, and in early 1940 bought a large, attractive
villa, standing in its own extensive grounds, in the village of Laren
not far from the city. This must have taken a good part of the
money he had left, but he did not yet sell the *Cardplayers*, though
he must have had it with him.

Van Meegeren had left behind in Nice much of his equipment,
in particular (it is supposed) the oven or ovens in which he had
aged his canvases, though none was to be found there. This may
seem curious because the one used for the first *Last Supper* must
have been really immense: the canvas was $57\frac{1}{2}'' \times 105\frac{1}{4}''$ and the
oven must therefore have been about nine feet long by five feet
wide, and four to five feet deep. However, on reflection its
disappearance becomes acceptable: it would have been out of the
question to try to export this huge, inexplicable and therefore
incriminating article, as it would have been to hide it. It may
therefore be supposed that van Meegeren had dismantled it, and
disposed of it as scrap, before leaving Nice. Although this would
seem to indicate that at the time of his departure he had no intention
of returning, other evidence (such as abandonment of important
canvases and his failure to let the villa) must suggest otherwise, and
it may be that he happened to have disposed of it at that time with
the intention of constructing an improved and more sophisticated
model which would have the full benefit of all his great experience.
Or he may have written to a confederate after the outbreak of war
instructing him to get rid of the old one quietly.

A new oven, in any case, he would now have to build in Laren,
where he was soon to start work again. I have taken it as certain
that he already had painted a rather mediocre *Last Supper* and left
it behind in Nice. He would now have decided on a better one—

---

* *sic*. It is amusing to note that he was accustomed to describe himself, therefore,
as *maître*. In the 1950 certificate he is demoted to *monsieur*.

† S.R. signifies *service routier*, meaning that the crates went by lorry.

better than the work he had described in his letter to Boon as 'the most beautiful and most important ever painted'. Perhaps to get his hand in, perhaps to try out, on a small and unambitious canvas, the new equipment and materials that he had assembled at Laren, he began by painting the small *Head of Christ* (plate 26), which he was to copy almost exactly in painting his second *Last Supper*. (As Decoen would have it, the latter, which was genuine, was already in his possession, though still deposited with Tailleur in Paris; the *Head* would be based on a sketch made from it.) As ever, he took much technical care—he may have been experimenting with refinements to his technique—though the paint structure was rather less complex: in the laboratory, only three layers were detected, of which the topmost comprised two sublayers. The bottommost, as always, was the old ground: as with several others, it contained ochre and oil. The next, as the Coremans Commission put it, was 'blackish; only the oil was detected'. Of the surface layer, the Commission reported: 'Layer 1A, bluish, contained white lead, natural ultramarine and artificial resin. Layer 1B, greyish-blue, was of the same composition, with the probable addition of indigo.'* It is curious that van Meegeren signed this sketch with Vermeer's name, as before, though Vermeer so often omitted his signature and would have been very likely to do so in a small sketch such as this.

Although he took considerable trouble with this fake, it was to be technically the least successful of all and has seriously deteriorated in the years since it was painted. It may not have been van Meegeren's original intention to offer it for sale; he may have been only practising. Anyway it was almost a year before he did so. In the meantime he was at work on his second *Supper*. In May 1940, probably before the *Head* had been completed, he would have bought the Hondius over which it would be painted. This was to be the most ambitious of all his forgeries; as already mentioned, the composition and the figures are extremely similar, often almost identical, to those of the canvas left behind in Nice. (According to Decoen, the latter did not yet exist but was made by an unknown copyist to the orders of Coremans from the allegedly authentic *Supper* of van Beuningen's.) Christ's head is almost exactly a copy of that in the small trial canvas;† it is similar, but less

---

* Quoted by Coremans, op. cit., page 17.
† Compare plates 26 and 27.

Plate 28 (above) is the photograph of the Hondius *Hunting Scene* found in their archives by Douwes Brothers after van Meegeren's death. It should be compared with the relevant area of the radiograph of the second *Last Supper* (plate 29, below).

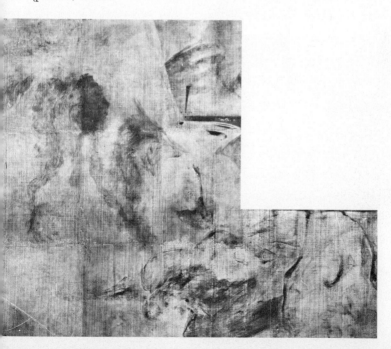

Plate 30. *Isaac Blessing Jacob*.

Plate 31. *The Washing of Christ's Feet.*

Plate 32. *Christ with the Woman Taken in Adultery.*

In both these radiographs, taken after van Meegeren's confession, clear traces of underpaintings may be seen. Beneath the *Adulteress* (plate 33, above) a battle scene was detectable, whilst the *Footwashing* (plate 34, below) had been painted over *Horses and Riders*.

Two authentic Vermeers:
the *Music Lesson* (plate
35, above) and the
Girl with Pearl Eardrops
(plate 36, right).

Plate 37. Van Meegeren at work on the *Young Christ*.

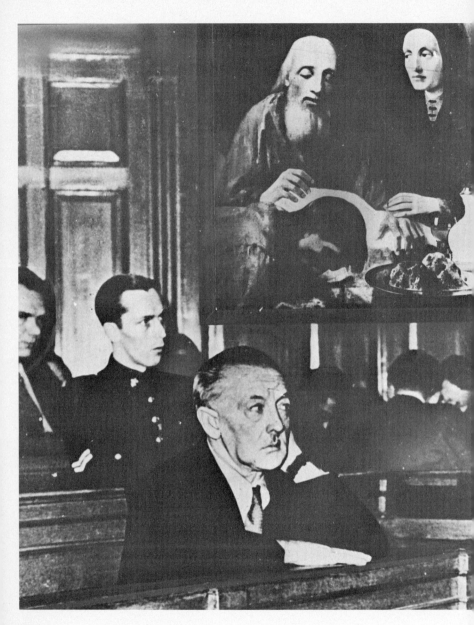

Plate 38. Van Meegeren in the dock, 29 October 1947, two months before his death. One of his forgeries, *Isaac Blessing Jacob*, hangs in the background.

so, to that in the Nice one. Although it is in almost every way superior to the latter, a new problem arose through the different proportions of the canvas now used ($68\frac{1}{2}'' \times 96''$, compared with $57\frac{1}{2}'' \times 105\frac{1}{4}''$). As with the earlier forgery, van Meegeren tackled the problems implicit in depicting thirteen at a table by having four of the apostles standing behind it, two to the left and two to the right; two more are seated on either side of Christ; there is one at the foot and one at the head of the table; and two apostles are seated opposite Christ, their faces almost unseen. None the less, even the Nice canvas had tended to be overcrowded; with the new dimensions, this problem became even more acute, since van Meegeren was to give his new work very little additional vertical space.

Coremans comments:

The lack of space is obvious. To be convinced of this, it is only necessary to attempt to place thirteen persons round the table. This work is in no way comparable to Vermeer's, in which it is said that the master painted atmospheres flooded with light, and breathing serenity.

The same general modelling of the faces is noticed in all cases. One need only observe in the various forgeries the practically identical shadow-play and the light around the eyes, nose and mouth (very large), and the neck, and only glance at the static and set representation of the figures to agree that the same hand may have painted them.

The faces are about five centimetres [two inches] larger than life-size,* which increases the falsely dramatic appearance. The hair gives the impression of having been just washed and combed.

The only way of explaining the play of light is by the presence of two or more luminous sources—which, once again, augments the general dramatic atmosphere.†

It does not strike me as remarkable that Christ and the apostles should have clean and tidy hair when sitting down to supper, but otherwise the critique is a good one. It no longer seems absurd that Coremans should describe as 'in no way comparable to Vermeer's' a work that had been very widely accepted as such, and is still so accepted by some, since it has been seen that many such judgments, however certainly expressed, are no more than a matter of opinion.

On the technical side, van Meegeren for the first time showed

---

* And five centimetres larger than those in the *Emmaus*.
† Coremans, op. cit., pages 36–7.

his contempt for those who would judge his work, his supreme confidence—it should have amounted to over-confidence—and his departure from previous perfectionist standards, by not bothering to remove large areas of the Hondius (plate 29). On the other hand the paint structure was as complex and painstaking as ever. Five separate layers were to be identified but of these the two bottommost belonged to the *Hunting Scene*—its original ground, which was reddish, and parts of its upper paint layer (depicting the horses, dogs, huntsmen and so on). To this van Meegeren applied a grey 'cellular' layer,* composed of white lead, chalk and oil. Above this was a blackish one, also containing oil; the topmost layer was whitish and it was here that traces of phenolformaldehyde were to be found eventually. In between the two last layers, traces of a homogeneous black substance were later to be detected: this was the ink with which van Meegeren would, as usual, cover the whole finished surface area in the manner, and for the purpose, already described. Some of it must have seeped through the crackle in the surface paint layer and dried between it and the next one.

Coremans writes that 'such a peculiar composition as that of the cellular layer is not encountered in the paint strata of seventeenth-century pictures. This might indicate the insertion of a film of paint intended to permit the continuity of the old crackle upwards through the overlying paint'.† This is very true, but it may also be remarked that this 'peculiar' cellular layer was no more noted by any expert who examined the work before van Meegeren's confession than was the clearly visible underpainting. And neither is taken as proving falseness by Decoen.

When van Meegeren had completed this second version of the *Last Supper*, he would still have had two other forgeries on his hands, the *Cardplayers* (a de Hoogh) and the recent *Head of Christ*. The amazing fact, which no novelist would dare expect his reader to believe, is that all three were sold within six months after passing through the hands of the same agent and the same dealer. Two, moreover, went to the same buyer.

Boon had fled Europe in the face of the German advance; his place as van Meegeren's first intermediary was now to be taken (1941) by the house-agent, R. Strijbis. He hailed from Apeldoorn, a small town near Deventer, and may therefore have been a

* See above, page 29.　　　† Coremans, op. cit., page 17.

childhood friend of van Meegeren's; in any case they were 'already acquainted', as he would put it at the trial, when van Meegeren proposed a means to him by which he might 'obtain a worth-while sum'. The forger told the house-agent that he had bought a number of paintings from an old Dutch family in The Hague which, he said, had fallen on hard times. On examining them carefully, he had reached the conclusion that several were very important and could fetch far more than he had paid for them. He explained that he did not wish to be identified with their re-sale, giving precisely the reasons offered to Dr Boon. The canvases might well be worth several million guilders. If Strijbis would act for him without mentioning his name, he would pay him one-sixth of the proceeds.

Strijbis, who had never dealt in pictures before, jumped at the opportunity. (He was to say at the trial that he 'knew nothing about art' and 'would not allow into his house' pictures such as he was now to offer for sale.) Van Meegeren first showed him the *Head*, for he had come to realize that if he himself had found it helpful to paint a trial study of his central figure before embarking on the *Supper*, it could well be accepted that Vermeer had done the same. He suggested that Strijbis should offer it to Hoogendijk (who had already been involved in the *Emmaus* sale) at the round figure of half a million guilders, which seemed so ridiculous to the house-agent that he could hardly muster the nerve to ask for it. As Hoogendijk was to put it at the trial, he 'at once thought of the *Emmaus*' when he saw it, just as van Meegeren had hoped he would, and then fell into the second prepared trap of thinking it a preliminary study, as indeed it was, for an unknown major work that had not yet been found. When he asked Strijbis how and where he had obtained it, the latter replied along the lines agreed, that the owner did not wish to be identified since this would make it known that he was forced to sell an heirloom. Hoogendijk took the *Head* to van Beuningen (who had already bought the *Drinkers*) and a sale was speedily made. At the trial, somewhat conflicting statements were made by those involved as to the price paid and the sums retained in commission by Strijbis and Hoogendijk, but the most likely estimate is that van Beuningen put up 475,000 guilders, of which Hoogendijk retained the 'odd' 75,000. Strijbis would presumably have kept one-sixth of the net sum handed to him, but this cannot be said with certainty, since he was to assert at the trial with splendid nonchalance that he 'kept no records' and 'now no longer remembered' how much he had been paid.

Thus for this small and unimportant work, van Meegeren received a reward of some 330,000 guilders—the equivalent of over £75,000 today.

Only a month or two later, in April, Strijbis returned to Hoogendijk with the story that he had now obtained, from the same collection, the particular Vermeer for which the *Head* must have been the study. Van Meegeren thus repeated his *Emmaus* trick of producing the canvas that a particular expert was in a way expecting, though with none of his previous finesse. Indeed it must be thought extremely foolhardy of him, if nothing more, to have produced it so quickly like a rabbit out of a hat. Happily, no-one could have been more gullible than Hoogendijk: 'My first impression was that this was the most extraordinary work,' he was to say in evidence at the trial. Then he added regretfully: 'But I again allowed myself to be influenced by the *Emmaus*. It seems quite beyond understanding now. At the time, you know, all was done secretly.' Secretly, therefore, he went back to van Beuningen, to show him the work and to suggest a price of 'perhaps two million guilders'. It will be noticed that Hoogendijk so completely accepted the fact that these two should have materialized within a couple of months that he did not think it necessary to go to a different collector.

Van Beuningen was an extremely wealthy man, but even for him this was certainly no trifle. It would have been about £200,000 then, or the equivalent of half a million today. He at first demurred; but Hoogendijk referred to the danger of the Nazis getting it and soon the haggling began. Eventually it was agreed that he would pay for the *Last Supper* by making over to Hoogendijk some half-dozen less important works from his collection. Their combined value was put at no less than 1,600,000 guilders.

The interesting fact is that one of these was the recently purchased *Head of Christ*, and it was still on Hoogendijk's hands at the time of van Meegeren's confession. Herein lies the most convincing evidence that Hoogendijk, amazing as it may seem, was not criminally implicated. It may be that he liked the work and wished to keep it for himself, but this would seem very unlikely. It is more likely that he found it impossible to find a buyer at what he thought the right price. What must be absolutely sure is that if he had known it to be a forgery, he would not have kept it for four years on his premises or allowed it to be discovered there by the police.

Less than three months later, van Meegeren told the house-agent of the *Cardplayers*. Strijbis went straight back to Hoogendijk. As previously, no serious attempt was made to explain the discovery, but it seems to have been suggested that it, too, came from the same remarkable collection. Hoogendijk would say at the trial: 'There was only vague talk about an old Dutch family.' The *Cardplayers* appeared to be an entirely typical de Hoogh—except that de Hoogh might never have copied so slavishly from previous works of his—and was beautifully signed with his initials. Having bled van Beuningen dry, Hoogendijk took this one to van der Vorm, who had put up most of the *Emmaus* money and was later to buy *Isaac Blessing Jacob*. The price, 219,000 guilders, was much the same as van Beuningen had paid in 1939 for the first fake de Hoogh, the *Drinkers*.

Van Meegeren was by now an extremely wealthy man (and Hoogendijk and Strijbis were doing far from badly). The three forgeries sold in 1941 had fetched a total of some 2,300,000 guilders, the equivalent of £230,000 then or of well over twice that sum today. Van Meegeren had received about two-thirds of it. He was fifty-two; he had enough to live in perfect luxury for all the rest of his life, and it might be imagined that he would now have been content to rest safely on his laurels; with each new fake, the risk of discovery would grow. On the contrary, however, he now entered his most prolific period: in less than two years, he was to complete three major forgeries.

According to his own evidence, his reason was quite simply that he found the work so satisfying and absorbing. He was to say at the trial when asked why he continued: 'Because I enjoyed painting them [the later forgeries] so much. I came to a condition in which I was no more master of myself. I became without will, powerless. I was forced to continue.' This may well have been so, for it must certainly have been giving him the most intense satisfaction that for the first time in his life the most eminent collectors wanted to buy his work and were paying outlandish prices for it. Again he would say at the trial: 'I had been so belittled by the critics that I could no longer exhibit anywhere. I acted only from a desire to paint. I decided to carry on after the *Emmaus* not primarily from a desire to turn out forgeries but to make the best use of the technique I had discovered.' This he certainly did; but he failed to mention that the purpose of that technique was *solely* to persuade the technical examiner that his work had been painted in the mid-seventeenth century. Thus it was absolutely fraudulent and of no artistic value whatever.

He enjoyed wealth no less than the next man—more, indeed, than many would. He must have long since given up any thought, at any level of conscience or consciousness, of ever repaying any part of the money. He would have convinced himself by now that it was no less than his due, that it had been paid for major masterpieces of which he had been the author, that they gave as much aesthetic delight as if they were Vermeers, that he was thus defrauding no one. Whether or not he reached such a pitch of self-deception, he began spending more heavily than ever when the *Head of Christ* put money back in his pocket, and ran completely riot when the next two forgeries brought him such stacks of banknotes—he always insisted on cash—that they began to be an embarrassment. To safeguard some part of his wealth, he began buying real estate, probably through Strijbis—by the time of his confession he owned fifty houses, hotels and night-clubs, mostly in Amsterdam and Laren—and works of art (genuine ones). Like those he was defrauding, he sought a hedge against inflation—the same hedge—to protect the capital he was receiving from them. To his friends, he justified his overflowing wealth either by saying that he had made a big profit on a picture sale (very true) or by harking back to his old story of the *Loterie Nationale*. In fact at about this time he put round the word that he had won the *gros lot* twice; nobody questioned his assertion.

The villa was furnished and decorated with the greatest luxury imaginable, and van Meegeren began a life of wild and reckless debauchery. Indeed it is rather surprising that he ever sobered up enought to paint another fake, especially when more money was totally unnecessary. But his creative instinct and artistic drive, now so falsely twisted, still ran so strongly in him that he simply could not stop. Within a few months of the *Cardplayers* sale, he was again at work with his resin and his oven.

Here should be emphasized the unreliability of the evidence owing to the conditions of the Occupation and to van Meegeren's own devious nature. He was to weave an intentional fabric of lies, half-truths and mis-statements which has never been untangled and now never will be. He consciously planned that if ever his handiwork were suspected, the investigator would find only a series of dead ends, of contradictory statements. Even after his confession, even when he knew that his conviction—which none wanted more than he did—was certainly assured, he continued to lay the trail of deception, as much from habit and a perverse sense of humour as for any rational reason. He had become completely irresponsible, uncaring for the world and its opinions, a man who believed only in himself and cared only for his own tattered destiny. Deception absorbed him; after all, it was his trade. In telling of his achievements, he would add the things that might have happened or that nearly happened until he may well have believed they *did* happen. Another day, before another audience, he would tell a different story.

However, it seems likely that towards the end of 1941, in which year he had already garnered two million guilders, he began work on two forgeries, *Isaac and Jacob* and the *Adulteress* (plates 30 and 32), which were to occupy him, sometimes concurrently, for nine or ten months. Both were sold in 1942, the former in April, the latter in October.

One has only to glance at either of them to see how his standards had fallen since the *Emmaus* and the *Supper*. These had been executed with love, skill and inspiration. This cannot be said of the *Isaac* and the *Adulteress*: their compositions are unpleasing, their artistic quality far lower, their scope greatly diminished. The *Isaac* canvas has almost the same dimensions as the *Emmaus* would have if up-ended, $49\frac{1}{4}'' \times 45\frac{1}{2}''$; the *Adulteress* is considerably smaller—$38\frac{1}{4}'' \times 33''$. From a technical point of view, van Meegeren took as much care with *Isaac and Jacob* as ever: he removed the underpainting—its subject is unknown—much more completely than in the case of the *Last Supper* or even of the *Emmaus*. The paint structure was less complex, though still adequate to evince convincing crackle: it consisted of three layers, of which the bottommost, as before, was the original ground, employed in the usual way. The middle one—blackish with an oil base—was the cellular layer; in the topmost, traces of phenol and formaldehyde were to be found.

The *Adulteress* is much less accomplished technically. It has already been mentioned that van Meegeren left large areas of the underpainting—a battle scene with warriors and horses (plate 33)—which are clearly visible to X-rays, and that through forgetfulness, hangover or general confusion he used cobalt blue as well as ultramarine. The paint structure was similar to that of the *Isaac*: the original ground (reddish, containing oil and ochre), the cellular layer (whitish, with chalk and glue) and the surface layer in which traces of the artificial resin were again to be discovered by the Commission.

There are familiar faces in both canvases. The head of Isaac is a composite, drawn from two *Last Supper* apostles: the brow, eyebrows, eyes and most of the nose are almost identical to those of the unidentified saint who was also to serve van Meegeren as a model for his *Mother and Child* (plate 22), whilst the beard is the beard of St Peter (on Christ's immediate right). The Christ of the *Adulteress* has much in common with Isaac and with all the earlier van Meegeren Christs. As for the sinner herself, she is copied closely from the authentic Vermeer, *Woman in Blue* at the Rijksmuseum, which had also served as a model for his earlier, unsold forgery, *Woman Reading Music*.* It is widely believed that the model for *Woman in Blue* was Vermeer's wife; it might at first be imagined that he would have been thought unlikely to have used her as a model for the woman taken in adultery, but in fact it is believed by many that she also sat for the harlot in his undisputed *Procuress* (which, if true, throws an interesting sidelight on his character), so this would have been no more remarkable and might indeed be thought in keeping with Vermeer's known personality.

The jug and wineglass in the *Isaac* are almost identical to those depicted ˙previously. In both canvases there is a prominent Vermeer signature, with which the forger, as always, took much loving care.

The sale of the *Adulteress*, being of particular importance, is considered separately in the next chapter. Here it need only be mentioned that it found its way to Goering by a completely different route. For *Isaac Blessing Jacob*, however, which was almost certainly the first of the pair completed, van Meegeren once again used Strijbis, who again went to Hoogendijk—the fourth time these two had been involved in little over a year—

* Compare plates 1–3.

who once more went to van der Vorm. The price extracted from him was 1,270,000 guilders—the equivalent today of over £300,000.

This was to be the last time either Strijbis or Hoogendijk was involved in a sale. After van Meegeren's confession, Hoogendijk returned to the buyers at least part of the commissions paid by them, which had totalled some half-million guilders, in respect of the five forgeries he had sold: the *Emmaus*, the *Cardplayers*, the *Head*, the *Supper* and the *Isaac*. No charges of any kind were ever preferred against him; he had declared his commissions for tax purposes as he regularly did with any sale. Strijbis was less lucky. He had said that he kept no records, but it was estimated that he had received a total of 540,000 guilders; this he had never declared and he now owed so much tax that he had no hope of paying it. Like van Meegeren, he would face bankruptcy.

Even before the deal with Goering had been completed, van Meegeren was probably at work on what would be his last forgery, the unpleasant and uninspired *Footwashing* (plate 31). Thus he was to turn from Christ's rescue of an adulteress to his forgiveness of a prostitute, subjects which it is easy to imagine had much appeal to van Meegeren.* The *Washing of Christ's Feet* ($45\frac{1}{2}'' \times 37\frac{1}{2}''$) is terribly overcrowded, badly drawn and badly composed. Christ is understandably declining what appears to be a large pudding offered by a servant woman. The same old wine jug is as prominent as ever. One Pharisee, based on the Judas in the *Last Supper*, stands in the background and takes no notice of the proceedings; another, a pure van Meegeren portrait, who (like his St John) might equally well be man or woman, is regarding Christ with love and admiration, the very opposite of the sentiments expressed by the Pharisee in the gospel. Mary Magdalene, with downcast eyes, is bathing Christ's right foot; the left foot is not seen.

Moreover the technical side was very careless and slapdash. As

* He seems to have had much sympathy—even to have identified—with prostitutes. Moiseiwitsch tells (op. cit., page 157) that he recounted to a friend how he had prevailed upon one such girl to allow him to have her without payment (as would have been very desirable to his need for acceptance). He accounted for her consent with the words: 'Well, she must have recognized a fellow-whore, that's how I explain it.' This would have been soon after the *Emmaus* sale; if not apocryphal, it would be a most revealing statement.

in the *Adulteress*, van Meegeren left visible large areas of the under-painting—*Horses and Riders* by an unknown hand (plate 34)—and he also made a serious mistake in his final baking of the forgery. As he would later agree, he either left it too long in the oven or exposed it to too high a temperature (he could not remember which); numerous small craters appeared in several areas of the surface paint layer because the oil had volatilized too rapidly; he clumsily restored them and hoped for the best. (The best, as usual, happened; they were never once noticed.) The paint structure, besides, is much less complex than before. Over much of the canvas, there are only two paint layers, one of which is the ground of *Horses and Riders*. This as often before was found to be brownish, of ochre and oil; its undersurface was impregnated with glue. The upper (modern) layer consisted of two sub-layers: layer 1A, which 'was bluish, containing white lead, natural ultramarine and artificial resin', and 1B which was greyish-blue and 'probably contained indigo in addition'.* In certain areas only, particularly under Christ's robe, a cellular layer of white lead, chalk and oil was found. This painting must have cost van Meegeren dear in lapis lazuli, since the robe, which is ultramarine, occupies more than one-third of the canvas, but by now he could well afford it.

Because the *Footwashing* was sold to the Netherlands State, its sale is better documented than any of the other war-time forgeries. Van Meegeren at last grew wary of the well-worn Strijbis–Hoogendijk pipeline; instead he asked an old schoolfriend, Jan Kok of Deventer, if he would help him to sell an old picture. Kok, who had been a Government official in the Dutch East Indies until they were overrun, knew nothing whatever about painting—even less than Strijbis. He was to say at the trial, to the pained dismay of his hearers, that he had *never heard of Vermeer* until van Meegeren approached him with the story that he had found the *Footwashing* 'in an old collection'. No further particulars were provided except that he had bought it cheaply, thought it a Vermeer, and believed it 'should fetch over a million guilders'. Because of his bad relations with dealers and experts, he could not himself handle the sale or be mentioned in connection with it, so perhaps his friend would say that he himself had found it. Much the same old story. Kok agreed; he took the thing in a wooden crate to de Boer, the

* From the Commission's report, quoted by Coremans, op. cit., page 18.

Amsterdam dealer who had handled an earlier fake, but that had been the 'de Hoogh' brought to him by Boon before the war, so there was no reason why the two should be associated. He said he believed he had found a valuable Old Master; when de Boer asked whose work it was, Kok replied (according to his own evidence at the trial) that de Boer would know this 'the very moment he saw it'. As soon as the crate was opened, de Boer, like Hoogendijk before him, at once thought of the *Emmaus*, just as van Meegeren had planned; when he asked Kok where he had found it, the latter gave a reply of the same kind as Strijbis had given. De Boer thought the *Footwashing* of such potential importance that it should be offered to the State—he was fully aware of the danger that the Germans might get to know about it, and realized that he could use this as a lever—and he got in touch with the Rijksmuseum.

The forgery was first examined by Dr A. M. de Wild, who was to serve on the Coremans Commission, and also by Luitwieler, the restorer to whom the *Emmaus* had been entrusted. This was lucky because it made it the more likely that this forgery would be compared with the earlier one. Both expressed a *prima facie* opinion in favour of buying it; they telephoned Dr Hannema and asked him to come at once on a highly important and confidential matter. Hannema, the Director of the Boymans, had been more responsible than anyone for its acquisition of the *Emmaus*; he drove over from Rotterdam and, as he was to admit in evidence, 'immediately got the impression that the picture was a Vermeer'. A Government Committee was set up to examine it and then decide whether the State should purchase.

If van Meegeren's aim had been to deceive and discredit the established art world, he himself could hardly have chosen a more representative septet than those who met together a few days later in the Rijksmuseum. Besides those already named, there were present Dr C. D. Roell and Dr A. van Schendel, respectively Director General and Curator of the Museum; Dr J. Q. van Regteren Altena, a Professor at Amsterdam University who, like de Wild, was to serve on the Coremans Commission; and Dr J. G. van Gelder, a Professor at Utrecht and acting Director of the Museum. Van Meegeren would not have been extremely pleased, however, if he could have heard their deliberations, which seem to have been absolutely extraordinary.

Altena, as all the others subsequently agreed, at once denounced the picture as a forgery.* According to their evidence moreover, none of the others admired the picture though all thought it authentic. Van Gelder was to admit that he 'never doubted its genuineness; I thought it ugly, but still a real Vermeer'. Hannema would recall: 'None of us liked it very much but we were afraid it would go to Germany.'

The preposterous outcome was that these seven great experts, of whom one was convinced that the picture was a fake and the others did not like it, recommended to the Government that it be acquired for the Rijksmuseum (where, however, it could not yet be exhibited owing to the Occupation) at the outrageous asking price of 1,300,000 guilders. This is the more unbelievable if one can credit the evidence of de Wild, as I suppose one must, that de Boer refused their request to X-ray it, which must surely have suggested to them not merely that it was more doubtful than ever but also that de Boer felt certain doubts himself. It was finally shown to Professor J. van Dam, who agreed at the trial that as Secretary General of the Ministry of Education it was his sole final responsibility, acting on the advice of the *ad hoc* committee, to authorize the purchase.

De Boer's usual commission was a flat ten per cent. Because this was a sale to the State, he agreed to settle for five. That would have been 65,000 guilders (about £6,500 in 1943). Kok received more: there are several different estimates but 80,000 guilders seems the most likely figure. Certainly van Meegeren cleared well over a million.

The honest Kok seems to have been genuinely dumbfounded by the fee offered him. He said he had done next to nothing; he had never expected a reward on anything like such a scale. However, he accepted it. But it has to be said in his favour that he repaid the greater part of his fine fee when the picture was later proved a fake.

From his evidence at the trial, it is clear that Hoogendijk saw the *Footwashing* before its sale, though he was not this time professionally involved. He had thus seen all the false Vermeers except

---

* Coremans writes that 'this is worth recording'—a considerable understatement—'since Dr Altena was the first to react in the direction of the truth' (op. cit., page 37). In fact he was by no means the first: it will be recalled that the *Emmaus* itself was denounced with contempt as a 'rotten fake' by Duveen's man in Paris six years earlier.

the *Adulteress*, and one or both of the false de Hooghs. He did not however feel the smallest whisper of suspicion.

The most important aspect of the whole van Meegeren case is not his skill, nor the acclaim accorded the *Emmaus*, but the ease and virtual unanimity with which these later forgeries secured acceptance and were sold. Perhaps the only standards by which a picture's value should be judged is its artistic merit; if this were the case, such prices would never have been paid, so it certainly cannot be. But if a man is to pay a fortune for a signature, for a work that derives its supposed value from the identity of its supposed creator more than from any other factor, he might be expected to take some little trouble to confirm that identity. One would imagine that two obvious questions would at once spring to mind: where has this painting been found and how has its authenticity been tested? Yet if these were so much as asked, it may be said with complete certainty that on no occasion could either have received a remotely satisfactory answer. It might be imagined that whenever van Meegeren produced a new forgery he would concoct as convincing a story as possible to account for its discovery and to explain why such a masterpiece had been lost and unacknowledged for three centuries; that if dealers such as Hoogendijk had been prepared on the first occasion to forego such full details, their suspicions would be aroused on the second or surely the third; that if they were again refused any information that could be checked as to previous history, they would insist upon the most searching scientific tests. Then, as we now know, the falseness of the later forgeries might well have been established. But, as has been seen, nothing of the kind happened, and indeed de Boer, so far from making any attempt to satisfy himself as to the authenticity of the *Footwashing* before offering it for sale, refused to allow the State officials to carry out the elementary test to which they sought his agreement. Yet, despite van Meegeren, almost exactly the same state of affairs again exists today—the same fine nonchalance, the same pretence of omniscience, the same total neglect of scientific research. It is only after they have been sold, for example, that some hundreds of modern canvases are now, as I write, being radiographed in the United States because the likelihood that they are fakes has arisen on circumstantial grounds. It is already known that thousands of forgeries and wrong ascriptions remain undetected; it has been said with some cynicism but a great deal of truth that of the 2,500 paintings that Corot might have painted in his lifetime 'almost 8,000 are to be found in America'. Yet the judges through the centuries have retained their dignity, the critics their self-esteem and poise. It cannot be seriously pretended that those concerned in the van Meegeren case were a small, incompetent clique, hypnotized by circumstances, suddenly deprived of their critical faculties, the exception to the rule. They were in fact the most eminent critics, dealers, collectors, art historians in Holland—the native land of Jan Vermeer and Pieter de Hoogh, where most should be known of them. And yet the van Meegeren case, which in the end did prove, just as he had planned, either that they were totally incompetent or else that it is impossible to distinguish between a genuine Old Master and a modern fake, has had no lasting effect whatever.

By the middle of 1943, Han van Meegeren was an extremely wealthy man with a large private income from investments. He had accumulated a fortune of about five million guilders and no longer had the smallest intention of repaying it.* It was not only that he had spent and lost so much that repayment would have been possible no longer; he had tasted the enjoyment of great wealth, had become used to spending money as he liked and was not able to surrender this power when at last he had attained it. This was his failure; he had set out with a purpose, an ideal of its own strange kind, and having come within reach of its achievement had allowed himself to be turned aside to more material ends. He had never been afraid of spending and it is certain that a great proportion of the one and a half million guilders that could not be otherwise accounted for in his bankruptcy had been spent on personal outgoings during the eight years between the sale of the *Emmaus* and his confession.

It may thus be estimated that during this period he was getting through some £20,000 a year at a time when prices were one-half to one-quarter of today's, quite apart from his expenditure on property such as houses, pictures and antiques, which remained after his death and were sold to repay part of his liability, and the very considerable sums which he hid and could not find. It was

---

* In 1950 the Statute of Limitations would have come into effect if he sold no further forgeries and none of his illicit gains would have been any longer at stake.

easy to spend money in Holland during the war; everything was controlled, everything in short supply, everything had its flourishing black market. Besides spending money on himself and his wife, van Meegeren was a magnet to countless sycophants and a few friends whom he entertained on a lavish and always increasing scale. To be host in this way pleased him immensely; he loved to throw large and extravagant parties where he would see himself as the centre and inspiration. Night after night, in a favourite café or at the villa, he would gather with fifteen or twenty others: there would be drinking and argument and song, or intellectual discussion, as the spirit moved him. All were at ease when Han was the host.

His growing investment in houses and hotels has already been mentioned—he now owned over fifty. He was also adding to his collection of Old Masters. He still engaged from time to time in dealing and would often retain a canvas if it pleased him; this *penchant* alone must have accounted for tens of thousands. And he now acquired the extraordinary habit of hiding stacks of bank-notes—in the pipes of the central heating system, beneath the floorboards of a bedroom, buried in the garden—and then moving them round from one hiding place to another. Still imagining that the world was against him, he assumed that a conspiracy might take away his wealth, and the same cache must not be used too long. He might then lose track of a hoard; he was later to tell his son and daughter that several were still hidden at Laren but he couldn't quite remember where.

He had one nasty moment. Towards the end of the war, the Government called in all thousand-guilder (£100) notes; those who possessed large quantities were invited to explain just how they had been acquired. Van Meegeren went round all his hiding places and managed to find about 1,500. He had no option but to turn them in, stating blandly that he had sold several Old Masters, which was very nearly true. The authorities became suspicious, however, and retained the equivalent of £90,000—almost two-thirds of the total—pending enquiries; this was never returned. Thus van Meegeren was suspected by the revenue authorities, as he was to be suspected by the political police: by the art world, never. He must now have realized that his activities might be closely watched and this may have contributed to his decision that he had painted his last forgery.

His life became without any aim; money and his own crooked genius had destroyed him. Before the war he had been daunted by opposition and poverty, now by weakness and wealth. His health began to fail through the many excesses to which he subjected himself, but the tempo never slowed. Under the strain of the life he was leading he had begun to take morphia; soon it was a habit and he used the drug heavily. Meanwhile his marriage was ending; he had returned in his fifties to the promiscuity of his twenties. Morphia, sexual abandonment and the stresses of war and secrecy were stealing from him such little talent as remained and plundering his last coins of integrity.

In 1943, after the *Footwashing* sale, van Meegeren let the villa and moved to Amsterdam, where he bought a large four-floored house on the Keizergracht, a quiet, fashionable street, running beside a tree-lined canal through the centre of the city. That same year, his wife divorced him. It is a curious fact, however, that they continued living in the same house, though in different parts of it. At this time van Meegeren made a settlement in her favour of 800,000 guilders; when he went bankrupt this remained intact because they were not married.

Now it must be supposed that he dismantled his oven and disposed of it, that he cast out his pigments and poured his resins away. As he planned it, that was the end of the story. The revels were ended:

> *Deeper than did ever plummet sound*
> *I'll drown my book.*

But the past is seldom drowned and before too long, many miles away, half-forgotten fragments of it began to float to the surface.

8
Dénouement

VAN MEEGEREN's downfall, which led to his triumph, came
about eventually from no sudden, unwonted insight or intuition
of the experts, nor from a willing decision on his own part to
claim authorship of the fakes, but through the completely fortuitous circumstance that the *Adulteress* had ended up with
Goering. This would force him to an unwise, unplanned confession when it was traced to him and he was accused—not of
forgery—but of trading with the enemy.

If the *Adulteress* had stayed in Holland as he had planned, the
facts would quite probably never have come to light, certainly not
fully to light, at any rate in his lifetime. It is true that two or three
of the fakes, in particular the *Head of Christ*, have now so deteriorated
in the quarter-century since they were painted that serious doubts
would by now have arisen in respect of them. However, the agent
concerned could well have maintained his perfectly tenable position, if a work had become suspect and been traced to him and if
he had been traced, that he had undertaken not to reveal its source,
that this had been an agreed condition of sale and must therefore
be respected. By now the *Footwashing* might well have been
transferred discreetly to the vaults of the Rijksmuseum, where it
would be shown with a wry smile to each succeeding Director but
perhaps to no-one else. The van der Vorms might still be maintaining that the *Isaac* was a Vermeer—not one of his best, they
might admit, but of much historic interest—although those to
whom they showed it might here exchange a wink. Hoogendijk
would have despaired of ever re-selling the *Head* and would have
written it off as a tax loss. There seems very little doubt, however,
that Vermeer's *Last Supper* and de Hoogh's *Drinking Party* would
have been among the canvases willed by van Beuningen to public
institutions where they would now be much appreciated, that the
Cardplayers would have been welcomed into the accepted *oeuvre*
of de Hoogh, and above all that the *Emmaus* would still be

the pride of the Boymans. It was solely for political reasons that their inauthenticity came to light; never at any time was any new suspicion aroused on aesthetic or scientific grounds and never did van Meegeren make a serious enough artistic or technical error for questions to be asked. Such must always be likely, for once a great work of art has been publicly exhibited, or hung in a well-known private collection, with a firm attribution, there is often no good reason why it should not hang there for ever.

The sale to Goering had not merely been accidental but contrary to van Meegeren's very specific instructions. He had been aware of the dangers of trading with the enemy, and realized that any canvas found after the war in enemy hands would be liable to detailed investigation. He had therefore specified to Rienstra van Strijvesande, the agent to whom he had entrusted the *Adulteress*, that on no account should it end in German hands. (This was particularly necessary because van Strijvesande was known to have dealings with a Bavarian banker, Aloys Miedl, who had an office in Amsterdam.) The fact that it did so was van Meegeren's one piece of bad luck—it can hardly be called a mistake—in all the years of deception. Once it had reached the hands of van Strijvesande, its destination passed from his personal control. The existence of 'a newly-discovered Vermeer' did come to Miedl's knowledge, and thence to that of Dr Walter Hofer, one of many agents used by Goering and other Nazi leaders for the acquisition of major works of art. If only from self-interest, van Meegeren would have opposed the sale to Hofer if he had been in a position to do so; once Miedl knew of the canvas it was already too late and he could only hope for the best.

The best, for once, did not happen. The post-war Allied Art Commission, whose duties were to seek out and investigate the accumulated treasures of the Nazi leaders with a view to returning them, where appropriate, to their owners, and to trace and punish the collaborators who had handled them, must soon have become accustomed to finding important works of art. None the less, this particular canvas must have been of very special interest to them when they unearthed it at the famous salt mine outside Alt-Aussee in Austria. It bore a prominent Vermeer signature—the usual *I. V. Meer*—in the top left-hand corner, and must at once have put them in mind of the greatly esteemed *Christ at Emmaus* whose discovery had caused such a stir in 1937. And yet it was unknown to them.

If it had been the supposed work of almost any other great master, this would not have been at all remarkable. Nobody would claim a personal knowledge of the entire *oeuvre* of Rembrandt or Tintoretto. But because so very few canvases are attributed to Vermeer, all would have been well known to several Commission members. (They had already found at Berchtesgarden his famous *A Painter in his Studio*, stolen by Hitler from the Kunsthistorisches Museum, Vienna.) It therefore became a find of quite particular interest and importance. It had been sold as a Vermeer; if so, it was an unknown Vermeer, and Goering had paid an unprecedented sum for it (as the well-kept Nazi records quickly showed). Thus one of the facts that had driven van Meegeren to choose Vermeer as his main victim was in the end to work against him.

Goering had agreed to pay the absurd figure of 1,650,000 guilders—fifty thousand more than van Beuningen had paid for the *Last Supper*, which was much larger and more pleasing, and by that amount the highest price paid for any of the forgeries. It would be the equivalent today of almost half a million pounds. It turned out that he had paid in kind (as had van Beuningen): he had handed over to Miedl more than two hundred paintings which had been stolen from the Netherlands by the occupying Nazis. Their total value was probably rather more than the agreed figure. It is not known precisely how much van Meegeren received— strangely enough, nobody who participated in this sale was called to give evidence at the trial—but it was certainly well over a million guilders.

Never before had any serious attempt been made to establish the previous history of a van Meegeren forgery. It is self-evident that no verifiable provenance could ever have been established for any of them, but on no occasion had any difficult questions been asked; purchasers were invariably satisfied, as they had to be, by the excessively vague stories told by van Meegeren's agents. Now the investigation was mounted, not because the authenticity of the canvas was in doubt—this question was never raised—but to settle two related questions, neither of which could ever previously have arisen: what traitor had been guilty of the very serious charge of collaboration, and what should become of the picture. These experts were deceived by the forgery no less than those who had preceded them; had they not fully accepted the *Adulteress* as a Vermeer, it would have been of no interest to them.

It was easy from captured records to trace it to Hofer, from Hofer to Miedl, from Miedl to van Strijvesande (though Miedl had fled and was sought in vain), and from van Strijvesande to van Meegeren. So it happened that at the end of May 1945 two uniformed officers of the Netherlands Field Security Service, a paramilitary force, presented themselves at the front door of the big house on the Keizergracht.

They were prepared to be diffident and respectful. They must have supposed that their visit to the eccentric, short-tempered, arrogant painter and collector, who seemed to be so well known in the neighbourhood, would be brief and straightforward, little more than a formality. They had no good reason to suspect him of trading with the enemy. It was known that he had been a very heavy spender during the war, but equally that he had won the *Loterie Nationale*—some even said he had won it twice—and made some memorable coups in legitimate picture deals. He had sold the *Adulteress* to a well-known Dutch colleague and could not be held responsible for its ending in enemy hands; it would be van Strijvesande who might have some explaining to do. But, they told him, in view of the work's undoubted importance, the high price paid and the identity of the buyer, they would have to know where he had obtained it. Such information, they assured him, would be strictly confidential.

It cannot be supposed that he would have been arrested next day if there had in fact been an 'old Italian family' from whom, as he now maintained, he had purchased the *Adulteress* before the war, and if the officers could therefore have confirmed that the sale had taken place and been legitimate. Its eventual purchase by Goering would have been accepted as not his responsibility. When he repeatedly and angrily refused to give any more information, on the usual grounds which had always previously been good enough but were now insufficient, the combination of circumstances became suspicious enough to justify his arrest. His inexplicable choice of an Italian provenance may have led the authorities to believe that he had acted as a middleman between Fascists and Nazis; or his downright refusal to identify his source may have made them suspect that the canvas had been stolen, as was the case with so many that had ended up in Germany, or obtained under duress. In any event his usual tale—that the seller, wishing it not to be known that bad times were forcing him to part with family treasures, had made it a condition of sale that his identity be not revealed—was now for the first time unacceptable. It was exactly the kind of story a collaborator would invent to avoid self-incrimination. It was also the kind of story that a forger would invent, but through six years and eight fakes it had never once been questioned.

Van Meegeren must have realized, as soon as the officers put their first question, that his whole position, which had seemed so perfectly secure, was suddenly most dangerous. He had taken little trouble since the *Emmaus* with inventing any provenance because none ever seemed of much importance to the buyer. Moreover it would not have mattered if one potential client had asked some hard questions. He could take it or leave it; van Meegeren could (and did) maintain that he had undertaken not to reveal the identity of the previous owner. This happens often: fine-arts auctioneers are frequently asked to do the same and the work appears in the catalogue as 'the property of a gentleman'. The Prado's Antonello had come from an unidentified 'native of Galicia'—nothing else was known, but that was quite enough. In no case had the buyers, or the dealers, or the agents insisted on more facts, though Hoogendijk had had knowledge of six of the fakes, Strijbis of four, van Beuningen of three. They had been in no position to do so.

Now the position was different. The Field Security men had simply wished to establish whether or not van Meegeren had been trading with the enemy. When he was faced with such a very serious charge, they found it unacceptable that he should flatly refuse the required information. On 29 May 1945, Han van Meegeren was arrested as a collaborator.

The irony of this baseless charge lies in the fact that, so far from being a traitor, van Meegeren had successfully (if unintentionally) duped Goering, by securing the return to their homeland of many authentic and valuable works of art, supplied to Goering by collaborators, in exchange for a valueless fake. Its inexplicable effect on him was that he now allowed himself to languish in jail for *six weeks*, derided as a traitor, when at any time, had he spoken four words, he could have become a hero.

It is possible to explain his arrest as resulting from the anti-Nazi hysteria that had understandably swept the Netherlands after Liberation; the Dutch people were out to find and punish those who had worked with the enemy and the smallest suspicion was very often enough. Van Meegeren's continuing silence in jail, however, seems so extraordinary—it might have been understandable if it had lasted a day or two whilst he thought things over—that it must be seen as totally irrational. He had become by now, at the age of fifty-six, extremely crochety and difficult—he was perverse, stubborn, self-centred—and the police and military, in their desire to extract information from him, refused him the morphia to which he was now addicted. From every point of view, this long and foolish silence, this refusal even to answer any questions, was unnecessary, kept him in prison under deep and increasing suspicion, and could only do him harm.

When on 12 July he did finally break down, for that is how it has to be regarded, and made what now seemed almost more a confession than a claim to immortal fame, his temperament and love of the dramatic compelled him to say far more than he need have said or was in his own interest. 'Fools!' he suddenly burst forth, as was faithfully recorded by his startled interrogators: 'You are fools like the rest of them! I sold no great national treasure—I painted it myself.' That's where he should have stopped. But his conceit and madness forced him to continue: he had also painted the Vermeer in the Boymans, the Vermeer and the de Hoogh in van Beuningen's collection, the Vermeer bought by the State—he was impelled to claim them all. He had made a fool of everyone; now—as he would later agree—he was being a fool himself.

If at this time he had confined his claim to the *Adulteress*—all that was necessary—it would have been far more credible and easily confirmed. He could have said: 'If you radiograph this great national treasure, you will find underneath it a painting of a battle scene which I bought from So-and-so's, for so much, in 1942. Go there and they will have a record of the sale.' Nothing more than that. Such facts could be checked at once; it would then have appeared, and he could have pretended, that he had performed a most daring and patriotic act by turning out a fake for the express purpose of duping a hated Nazi leader. Even if he had had to return the money received for it—but to whom, when no one deserved it more than he did?—he could very probably have kept the proceeds from the others. Whether he subsequently claimed them would have been a matter for his conscience. If he had done so, his story would then have been far more acceptable, besides being presented in a much more favourable light. This would have been so under any other conditions than those he now chose or were forced on him by destiny. There was no good reason why the others should have been associated with him. They had passed through the hands of different agents and no connection with them need have been seen. True, new suspicions might have been aroused when his story became widely known and the *Adulteress* was widely seen. Those who had been involved in the *Footwashing* sale, for example, might have noticed a similarity, instigated inquiries, and found that Jan Kok was an old friend of van Meegeren's; the conclusion would then have been obvious. But this, surely, would have been a risk worth taking. His needless cataract of words was certain to cost him all the millions he had made—or what was left of them—besides making it far less likely that anyone would believe him.

It may be suggested that he was now merely at last carrying out his original, long-abandoned plan of claiming the fakes as his own once they had been certified, sold, shown and fully acclaimed. This may have been the case. After six weeks of introspection—drugless, solitary, miserable—he may indeed have determined: 'To Hell with them! This is the time!' Or he may simply not have known what he was doing. Anyway, it was a most unwise course. So far from being accepted, his claim seemed so incredibly unlikely, so much more improbable than if he had confined it to the *Adulteress*, that the police at once supposed him either to be insane or to have invented this absurdly far-fetched story to escape conviction on a much more serious charge.

It was not very long before they began to change their minds. A radiograph of the *Adulteress* soon did reveal traces of the underpainting described by van Meegeren. This in itself need not have been conclusive evidence—he might himself have X-rayed it—but it was at once seen that the work bore a strong resemblance to the five other supposed Vermeers named by him, especially to the last two (the *Isaac* and the *Footwashing*). Moreover, now they all came to think of it, none of the six bore any resemblance at all to any Vermeer they had ever seen or heard of.

Until now the case was being handled by Field Security and the police. The fact that art experts had not yet been brought in is shown by the next step taken. It was put to van Meegeren that if he had painted the *Emmaus* he should now be able without much difficulty to make a copy of it. Only the police or army could have made so naïve a proposal: a copy of an existing work would prove nothing at all, since this would be within the capability of almost any skilled professional. Van Meegeren, having expressed his contempt, made a more interesting proposal. He asked to be given his freedom, the run of his studio, the materials (and the drugs) he needed. He would then create a new Vermeer before their eyes.

It was at just this time—late July—that the story reached the press. At once controversy on an unprecedented scale broke forth. It had at once been known that van Meegeren had been charged as a collaborator, that he had sold a Vermeer to Goering. His 'confession' provoked a first-class sensation: everyone was talking about it, everyone taking sides. *Was* he a collaborator? (It was well remembered that there had never been shortages in his household during the war.) Had he indeed painted the *Emmaus* and the rest? If so, what did it prove about his artistic skill, about the expertise—or foolishness—of those who had acclaimed them? Was he hero or villain, charlatan or genius? The creation of a new Vermeer before police witnesses was of special delight to the newspapers: HE PAINTS FOR HIS LIFE ran one eager headline.

The subject chosen by van Meegeren for this his tenth Vermeer* was the *Young Christ Teaching in the Temple* (also called *Jesus Among the Doctors*). This, it may be remembered, was a subject he had depicted during his own religious phase (1918). The *Young Christ*† is by no means impressive, though perhaps it is more pleasing aesthetically than the three preceding fakes; moreover, as it neared completion, van Meegeren learned that other charges— of fraud—would almost certainly be substituted and he therefore refused either to sign or to age it. However, no artist might give of his best in the ever-watching presence of Field Security, at least two members of which were never absent from his studio as he painted, and in a general atmosphere of suspicion, tension and mistrust. The canvas was a large one—$58\frac{3}{4}'' \times 75\frac{1}{2}''$, so that only the two *Suppers* had been bigger—but occupied him for only two

---

* Counting both his *Last Suppers* and the two early trial canvases.
† See plate 37.

months. All his requirements—the Vermeer pigments, oil of lilacs, phenol and formaldehyde, Bols and morphia—were provided by the police and it soon became obvious that he could indeed have been author of the others.

The authorities now found themselves in a very difficult position. It was perfectly obvious that there were no longer any grounds for holding van Meegeren as a collaborator and that charge was very quickly dropped. When it became a question of charging him with forgery, serious and most embarrassing problems were at once only too visible. It was not just that it might be very hard, in any event, to prove his guilt judicially, because, however much he wanted to be found to have painted all eight forgeries, his simple admission in this case might not be enough: it could well be disputed—as it was—by one who had been duped. But also the case would inevitably draw worldwide attention to the incompetence, perhaps the guilt, of many eminent personages who had been deeply involved in the negotiations and sales. It would have to be admitted that the State had paid well over a million guilders of the taxpayers' money for the purchase of a valueless van Meegeren. The experts called to give evidence would be those who had been deceived. They were far from anxious to be called; they might indeed be witnesses for the prosecution but would in fact be testifying to their own foolishness and to the great skill—if nothing more—of the defendant. If they disputed the latter, they would at the same time be underlining the former. It is not surprising that the trial was several times postponed. It was first set for May 1946 (ten months after van Meegeren's confession) but did not finally come to court till October of the year following. And then it would be a most Gilbertian, Alice in Wonderland trial, with the defendant wishing above all to be found guilty, thus—he maintained—to prove himself a genius.

Everything possible was done to play down the case, though with very little success. The suspect canvases were moved by the police from their owners' possession; it became virtually impossible for any outsider to see them. Questions by the press and others were unanswered and ignored. This had the predictable effect of vastly increasing public speculation and rumour, till soon it might almost have been imagined that van Meegeren had painted every known Vermeer.

Although all charges of collaboration were dropped, it was
held for many years, and is an opinion still heard in Holland today,
that he was indeed a Nazi or had at least had many dealings with
the enemy. Nothing could be more untrue or unfair. It has no
foundation on fact. The belief presumably resulted from the six
weeks he allowed to go by between his arrest and his confession,
when the nature of the charges brought were widely known and
many whose judgment was affected by the general anti-Nazi
hysteria made a number of false inferences. It was suggested that
he could never have entertained so lavishly unless he had been one
of 'them'; it was forgotten that he was an exceedingly wealthy
man and that almost anything could be obtained on the black
market if the right price were offered. Much importance and
publicity was given to the fact that a book of his drawings, which
had been on general sale during the war, was to be found at
Berchtesgarden with the inscription: '*Dem geliebten Fuerher in
dankbarer Anerkennung**—*Han van Meegeren.*' It was conclusively
proved that only the signature was in his handwriting—as is a
common practice, he had autographed fifty or a hundred copies,
one of which had been bought by an ardent Nazi, whose identity
has not been established, and dedicated by him—but the rumour
did not die. Even the van Meegerens' visit to Berlin for Hitler's
Olympic Games in 1936 was used as evidence against him,
but he would hardly have been the only non-Nazi who attended.
A moment's thought would have shown that the sale to Goering,
so far from indicating a pro-German sentiment, in fact proves the
opposite: it is absurd to imagine that if he had been a collaborator,
let alone a personal friend of Goering's as has sometimes been
suggested, he would have countenanced the sale to him of any
forgery under any circumstances, certainly not such a thoroughly
bad one at such an outrageous price. (Or, if the sale did go through
against his will, if it were beyond his power to prevent it once
Hofer knew of the existence of the fake, it would be a very strange
coincidence if it happened just by chance to end up in the possession of his friend or hero.) It is also clear that if van Meegeren had
in fact been a collaborator, he would have been prosecuted for
this very serious offence—his many enemies would have seen to it.
It may only be supposed that the calumny remains because there
was so much speculation and gossip in the weeks after his arrest,

* To the beloved Fuerher in grateful respect.

when he remained a target for spite and derision much longer than was necessary owing to his own pig-headedness.

After the substance of his confession had been proved, an adverse opinion was held of him by only very few. To the public at large, he became almost immediately the kind of national hero he had always hoped to be. Few have more appeal than one who has deflated pomposity and conceit, has shown the fallibility of the infallible, has destroyed the unjustified self-esteem of established authority and at the same time gained the professional reputation—as was now often held to have been the case—that *he* had always held to be due to him, that *they* had always denied.

Although it was generally assumed that he had indeed painted all eight forgeries, it was very soon suggested that van Meegeren might be claiming more than he had achieved and that the *Emmaus*, at least, might be a Vermeer. Decoen quotes from an article of his, published in *La Lanterne* as early as 5 November 1945. At this time he had seen none of the forgeries but based his remarks on the many reports already published in newspapers and learned journals. 'The arguments and proofs adduced have by no means convinced me,' he wrote. 'I should like to give at once, without waiting to examine [the *Emmaus*], the reasons which lead me to doubt the correctness of the statements of van Meegeren.' (It would be interesting to know what these reasons were, but Decoen, though reprinting all the rest of his article, completely omits them in his book—their place is taken by a row of dots in the text—which must indicate that he later thought better of them or that they were to prove incompatible with his eventual thesis.) He went on to write: 'Of [any] faked Vermeers that I have ever been able to view, none can be compared with the *Disciples at Emmaus*, and if van Meegeren is the maker of it, I take off my hat to him. The case would be unique in the history of painting, for the celebrated frauds which have become famous have invariably been objects such as sculptures and pieces of furniture, never a painting.'*

Decoen could not obtain a permit to visit Holland until the following February (1946). He was then able to inspect only the *Emmaus* and the *Young Christ*; at this time, as now, the authorities and owners were making it difficult for the forgeries to be seen.

---

* He should have written 'never an *old* painting'. The forgery of modern works is relatively commonplace.

The same month, he wrote in *La Lanterne*: 'The least that can be said of this affair is that we are here dealing with a sinister hoax. The picture in the Boymans [i.e., the *Emmaus*] is a genuine work of the 17th Century and is by Jan Vermeer of Delft. By painting the *Young Christ*, van Meegeren proved decisively that it was not he who had executed the *Emmaus*.'

The significance of these two articles is twofold. Firstly, Decoen had not yet established contact with van Beuningen. Latterly he was strongly backed and financed by him, owing to his personal interest in proving the *Supper* authentic, and his (Decoen's) opinions might therefore be suspect; he now had no axe to grind and reached his conclusion independently of any known external influence. Secondly it shows that Decoen's opinions were already widely known before the Coremans Commission began its investigations, which would not be for another four months. It is sometimes thought that when the Commission began its enquiry it was more or less assuming, since it had no reason to think otherwise, that all eight canvases were fakes, which might have hypnotized them into being deceived by van Meegeren if two of them (the *Emmaus* and the *Supper*) were in fact Vermeers. Having reached this erroneous decision, they would then have been too proud to admit they had been wrong when Decoen and others later thought otherwise—and were then prepared to take action of a most unscrupulous and dishonest kind, the faking of the Hondius and of the 'first' *Last Supper*, to support the untenable or shaky thesis to which they were now committed. These early Decoen articles prove this was not so. The Commission would have been perfectly well aware that at least one of the alleged fakes was held by some to be genuine and would therefore have been on their guard and given due weight to that belief. They could have had no sinister reason for finding that the *Emmaus* was certainly a fake if any evidence gave them any reason at all for feeling doubt. Rather, it must be imagined, they would have preferred to show that in this case, at least, their professional colleagues had not been deceived or might not have been deceived. They were to have no vested interest in reaching their decision, but rather the reverse.

The Coremans Commission was set up by the Minister of Justice on 11 June 1946. The inquiry was under the chairmanship of Judge G. J. Wiarda, who would, however, be no more than a

DÉNOUEMENT 163

figurehead. He nominated a committee of four to consider the available evidence and to submit all the works to complete technical and aesthetic examination. The technicians were Coremans himself and Dr W. Froentjes, official adviser on chemistry to the Ministry of Justice; the aestheticians were two leading art historians, Dr J. Q. van Regteren Altena (who, it will be remembered, had expressed it as his positive opinion that the *Footwashing* was a fake when its purchase by the State was being considered) and Dr H. Schneider, former Director of the State Department of the History of Art. Shortly afterwards, Dr A. M. de Wild was co-opted as an additional technician. This was a rather unkind choice, since he had been amongst those who had advised the State to buy the *Footwashing* and would therefore be testifying to his own error.

Van Meegeren offered full collaboration. He provided the salient details of his technique, which very greatly assisted the technicians in identifying the substances used, and such details as he could recall about the underpaintings. He had kept no written records and his memory was failing (along with other faculties), so that sometimes his recollections were inaccurate or confused. In the case of the *Emmaus* he was positive that the original painting had been a *Raising of Lazarus*; on 24 July he made an interesting sketch (plate 9) showing such details as he remembered of it with the *Emmaus* superimposed on them. In particular this included his estimate of the exact position of the *Lazarus* head which, it will be remembered, he had not been able to remove and which would therefore be alone visible in a radiograph. Coremans reproduces his sketch side by side with the radiograph that was now taken (plate 10) and comments that the head 'is in the position and of the dimensions [that van Meegeren] declared'.* As a matter of fact, it may be seen that this was something of an exaggeration: van Meegeren indicated that the head was just above and to the right of the wine jug, whereas the X-ray showed it to be just above and to the left of it. This, however, amounted to an error in recollection of only five or six inches after an interval of a decade.

Decoen states categorically, but without providing any confirmatory evidence at all, that van Meegeren was shown the radiograph before he made the sketch.† It is an absurd suggestion. If it were true there would have been no point whatever in the

* Coremans, op. cit., plate 52, caption.　　† Decoen, op. cit., page 25.

Commission asking him to make the sketch; and, besides, he would obviously have located the all-important head in exactly the right position. The Commission had no reason to wish to help van Meegeren. It has again to be emphasized that they would have had no desire, but rather the opposite, to prove he painted the *Emmaus* (or, for that matter, any other of the fakes), and were well aware of the opinion held by Decoen and others, which it would have been more in their interest to find confirmed.

The police investigation was handed to Inspector Wooning, who by all accounts pursued the case with very great zeal and skill. He found some confirmatory evidence in the forger's studio in Amsterdam, and also at Laren, but it was at the long-abandoned Villa Estate in Nice that his most important discoveries were made. It is indeed remarkable that van Meegeren—quite unnecessarily—had left behind so much relevant evidence which would certainly have cast deep suspicion if found earlier by accident. In most cases, on attempt had been made to hide it, and Wooning returned with a mass of vital material. This included the four unsold 'trial' forgeries, several uncompleted ones including a promising 'de Hoogh', and a canvas to which only the levelling layer had been applied (and admirable crackle induced in it). He also found various phenolic solutions and seventeenth-century 'props'. It is curious—as Decoen never tires of mentioning—that he missed the 'first' *Last Supper*, despite its immense size, which was to be found much later by Coremans.

As has been mentioned, he failed to discover the important strip of canvas that van Meegeren said he had cut from the *Lazarus*, and one of the two pieces cut by him from the stretcher. Here must be emphasized, however, the very great significance of the piece of stretcher he *did* find. This could be proved beyond any argument or doubt to be indeed a continuation to the left of the upper horizontal arm of the original *Lazarus* stretcher which had happily been preserved by the Boymans. It is at once obvious that the lines in the timber, which are the annual rings seen in cross section, coincide exactly. Moreover when van Meegeren cut the stretcher, it happened that his saw bisected a worm-hole in the timber; this is clearly visible when the two pieces are seen end-on.

This proved beyond any doubt whatever that the original stretcher had been cut down by 49·6 centimetres (the length of the fragment found in Nice) and therefore, with almost equal certainty, that the canvas had been cut down similarly. This in turn would clearly imply that the *Emmaus* was a forgery—and also, though this is not relevant to present considerations, that van Meegeren was intending to claim authorship. It would therefore be necessary for Decoen to dispute its validity. It is noticeable, and significant, that nowhere in his book does he make any attempt to do so. He ignores this evidence completely, though he goes into great detail on less important matters—a fact which testifies strongly to its high significance.

In fact, it is conclusive. It is a necessary implication of the Decoen thesis that the stretcher fragment found by Wooning is none other than a completely dishonest fabrication to give force to the Commission's verdict that the *Emmaus* is a modern work—just as he would later hold the Hondius photograph and the 'first' *Last Supper* to be. In this case, such a position simply cannot be held. In the first place, it would be to all intents and purposes absolutely impossible to find a piece of timber, new or old, in which the annual rings corresponded exactly (quite apart from the colour and texture) with those of the *Emmaus* stretcher. Moreover, if by some miracle such a piece of timber had been found, Decoen's line would necessarily imply that a member of the Commission had had it fashioned into an apparent continuation of the stretcher arm (but how about the worm-hole?) and then prevailed on Wooning to pretend he had found it in Nice—unless it be suggested that it was 'planted' there by a third party without the Inspector's knowledge. It is not unknown for the police of any country to connive in the fabrication of incriminating evidence, but on this occasion there was absolutely no reason for any such course. It would have been better by far for everyone—for all those who had hailed the *Emmaus* as a great Vermeer, for the Boymans, for the sacred memory of the now-lamented Bredius, for Dr Hannema and all—to show that van Meegeren's claim was in this instance untrue, that the *Emmaus* was genuine. Once the Commission had announced its verdict, it might just be conceivable—it would at least be within the bounds of human possibility, however unlikely—that evidence should be fabricated to give it additional weight. At this time no verdict had been reached and there could have been no conceivable justification for an act of such total dishonesty which in any case would have been technically impossible.

The Coremans Commission was to announce its findings in March 1947. It would thus give nine months to examining all the evidence—not only the eight sold forgeries and the *Young Christ*, but also the four trial fakes brought back by Wooning from Nice, together with the pigments, resins, oils, scraps of canvas and stretcher fragments found there, and the various seventeenth-century props found in van Meegeren's possession. These included the map that appears in the *Drinkers*, the wine glasses that assisted him in both *Last Suppers* and in *Isaac Blessing Jacob*;* two pewter plates similar to those in the *Emmaus*, both *Last Suppers*, *Isaac Blessing Jacob* and the *Footwashing*; and the famous white wine jug which appears, more or less adapted to suit his need, in five of the eight fakes sold. It was Coremans, with an assistant, who began examining the technical evidence, at the end of June in the Rijksmuseum. On 14 August he submitted his first findings to Judge Wiarda, and to the two other technicians, Froentjes and de Wild. The paintings were then transferred to a State laboratory in The Hague, where Froentjes and de Wild subjected them to a long series of chemical tests. Meanwhile, microchemical experiments were performed by Coremans in Brussels which primarily investigated the composition of the paint layers; radiographs were taken and evaluated. For a week in January (1947), all the technical evidence was collated and re-examined by the three chemists together, in collaboration with two British experts who were invited to check their findings: Professor H. J. Plenderleith, who was in charge of the Research Laboratory at the British Museum, and Mr F. I. G. Rawlins of the National Gallery Laboratory.

The Commission had set itself the task of finding answers to two specific questions. Were the eight paintings indisputably modern? If so, could they be the work of Han van Meegeren? In March, all seven experts reached the unanimous verdict that in both cases their answer was affirmative.

The principal techniques used had been those of visual inspection, radiography, ultra-violet and infra-red photography, spectrography and microchemistry. It had quickly been obvious that

---

* But not in the *Emmaus*, as Decoen says, completely mistakenly, was suggested by van Meegeren and the Commission. He prints side by side (op. cit., plates 84 and 85) a photograph of a glass found in van Meegeren's possession and a reproduction of one of the glasses in the *Emmaus*, which it does not at all resemble, thus disproving a theory that has never existed.

original seventeenth-century canvases had been used, and also—with the exception of the cobalt blue in the *Adulteress* and *Woman Reading Music*—authentic seventeenth-century pigments (though surprisingly, in several cases, pigments could not be identified.) Traces of underpaintings were found in most cases. It was established to the satisfaction of all that the *Emmaus* canvas had recently been cut down. None of these provided proof as to authorship or age of a completely positive kind. Apart from aesthetics, the Commission's unanimous verdict would be based on four principal findings. The presence of phenol and formaldehyde was in each case identified in at least the surface paint layer; these were unknown till the nineteenth century. The substance found in the crackle was too homogeneous to be dust or dirt. It was identified as ink; in at least two cases, this had seeped beneath the surface paint layer and dried between it and an undercoat. The paint had been so hardened that it was often not attacked by the most powerful solvents (even those that will completely destroy a genuine old painting) and had a dullness and porosity not normally found. Finally the crackle, when checked by macroscopy and radiography, was held to have been artificially induced: in some cases, notably the *Emmaus* and the *Supper*, the surface appearance was excellent, but the undercoats gave incriminating evidence.*

No-one has ever questioned that six of the eight are forgeries, but Decoen and his supporters have refused to accept the applicability or relevance of any of these four findings to the *Emmaus* and the *Supper*. Decoen's objections have already for the most part been considered. He explains the undisputed presence of artificial resin by suggesting that it was used by a latter-day restorer—in all probability van Meegeren himself; in the whole history of painting and restoring, there is no other record of such use. He disputes the allegation that the substance in the crackle was over-homogeneous. He does indeed seem to have shown that the conclusions of the Commission as to the over-hardness of the paint were erroneous.† He dismisses as inconclusive their findings on crackle in the case of the two disputed works.

---

* 'Van Meegeren achieved his aim on the surface, but did not succeed in imitating the *inside* aspect of genuine age-crackle.' Coremans, op. cit., page 23.

† See above, page 24.

Each must form his own conclusion on the basis of the facts available. It should be borne in mind that forgeries are said to have a mysterious tendency to reveal themselves with time: they may deceive when first they are painted, but soon deteriorate and eventually, it is suggested, the truth of its own accord makes itself known. This has indeed now happened, or so some say, with all but the *Emmaus* and the *Supper*; these two have remained unchanged. (It is to be remembered that they were the first false Vermeers and greater pains would have been taken with them.) I myself have no doubt whatever that van Meegeren painted van Beuningen's *Last Supper*; apart from anything else, I accept as absolutely conclusive the evidence of the Hondius. As to the *Emmaus*, I feel that there is perhaps one chance in ten thousand that it was painted by Vermeer. There is a final scrap of evidence that points in this direction. Van Beuningen, holding his *Last Supper* to be authentic, had *a fortiori* to hold the same of the *Emmaus*. After van Meegeren's death, he offered to buy it at the price paid in 1937. And the Boymans—though they keep it in the cellar, discourage all enquiries and seldom let it be seen—politely declined to sell.

Van Beuningen had at first refused to accept that his *Last Supper* was a fake. This was a completely natural reaction from one who had paid such a very enormous sum—the equivalent of almost half a million pounds today—for a large, splendid canvas which had been accepted almost universally as a work of beauty and of surpassing importance and significance. As the evidence piled up against it, he came to accept that his judgment had been at fault, that he had been terribly deceived. At the first meeting of creditors in February 1947, he entered his claim against the van Meegeren estate—as did every purchaser—for the return of all his purchase money. He could not yet have been sufficiently convinced by the arguments of Decoen and others that it might be a Vermeer. Decoen had approached him six months earlier and asked if he could see it; van Beuningen had been agreeable to this, but it was in the hands of the public prosecutor, who refused van Beuningen's specific request that Decoen be permitted to examine it. It appears that he was unable to do so until shortly before the trial, when van Beuningen appeared to accept the verdict with good grace. He never suggested in Court, nor was the suggestion ever heard there, that there were the smallest grounds for suspecting or hoping that the *Supper* (or the *Emmaus*) might be authentic. After the trial, the canvas was returned to him; it had been thought that the forgeries might be destroyed, as is usually required under Netherlands law, and it may have been (as Decoen claims) that it was because a possibility existed, however small, of two being authentic that this course was not taken. Van Beuningen, having considered the evidence of the Commission and Decoen's opinion on it, finally came to realize that it might not be conclusive, and put his great financial resources behind an all-out attempt to prove the *Supper* a Vermeer. He gave Decoen a completely free rein and hired two clever art dealers, the Krijnen brothers of Utrecht, to seek evidence in his favour. According to their later statement, their orders were to secure conclusive proof that the *Supper* was not a van Meegeren; to this end, they would spend three years in Belgium, France, Italy and Canada at van Beuningen's expense. As they told it, van Beuningen 'had been promised half a million dollars if the picture, once authenticated, could be shown in the United States; this sum would be shared between them and Decoen'.* Van Meegeren's widow would testify that they spoke in her presence of a £20,000 reward which would be paid for 'conclusive evidence' that the *Supper* was not her late husband's work.

These investigations did not bear fruit, for all their financial backing. None the less, van Beuningen came slowly to the point of full conviction that his *Supper* (once more) was a great Vermeer. Being of a logical frame of mind, he was led to three consequent decisions. He entirely withdrew his claim in respect of it against van Meegeren's estate. He offered to buy the *Emmaus*. And he initiated legal action against Coremans, claiming damages from the Belgian expert of £500,000 on the grounds that his faulty judgment had impaired his reputation as a collector and detracted from the value of his magnificent Vermeer.

The case was about to be heard in Brussels in June 1955 when van Beuningen had a heart attack and died. His heirs eventually decided to go ahead and it came to court some seven months later. In order to succeed in this over-optimistic litigation, it would be necessary for them to show that Coremans, and all the fellow members of his Commission, had arrived—if possible that they

* Quoted by John Russell in his article 'Revenge Keeps its Colour', *The Sunday Times*, 23 October 1955.

had arrived maliciously—at a completely false conclusion in attributing the second *Last Supper* to van Meegeren. All possible evidence was adduced, but the action failed. Coremans was once more fully vindicated; he was awarded damages and costs.

Van Meegeren was declared bankrupt in December 1945. This was a necessary step for the fiscal authorities to take when claims against him amounted to three or four times the estimated value of his remaining assets. It did not amount, as might at first appear, to a prejudgment of his case. It did not yet mean on the one hand that he would necessarily be found guilty, as he ardently desired, of having painted all eight forgeries if this should be disputed; nor, on the other, that he might not succeed if he contested the claims made by those deceived that they were entitled in each case to damages of nothing less than the full sums paid, and by the State for unpaid taxes. The fact was that these claims had been made— the State alone sought over four million guilders—and amounted to very much more than the total value of his assets. Some effective control had therefore to be placed on his spending and sale of property.

The finances are both complex and extraordinary.* It is best to start with the total paid for the eight forgeries sold. The most likely figure is 7,254,000 guilders (see Appendix 1). Of this van Meegeren is believed to have received something over five millions. Three-fifths of this had gone. The State, as already mentioned, had confiscated 900,000 guilders when they called in all thousand-guilder notes, van Meegeren had settled 800,000 on Jo at the time of their divorce, and he claimed to have lost about 300,000 guilders which he had hidden in bank notes at Laren and hadn't been able to find. His estimated personal expenditure over the eight years since the *Emmaus* sale was some one and a half million guilders. This left him with an estate that was valued at about two millions in 1945—mostly in houses, hotels, night-clubs and works of art.

The claims against this amounted originally to over seven millions. It may at first seem impossible that this should be very considerably greater than the total (five millions) received by him, but those who had bought the forgeries all began by claiming

---

* They are here expressed in guilders, which should be divided by ten to give an approximation of pounds sterling at then-current exchange rates.

every penny paid; in the case of the *Adulteress*, the Netherlands State presumed to take the line, without any justification that can readily be seen (although it would succeed), that *they* would claim in damages the whole sum paid by Goering. On top of this, the State demanded payment of income tax and capital gains tax in respect of van Meegeren's undeclared earnings and profits as a forger since 1937.

The first petitions were filed, by the Netherlands State and the Boymans, on 28 November 1945. These alone amounted to over five million guilders. The Boymans claimed the full purchase price, 520,000 guilders, in respect of the *Emmaus*. The State claimed almost three million guilders for the *Footwashing* and the *Adulteress*, and over two million for unpaid taxes, in addition to the 900,000 already confiscated.

Again, it is hard to see how the State could justify this. Tax is payable on net income. If those who claimed damages won their case, van Meegeren would be required to repay every penny received (though this would depend on it being demonstrated that the same work of art could be worth a million one day and nothing the next). It would be impossible for him to do this, but it might be imagined that his net income over these years on which tax might be payable could not be more than he had spent, lost, or made over to his wife—in other words the difference between what he had received and what might now be available to pay back those defrauded. The State thought differently: they claimed that he owed tax on the five million received by him, and moreover that this should take precedence over all other claims (including their own as purchasers of the *Footwashing* and—indirectly—of the *Adulteress*).

The complete unfairness of this may be seen if one considers, in isolation, the case of the *Footwashing*. The State were in fact saying to him: 'We were so extremely foolish as to pay Mr de Boer 1,300,000 guilders for this fake. Of this you received about a million. It is worth absolutely nothing. We now expect you to return the million and to pay tax on it though it will have earned you nothing.' The case of the *Adulteress* is even more absurd. Here the State were saying: 'You prevailed upon Goering to return stolen property to a value of 1,650,000 guilders in exchange for a valueless forgery. This was an illegal act since it involved trading with the enemy. The outcome of the transaction was that you

received over a million. Were it not for the fact that the Field
Marshall is a war criminal, at present languishing in jail, he would
be entitled to claim this from you. As custodians of enemy
property, *we* intend to claim it, and we also claim tax on your
profit even though, if you repay the purchase money, you will not
have made any.'

When the matter was considered more carefully, certain factors
began to come to light which would favour van Meegeren though
they could not possibly lead to solvency. In the case of the
Emmaus, just over seven years had gone by since the sale, and the
Statute of Limitations would therefore take effect; the Boymans
Museum was forced to withdraw its claim. In any event it could
hardly have succeeded if van Beuningen's offer to buy the *Emmaus*
at the price paid in 1937 had been refused. Then van Beuningen
came to realize that if he were stoutly maintaining that his *Last
Supper* were authentic, he could not also maintain that he had been
defrauded, and he too withdrew his claim. If he had had any
interest in doing so, van Meegeren could have tried to prove that
the State had no right whatever to claim for themselves what
Goering had paid, and might even have succeeded. But it would
not have helped him in any way to do so: even without the
Adulteress, the *Supper*, the *Emmaus*, he had received over two
million guilders for the others. This was more than remained to
him before paying any arrears of tax; his financial situation was
obviously impossible and there would be no point in disputing
the fact of his insolvency.

It would be fully ten years before the bankruptcy was settled.
There is something of a conspiracy amongst all those involved,
especially the State, to keep details hidden, but the final outcome
was more satisfactory to those who had been deceived than had at
first seemed possible. In 1945, with van Meegeren's estate valued
at two millions and the prior claim for unpaid taxes amounting to
about that sum, it seemed unlikely that they would ever receive a
cent. Two factors helped them. The necessary withdrawal of the
Boymans claim, and of van Beuningen's in respect of the *Last
Supper*, reduced the liability by almost two millions. It was then
to be found that van Meegeren's assets, which had happily been
well invested by the Receiver, had almost doubled in the years
since his bankruptcy. Even allowing for the fact that the State
would have charged interest on the tax arrears, there was enough

left after payment of tax in full for a dividend of 28 per cent to all claimants. The most important was the State itself, who had sought over two millions for the *Footwashing* and the *Adulteress*. The State would thus receive back from van Meegeren an aggregate of some 3,500,000 guilders: the nine hundred thousand that had been confiscated, some two millions in tax, and some half-million in damages. This would more than compensate their loss of public funds, but not their public reputation, in having paid over a million for the worst of all the fakes.

These financial gymnastics were of no interest to van Meegeren, nor to his ex-wives and children, who could not benefit from them. His only possible hope would have been to show that the forgeries were worth what had been paid for them; he may have pretended to himself that this was so, but must have known well that there was no chance of maintaining it in a court of law. He never made the attempt nor showed any intention of doing so. It is true that if he had lived and survived his prison sentence, he might have made a most remarkable recovery: editors were clamouring for his story (which he could not tell so long as the case was *sub judice*) and moreover there was a sudden demand for authentic van Meegerens which must have greatly pleased him though he may have made one or two cynical comments. Dealers went through their store rooms in the hope of finding a forgotten work by him which would then be prominently displayed at a price ten or twenty times higher than could previously have been sought. Van Meegeren received a flood of commissions: in particular, he was offered a 'golden bridge' to the United States if he would go over and paint modern portraits, new Old Masters, in the style and technique of the forgeries. A story has been told that a showman offered to buy all eight fakes at their original prices in the belief that he could soon recoup his outlay by taking them on tour: it is a pleasant tale, but the fact that nothing came of it must prove it apocryphal, since it could not have been in anyone's interest to turn the proposal down.

Claims for damages by those who had been deceived would be considered separately in civil proceedings. They would be irrelevant at his long-delayed trial on two criminal charges, forging signatures and obtaining money by fraud.

9
Endings

IT seems to have been tacitly agreed by everyone in authority that his case should be played down as far as humanly possible. The Court would be concerned to prove van Meegeren guilty—nothing else. But this was his own principal desire and there would be no-one to oppose it. Van Beuningen would prefer not to mention the possibility, nor allow any supporter of his to mention it, that his *Last Supper* might be a Vermeer, since this might be held against him in his claim for damages against van Meegeren if it were proved false eventually. Decoen therefore would not be called to give evidence. As to the *Emmaus*, it had just been realized that the Statute of Limitations had already taken effect and it could not be considered. This had brought some recompense to the Boymans and to the select ranks of the Rembrandt Society: their foolishness, at least, could not reach the limelight. More strangely, it seems to have been decided that the *Adulteress* need hardly be mentioned either. Goering, by now, had swallowed his bitter pill; the Netherlands State, though claiming the money he had paid for it, seemed with equal absence of logic to have no wish to embarrass those who had sold to the enemy what they believed to be a Vermeer. None of those involved was called. Yet this was not thought remarkable at the time; only one newspaper would criticize or even draw attention to the fact that 'the political side of the case was not publicly mentioned'.

The ignorance of the experts, the dealers, the collectors—this would not be raised. Perhaps it might be considered at some far-off later date (in fact, it never was), but at present it was only van Meegeren's that mattered. This was the official point of view, and van Meegeren himself, even had he retained the most aggressive defence counsel, would not have been able to influence it much. In the event his lawyer, Meester E. Heldring, was seldom heard from at all until he rose to make his closing speech. He hardly had any alternative. If he had attempted a hostile cross-examination of those who had been deceived, with a view to showing their irresponsibility and foolishness, it would at once have been ruled irrelevant and therefore out of order. Moreover, in one way, this would have been against his client's interests: van Meegeren's argument that he was a great master, even the greatest of his age or century, would gain nothing from showing the total fallibility of expert thought. It would hardly have helped him if Heldring had asked de Wild, Hannema or van Dam: 'You advised the State to purchase this daub, the *Footwashing*, as a Vermeer; how do you excuse this gross misuse of public funds?' If it were van Meegeren's contention that the *Footwashing* was a masterpiece, their deception would have been understandable and forgivable—even welcomed. And the prosecution would have no interest in drawing attention to it.

It is true that many eminent personages would have to take the stand. Although, unhappily, this could not be avoided, they would be allowed to suffer the least possible embarrassment. Many awkward questions to which answers were eagerly awaited would not be asked at all. The trial of van Meegeren would have taken several weeks if the guilty had been accused. Instead it took $5\frac{1}{2}$ hours, all on a single day; almost half the time was occupied by the closing speeches on both sides. A total of seventeen witnesses were called; their evidence was heard in just two hours—an average of seven minutes each.

However, this convenient attitude on the part of the authorities had not succeeded in preventing the trial from rousing worldwide interest on an unprecedented scale. Before dawn on 29 October 1947, a queue of would-be spectators was already forming outside the Fourth Chamber of the District Assize Court in Amsterdam. The press would be out *en masse*—from the United States, Britain, France, everywhere. Han van Meegeren, fifteen years (almost to the day) after starting his experiments at the faraway Primavera, was about to gain such glory as was allowed him.

He was in very bad health; indeed, as is now known, he was dying. Since his bankruptcy he had been necessarily restricted to a much less reckless life—he received only a very small allowance from the Receiver—but his physique had always been frail, his heart always weak, and the damage had been done. He was fifty-eight, very grey-haired, hollow-faced and a confirmed morphia addict. That summer he had collapsed. Specialists at the Valerium

Clinic had diagnosed angina; he had been released after a month's detention there, but had since had several further attacks. However, for his day of triumph, he was determined to seem at his best, to appear as jauntily confident as he could, to be dapper and debonair. He had shaved carefully that morning, trimmed his little moustache, and donned a pale blue shirt, a dark blue tie and an elegant dark blue suit. Then he had walked briskly from his house, surrounded by reporters and photographers, with whom he had talked and joked all the way to the court-house in the Prinsengracht.

The Fourth Chamber is the largest, and it was packed to over-flowing with over two hundred spectators. It had more the appearance of a picture gallery than a law court. The presiding judge, Meester V. G. A. Boll, would be seated at his large desk on a dais; behind him, as usual, would be the portrait of the Queen. Today it would be dwarfed by two huge canvases, on its left by the life-size *Emmaus*, on its right by the more-than-life-size *Last Supper*. The rest of the sold forgeries, and the *Young Christ*, decked the other walls. A canvas screen had been erected on the dais for the projection by Dr Coremans of his photographic evidence.

The experts were present in force. There were the members of the Commission: Coremans himself, Altena, Schneider, Froentjes, Plenderleith and Rawlins. There were those who had been deceived: van Beuningen, Hannema, de Boer, Hoogendijk, van Dam, van Gelder and van der Vorm. And then there was de Wild, in his unique, unhappy position as one of those deceived *and* as a member of the Commission. Bredius and Goering were dead. Waiting to give evidence were the agents Kok and Strijbis; Boon had been sought in vain, as had van Strijvesande and Miedl. A leading psychiatrist, Dr van der Horst, had prepared a report on his observations of the defendant.

At ten o'clock sharp, van Meegeren entered the courtroom and took his seat in the dock, facing the judge's desk, a police officer behind him. He gazed happily round the walls, admiring his handiwork: *Isaac Blessing Jacob* over his left shoulder, then the *Young Christ* and the *Head of Christ*. The *Supper* and the *Emmaus* both looked very well; the latter was still in its fine Boymans frame, the former on the same large sheet of plywood to which he had tacked it at Laren. He smiled and waved to his friends, to his son and daughter, to Jo, as photographers surrounded him; it was reported that he 'posed for them like an actor'—glasses off, glasses on—standing up, seated—turning this way and that as they called to him.

As soon as the presiding judge had entered and was seated, the clerk put the formal question: 'Are you Henricus Antonius van Meegeren?'* The defendant acknowledged the fact with a curt nod, and it was then agreed by his counsel that only the charge be read. (The full summons ran to eight typed pages.) This was done by the public prosecutor, Meester H. A. Wassenbergh. Its substance was that the defendant, firstly, had obtained money by fraud; secondly, that he had put false names or signatures 'on certain paintings' to make them appear the work of others, contrary to Articles 326 and 326B of the Penal Code.

The judge addressed van Meegeren: 'Accused, do you admit the charges?'

'I do.'

'Then let us proceed at once to the evidence of the experts.'

The seven members of the Commission took the oath and each in turn was asked two questions: whether in his opinion all the paintings were modern and whether 'they could be the work of van Meegeren'. All replied to both in the affirmative. The curtains were then drawn and Dr Coremans, on behalf of the whole Commission, showed with the aid of slides how these conclusions had been reached. His lecture took half an hour: he concentrated on the crackle, on cross sections of the paint layers, on the discovered presence of artificial resin and, briefly, on the fragment of the *Emmaus* stretcher. From time to time the President intervened to ask the defendant if he agreed and on every occasion van Meegeren, who listened with obvious interest and fascination, would answer 'Certainly' or 'I do', or 'That is perfectly correct'. When Coremans had done, he was again asked for his comment and caused a ripple of amusement with his sharply sardonic reply: 'I find this work excellent. Indeed it is phenomenal. It will never be possible to get away with forgery again. To me, such work seems much more clever than—for example—the painting of the *Emmaus*.'

It was now eleven o'clock; Coremans was flying to New York that day and was permitted to depart. The next witness was de

* There is this tendency in Holland to use the Latin form on occasions.

Wild—he who had advised the State to purchase the *Footwashing* and had then served on the Commission that found it false. The public prosecutor invited him to explain this, and it was now that he sought to excuse himself by saying that the dealer concerned, de Boer, had twice refused to allow it to be radiographed.

'Later, I could do so,' he continued. 'This brought me to my changed conclusion.'

De Wild did not mention how much later. The radiograph was in fact not taken till after van Meegeren's confession; it had then been two years in the possession of the Rijksmuseum. He was not asked about this. Nor was he asked why, at the time, he and his colleagues did not think it highly suspicious that de Boer refused this reasonable request.

Laughter swept the court when he actually went so far as to claim personal credit for the work of the man who had deceived him.

'For me, these tests were less difficult,' he said in his confident way. 'It soon became clear to me that the accused had borrowed a formula for the composition of his quasi-old paints from my treatise on the methods of Vermeer and de Hoogh. Even certain impurities that I mention as being found in Vermeer's paint are also found in van Meegeren's.'

De Boer was not asked why he had failed to notice this till after van Meegeren confessed.

Dr Froentjes and Dr Altena gave confirmatory evidence. The former concentrated on the chemical and microchemical analysis, with special reference to the artificial resin. The latter, who had been concerned only with aesthetic values, made his boast that he had condemned the *Footwashing* as an undoubted forgery before its sale, though in fact his opinion had no effect at all upon the decision to buy it.

The examination of Commission members had now been completed; the house agent, Strijbis, would be the next to take the stand. First, however, the judge had a question for van Meegeren—not a very difficult one: at what stage, he asked, would he add the signature?

'I did that last of all and it was much the hardest job,' replied the defendant. It was recorded that he gave a sigh as he remembered just how difficult it had been. 'It had to be done all in one stroke,' he said. 'Once I had begun it, there could be no going back.'

Strijbis had received over half a million guilders and had paid no taxes on it; he would be in trouble later, but today this was not mentioned.

'I was already acquainted with the accused when he asked me, in 1941, if I would sell a painting for him,' he said. 'I knew nothing about art but he offered me a handsome commission—one-sixth of whatever price I got. I took the work, a *Head of Christ*, to Hoogendijk.'

'Did you know it was a fake?'

'Certainly not. The accused said it was a Vermeer. He never told me where he obtained it. Later I sold three others for him, all to Hoogendijk: the *Last Supper*, a Pieter de Hoogh and the *Blessing of Jacob*. They were supposed to be all from the same collection.'

'What were the prices paid?'

'I no longer remember. I kept no record.'

The total paid for the four forgeries sold by him, of which he kept no record, was about three-and-a-half million guilders. Strijbis mentioned that Hoogendijk was as mysterious about his clients as he had been to Hoogendijk.

'He never told me who got the pictures,' he said.

Hoogendijk himself was the next witness. It was not to be suggested, as it had been to Strijbis, that he might have been a party to the fraud.

'I walked into the trap,' he admitted. 'When I saw the *Head of Christ*, it made me think of the *Emmaus*.'

'Did you not think it strange that more and more Vermeers were discovered?'

'No. The historians agree that there should be more, that the *Emmaus* could not be the only one of its kind. I sold the *Head of Christ* to Mr van Beuningen. That was in 1941, in Rotterdam. It was a much finer painting then that it is now.'

The President intervened to enquire if this really was the case. Hoogendijk was convinced of it. And van Meegeren agreed that its 'dull, lack-lustre appearance' did not give at all the same impression as when he put it on the market 'in Vermeer's name'.

Hoogendijk resumed his evidence.

'Van Beuningen also bought the *Last Supper*,' he said. 'My first impression was that this was an extraordinary painting. My first impression is often the best, but again I was allowing myself to be influenced by the *Emmaus*. It now seems beyond understanding; at the time, you know, all was done secretly. After the *Supper* I sold two more, including the strange one, the *Blessing of Jacob*.'

'How do you account for your acceptance of that one?'

Hoogendijk turned to have another look at it.

'Yes,' he agreed. 'It's difficult to explain. It is unbelievable that it fooled me. But we all slid downwards—from the *Emmaus* to the *Last Supper*, from the *Last Supper* to the *Blessing of Jacob*. When I look at them now, I do not understand how it could possibly have happened: a psychologist could explain it better than I can. But the atmosphere of war contributed to our blindness.'

He was speaking with his usual urbane charm but his frankness must be acknowledged.

'It should be remembered that the *Emmaus* was declared authentic by experts with a world-wide reputation,' he went on. 'The subsequent fakes were concatenated links of the same chain. That is why sales were more easy. There was also the desire to keep the paintings in Holland.'

Defence counsel questioned him: 'How about the pretended origins of these paintings? Was it not said that they came from a Countess, who had received them as a family heirloom?'

'No,' replied Hoogendijk. 'No Countess was mentioned. There was only some talk of an old Dutch family.'

Hoogendijk mentioned that he never bought from Strijbis until he had assured himself a sale. He claimed—and it was not disputed —that when he knew the works were false he returned his commission to his deceived clients.

The morning session, which had lasted a bare two hours, was completed by the evidence of the psychologist, van der Horst.

'The character of the defendant leads to sensitiveness to criticism, fed by a revenge complex which explains his anti-social attitude,' he stated. 'I would describe him as disequilibrated but fully responsible for his actions. A man of his personality would be greatly hurt by isolation; I would not advise imprisonment.'

After the adjournment, seven witnesses were called in less than an hour: de Boer, Kok, Hannema, van Dam, van Beuningen, van der Vorm, van Gelder. Their examination added little of importance that has not previously been quoted; on several occasions, the questions *not* asked are of greater significance. De Boer told of his visit from Jan Kok:

'In 1943, he came to offer me an old painting, the *Washing of Christ's Feet,* for which he asked over a million guilders.'

'Did he say who had painted it?'

'He did not; but he told me I would know this the very moment I saw it. As soon as he showed it to me, I said it was by the same master who painted the *Emmaus.* I added that it was probably not signed; when I examined it more carefully, however, I found Vermeer's signature.'

'Did you ever doubt its authenticity?'

'No, I didn't.'

He was not questioned at all about the fact alleged that morning by de Wild that he had, none the less, refused to allow a radiograph to be taken of it. Nor was his involvement in the prewar sale of the false de Hoogh mentioned.

Van Meegeren helped him by the assertion that he 'was sure he was perfectly honest' and had acted in good faith. Similarly, he helped Jan Kok, his former schoolfriend, whose evidence for some reason seemed to move him deeply, though, apart from admitting that he had never heard of Vermeer, he gave nothing more than a very factual account of the small part he had played.

'He is the most noble of all those who have given evidence in this case,' said van Meegeren.

Hannema and van Dam described the sale of the *Footwashing.* 'I immediately got the impression that it was a Vermeer,' said Hannema. 'It was examined by a Government committee which decided to advise its purchase. None of us liked it much but we were afraid it would go to Germany.'

'But you also bought it for its artistic value?'

'Of course. After all, Vermeers are scarce.'

'Did no one enquire about the origin of the work?'

'Yes, but it was all very vague.'

Van Beuningen came next. He described his purchase of three supposed Old Masters—a de Hoogh and two Vermeers. Of the first he said: 'I never had any doubts. Dr Boon enlightened me as to its alleged origins and it seemed a plausible tale.' He did not say what the tale was, nor that it must have been totally unverifiable. Of the Vermeers he again admitted that he had felt no doubts; he said he had been influenced by 'a statement of Dr Bredius in 1937,' thus giving the completely false impression that Bredius had believed the *Head* and the *Supper* authentic. In fact he is most unlikely even to have seen them; in 1937, anyway, they hadn't even been painted. He was in fact referring to the *Emmaus* certificate, meaning that it had added something by inference to the later fakes, but failed to make this clear.

Dr J. G. van Gelder, one of those who had advised the purchase of the *Footwashing*, contributed some rather curious evidence. Having admitted that he had never doubted its authenticity, although he found it 'ugly', he went on to say that during the war he had once been visited by two tax consultants, who were quite unknown to him, and whose unnamed client, an artist, wanted to sell 'some old paintings'.

'Somehow I had a presentiment that they were the work of the accused,' said van Gelder. 'I told them I thought their client was van Meegeren and invited them to return next day. I never saw them again. Afterwards, I always had a feeling that van Meegeren was not quite straight.'

Van Meegeren was suddenly on his feet. 'So you had a feeling?' he enquired.

'Yes,' replied van Gelder, and added amid laughter that it had appeared, later, to have been rather more than justified.

'And when did you first get this feeling of yours?' asked van Meegeren.

'In 1942.'

'Then I draw the attention of the Court to the fact that the *Footwashing* had not been offered for sale then—it didn't even exist. Despite this precious feeling, you would still accept it [a year later] as an undoubted Vermeer.'

It was 2.15 p.m. All witnesses had now been heard and Judge Boll questioned the defendant.

'You still admit that you painted all these fakes?'

'Yes, Mr President.'

'And also that you sold them, at a very high price?'

'I had no alternative,' said van Meegeren. And added, very reasonably: 'If I had sold them at a low price, it would have been an *a priori* indication that they were false.'

'Why did you continue after the *Emmaus*?'

'I found the process so beautiful. I came to a condition in which I was no longer my own master. I became without will, powerless. I was forced to continue.'

'That's all very well,' said the President. 'But at least you made a pleasant little profit.' This as a joke, without hostility.

'I had to, Mr President. I had been so belittled by the critics that I could no longer exhibit my work. I was systematically and maliciously damaged by the critics, who don't know the first thing about painting.'

'Perhaps the financial side had *some* influence on your actions?'

'It made little difference. The millions I earned from the later pictures were added to the millions I had earned already. I didn't do it for the money, which brought me nothing but trouble and unhappiness.'

'So you acted from no desire for financial gain?'

'Only from a desire to paint. I decided to carry on, not primarily from a wish to paint forgeries but to make the best use of the technique I had developed. I intend to continue using that technique. It's an excellent one. But I will never again age my paintings nor offer them as Old Masters.'

The dialogue was over; the Public Prosecutor now took his stand and spoke for something over an hour. But he said remarkably little and much of it favoured van Meegeren: it was clear that he had much regard for him despite everything and, though he would have some harsh words to say, cannot be thought to have pressed his case vigorously. He must have been well aware that public sympathy was strongly with his opponent.

'This court room, which is usually rather drab, has a colourful appearance this afternoon,' he began. 'These paintings, which have been regarded as Old Masters, are now judged somewhat differently. Even the earliest of them, this *Christ at Emmaus*, is only ten years old.' And he indicated it—it was close beside him—with a quick gesture.

'The defendant hoped to prove to the world that he is a great artist,' he went on. 'But by these falsifications he has in fact shown himself to be less of an artist than ever. The whole art world is in shock and one begins to doubt the very essence of artistic evaluation.'

To bring about just such a state of affairs had been van Meegeren's chief ambition. The Public Prosecutor now asserted that art arouses emotion; as evidence of this—excellent evidence—he read out several critiques of the *Emmaus*, dating from 1937, commenting with perfect logic—he was here again pleading his opponent's cause—that either these emotions had not been real, or else van Meegeren had been able to inspire 'pure artistic emotion' through his forgery. The question of whether he was a painter of genius had not yet been answered in Court, said the Prosecutor.

He could not accept van Meegeren's statement that he had acted as he did because he was a misunderstood genius who wished to prove himself a master. His reason for not accepting it was simply that the defendant had in fact failed to achieve that end. He had not managed to reach the goal of recognition and acclaim, his 'halo had faded' and 'only his self-enrichment now remained'. After commenting on the excellence of the signatures, which, he said, could not be distinguished from real ones, the Prosecutor remarked that at the time of the *Emmaus* sale the story of the 'noble Dutch family' which found itself 'on its beam ends' had been at once accepted; various intermediaries, 'some of them innocent, some very shrewd', had then taken over. He singled out Boon, 'our former Member of Parliament', for special mention, as one who—though acting 'to a certain extent in good faith'—deserved censure for his 'light-hearted behaviour' in such an important affair. After the *Emmaus*, 'the forgeries sold like cakes'.

Van Meegeren had damaged the Netherlands State and several private individuals, said Meester Wassenbergh. (He did not mention Goering.) It was to be regretted that so many experts had been deceived. He would not discuss further the question of whether van Meegeren was a master, which in any case would give no reason for justifying clemency.

'I hold that both parts of the charge have been proved,' he concluded. 'The maximum sentence allowed by the Penal Code is four years. Taking into account the defendant's health and sensitivity, the psychiatric report and certain other extenuating circumstances, I ask the Court for a sentence of half the maximum term. I recommend that the forgeries be returned to their owners though I should point out that it is within the Court's competence to order their destruction.'

Now it was Heldring's turn. He spoke for rather less than an hour. It was an intelligent, witty and persuasive speech, at times anecdotal: he told the story, for instance, of van Meegeren's visit to the Boymans in 1938 to see their new Vermeer, when he was reproved by an attendant for coming too close to it. He considered the psychiatric report, agreed with it in principle, and added his

own personal opinion of the defendant: quick and highly intelligent, a man of great charm (this he should have qualified with the
word 'sometimes'), childishly generous and 'wax in the hands of
parasites'. His client 'could not tolerate opposition'; this would
lead him to 'very violent reactions'. He had merely wished to
defend himself against the critics, who had condemned him
without mercy when he painted under his own name and had
then been 'quite beside themselves' with enthusiasm for the
Emmaus.

Heldring went on to examine each sale 'from a purely legal
viewpoint'. In no case could he find that fraud or false pretences
had led to the sale itself. Certain 'clever artifices' had been used in
the painting, but there had been 'no tricks' in the selling; it had
never been said that a canvas *was* a Vermeer or de Hoogh, or even
that it might be—in each case this had been left to the expert or
the dealer or the buyer to decide. There remained, it was true, the
little matter of the signatures, but really a signature was not so
very important as a guide to authenticity. On the charge of fraud
under Article 326, Heldring submitted that his client should be
found not guilty and asked for acquittal. On the charge of forging
signatures under Article 326B, which was admitted, he asked for
'conditional punishment'. He suggested 'utmost leniency'.

It was already known that judgment would be reserved, that
verdict and sentence (if any) would be announced two weeks later
on 12 November. The President asked van Meegeren if he had any
final question. He sat quite still, looking straight ahead, for several
long seconds, and then replied in a firm voice with the single word
'No'. The Court stood adjourned, and the crowds swirled
around him, and he made his way back, again on foot, to his
house in the Keizergracht.

On 12 November he was found guilty on both charges and
sentenced to a year's imprisonment. It was the minimum sentence
possible. He would have to be under medical supervision and it
was tacitly recognized that he would probably serve the greater
part of his sentence in a hospital or clinic. The Judge ordered that
all the forgeries be returned to their owners; the *Adulteress* would
become the property of the Crown. As for the *Young Christ*, it
was adjudged the property of van Meegeren; so were the early
trial fakes brought back by Wooning from Nice. They would

therefore be sold, along with all his other effects (except the house, which was in the name of his former wife) to go towards payment of his debts.* He was given two weeks in which to lodge an appeal, but did not do so. As subsequently became known, but was never announced officially, he would almost certainly have received a free pardon. His petition had gone to the Queen and the Public Prosecutor had let Heldring know informally that he would not oppose it. An unopposed application for the royal pardon is very usually granted.

But the Queen's mercy would not be needed; he was to go free anyway. On 26 November, the last day for lodging an appeal, he was again admitted to the Valerium clinic. It was widely supposed that authority was being kind, that he was tactfully being allowed to enter hospital instead of prison. In fact, however, he was desperately ill; he had collapsed that morning and was incapable of movement. He made something of a recovery and was allowed visitors for a week or two, though he was very weak and prostrate. On 29 December he had a last terrible heart attack and died next day.

Han van Meegeren, beyond doubt, had been the most successful known forger of all time. He still is. That, for what it's worth, is his claim for immortal glory.

It fails. His entire edifice had been constructed on a completely false value judgment. A man of integrity would have known this in his heart and it may be that van Meegeren knew it. He himself had been a fake, just as his Vermeers had been. He was far from being the only one. For a fake is any object, animate or inanimate, admired for valued qualities—beauty, knowledge, skill—that it once seemed to possess but are now proved absent or spurious. By the same token, many of his victims were shown to be equally false.

All this time, somewhere else, artists were at work, living and eating, making love to their girls, going about their business, painting as they wished to paint, remaining true to themselves, indifferent to the world. They were the true ones.

* The *Young Christ* was bought at public auction by a Hague dealer for 3,000 guilders (about £300); it was later sold to Sir Ernest Oppenheimer and is now in a church in Johannesburg. It may be thought of no small significance that only one of the eight sold forgeries has been offered for re-sale since van Meegeren's confession. This was the *Adulteress*, purchased for an unknown sum by the Stichting Nederlands Kunstbezit of The Hague.

APPENDIX I. CHRONOLOGY

1889 Han van Meegeren born at Deventer.

1907 Enters Delft Institute of Technology.

1912 Marries Anna de Voogt. Son born.

1913 Leaves Delft Institute. Takes degree in Art at Hague Academy. Starts career as painter.

1915 Daughter born.

1916 First one-man show. First meeting with Johanna Oerlemans.

1923 First divorce.

1929 Marries Johanna Oerlemans.

1932 Moves to Roquebrune. Begins research.

1936 Completes research, begins work on *Emmaus*.

1937 *Emmaus* completed and sold (December).

1938 Probably paints the *Drinkers*. Moves to Nice.

1938–9 Probably paints the first *Last Supper* and the *Cardplayers*. Returns to Holland (July).

1940–3 Probably paints the last five 'Vermeers'.

1943 Second divorce.

1945 *Adulteress* found at Alt-Aussee salt mine. 29 May, imprisoned as collaborator. 12 July, confesses. Autumn, paints *Young Christ*.

1946 June, Coremans Commission sworn in.

1947 March, Coremans Commission reports. 29 October, trial. 12 November, admitted to Valerium clinic. 30 December, dies.

APPENDIX 2. PRINCIPAL DATA ON THE FORGERIES

Subject	Style and size (inches)	Where painted and likely year of completion	Buyer and year of sale
1. *Woman Drinking*	Hals 30¾ × 26	Roquebrune 1935 or 1936	not sold
2. *Portrait of a Man*	Terborgh 12 × 9¾	,,	,,
3. *Woman Reading Music*	Vermeer 22½ × 19	,,	,,
4. *Woman Playing Music*	Vermeer 25 × 19¼	,,	,,
5. *Christ at Emmaus*	Vermeer 45½ × 50¼	Roquebrune 1937	Rembrandt Society 1937
6. *Interior with Drinkers*	de Hoogh 31½ × 27¼	Roquebrune 1938	van Beuningen 1939
7. *Interior with Cardplayers*	de Hoogh 29½ × 24½	Nice 1939	van der Vorm 1941
8. *Last Supper*	Vermeer 57½ × 105¼	Nice 1939	not sold
9. *Head of Christ*	Vermeer 19 × 12	Laren 1940	van Beuningen/ Hoogendijk 1941
10. *Last Supper*	Vermeer 68½ × 96	Laren 1941	van Beuningen 1941
11. *Isaac Blessing Jacob*	Vermeer 49¼ × 45½	Laren 1942	van der Vorm 1942
12. *Christ and the Adulteress*	Vermeer 38¼ × 33	Laren 1942	Goering 1942
13. *The Washing of Christ's Feet*	Vermeer 45½ × 37½	Laren 1943	Netherlands State
14. *Young Christ*	Vermeer 58¾ × 75½	Amsterdam 1945	Oppenheimer

Intermediaries	Best estimate of price paid (guilders)	Best estimate of the sterling equivalent	
		THEN	NOW
(1) —	—	—	—
(2) —	—	—	—
(3) —	—	—	—
(4) —	—	—	—
(5) Boon/Bredius/ Hoogendijk	520,000	£58,000 $286,520	£180,000 $504,000
(6) Boon/de Boer	220,000	£24,000 $117,360	£66,000 $184,800
(7) Strijbis/Hoogendijk	219,000	£22,000 $97,680	£55,000 $154,000
(8) —	—	—	—
(9) Strijbis/Hoogendijk	475,000	£47,500 $191,662.50	£120,000 $336,000
(10) Strijbis/Hoogendijk	1,600,000	£160,000 $645,600	£400,000 $1,120,000
(11) Strijbis/Hoogendijk	1,270,000	£127,000 $512,445	£315,000 $882,000
(12) van Strijvesande/ Miedl/Hofer	1,650,000	£165,000 $665,775	£400,000 $1,120,000
(13) Kok/de Boer	1,300,000	£130,000 $524,550	£320,000 $896,000
(14) —	3,000	£300 $1,210.50	£600 $1,680
	7,257,000	£733,800 $3,042,803.00	£1,856,600 $5,198,480

Index